AF583686

The Writer's PRESS

A book editor for more than twenty-five years, Craig Munro has published in a wide variety of books, newspapers and journals. He has edited a short-story anthology and a new edition of P. R. Stephensen's *The Foundations of Culture in Australia.* His Stephensen biography — *Wild Man of Letters* — won the Fellowship of Australian Writers Biography Prize and the Walter McCrae Russell Prize for Literary Scholarship.

UQP's first fiction editor, Craig Munro received the Barbara Ramsden Award for Editing in 1985 and won a Churchill Fellowship in 1991 to study publishing in Canada and the United States. He is currently co-editing the third volume of the forthcoming History of the Book in Australia, and is on the Editorial Board of the Academy Editions of Australian Literature. He was the founding chair of the Queensland Writers' Centre, and has been publishing manager at UQP since 1983.

The Writer's PRESS

1948 — 1998

EDITED BY CRAIG MUNRO

UNIVERSITY OF QUEENSLAND PRESS

First published 1998 by University of Queensland Press
Box 42, St Lucia, Queensland 4067 Australia

Copy-editing: Felicity Shea
Layout and design: Paul Rendle
Typesetting: Karen Lennard
Index: Neale Towart
Text set in $11^1/_2$ on $15^1/_2$ Bembo
Printed in Australia on Impress Matt Art paper by McPherson's Printing Group

Distributed in the USA and Canada by International Specialized Book Services, Inc., 5804 H.E. Hassalo Street, Portland, Oregon 97213–3640

This project has been assisted by the Commonwealth Government through the Australia Council, its arts funding and advisory body.

Sponsored by the Queensland Office of Arts and Cultural Development.

Cataloguing in Publication Data
National Library of Australia

UQP: the writer's press.
Includes index.

1. University of Queensland Press — History. 2. Publishers and publishing — Queensland — History — 20th century. I. Munro, Craig, 1950– .

070.5099431

ISBN 0 7022 3005 7

'... Publishers, a set of men who never scrupled to vend either Calumny or Blasphemy, as long as the Town would call for it.'

Alexander Pope, Introduction to *The Dunciad* (1728)

'A publisher is blamed if a book fails and ignored if it proves a success.'

Letter to Charles Scribner

'You need skin as thin as a cigarette paper to write a novel and the hide of an elephant to publish it.'

Frank Dalby Davison

Contents

Foreword

Fifty years in book publishing is not a particularly long period of time. In the centuries-old tradition of European universities and the dissemination of knowledge, it is but a brief span of years. In Aboriginal terms it is only a fleeting moment during forty thousand years or more of continuous cultural practice.

For half a century UQP has not only been inextricably bound up in the scholarly and literary life of the nation, it has played a crucial role in giving voice to emerging writers who now contribute so much to mainstream Australian cultural life. It has been very much a writer's press.

Born in 1948, in the aftermath of the Second World War, and nurtured in the heady and turbulent years of the sixties and seventies, UQP has been an intimate part of the evolution of modern Australia. Its extraordinary range of titles has reflected the preoccupations of a nation undergoing rapid, continuous change. Many UQP authors have been at the forefront of that change.

As a publisher UQP has always been prepared to take risks. It has had the courage to back its judgment as to the innate value of authors and subjects that, whilst not fashionable at the time, soon proved to be central to the needs of an increasingly eager reading public. UQP developed and sustained a remarkable track record as a pacesetter in Australian publishing and as a nurturer of new writing talent. It has consistently broken through, against the constraints of conservative thinking and timid editorial practice in Australian publishing.

What is equally remarkable is that UQP has achieved all of this from a small base, on a university campus at the geographical and cultural outer edge of the continent. Perhaps by not being at the centre of population, and therefore not so caught up in the daily machinations of big city life, UQP has had a vantage point, an acuteness of vision, that has provided a wider perspective on Australian life. Certainly this has better enabled UQP to respond to the regional differences in Australian writing and has allowed a greater empathy with the voice of the individual just starting out.

A university press should be a risk taker. It should be at the forefront of change. It should be involved with the difficult aspects of cultural expression and new writing. It should be concerned about standards and should also be a pacesetter and provide leadership. It should come as no surprise then that UQP strives conscientiously in all of these areas. As to the success of our endeavours, that is for others to judge.

This book attempts to chart our course to date and to provide some insight into the workings of UQP at critical times in its existence and to give personal voice to the individuals who developed UQP with passion and daring over the past half century. It does not attempt to be exhaustive or encyclopedic. Over the fifty years there have been many, many talented people who have made UQP into a publishing house that is respected and admired both nationally and internationally.

For those of us still rowing in the galleys of UQP we salute those who have been at the oars before us and we modestly hope that we have maintained and perhaps added to the proud legacy of UQP as an innovative and fiercely independent Australian publisher.

We hope too that whilst reading this somewhat unconventional history of UQP you not only enjoy it, but gain some inkling of the sense of achievement and pride in UQP's reputation as a writer's press.

Laurie Muller, A.M.
General Manager
September 1998

Acknowledgments

As a history with multiple voices and perspectives, this volume has been made possible by the encouragement and involvement of many colleagues, past and present. In particular, thanks are due to Laurie Muller and Frank Thompson for their enthusiasm and wide knowledge of the book trade. The University Librarian Janine Schmidt and her staff, including Fryer Librarian Ros Follett, supplied vital bibliographical data, and Cathy Leutenegger compiled the Appendix II guide to the UQP Archive in Fryer Library. Additional research and editorial assistance was provided by Joseph Crowley and Rebekah Scott as well as by principal editor Felicity Shea. By their efforts, the various contributors have created this history. Anne Galligan's advice and her patience in preparing the final overview chapter are also much appreciated.

Introduction and Chronology

CRAIG MUNRO

MY FAVOURITE UQP story actually predates the Press's formal establishment in 1948. In those far-away forties, the university published under its own coat of arms. This was the era of scorched-earth diplomacy, and the fabled 'Brisbane Line' probably bisected the St Lucia campus where the army had set up its Pacific headquarters. Just months before Pearl Harbour, and Japan's terrifying southward avalanche, the University of Queensland had the extraordinary foresight to issue a small insurance policy entitled, innocuously enough, *Japanese for Beginners* (1941).

The University of Queensland Press — UQP or, more familiarly, the Press — came of age as a publishing house much later than this. Officially constituted as a department in 1948, it continued to publish predominantly university materials until the 1960s. This academic tradition can be traced back to the First World War. Each year the university published an unexceptional trickle of books, lectures and journal offprints, with the most profitable lines being school exam papers.

Japanese for Beginners appealed to the Publications Committee but the lectures of respected painter and teacher Vida Lahey did not. (Twenty years later her niece, Ann Lahey, became the Press's first full-time editor.) A small anthology of Australian 'verse and literature', edited by Russian lecturer Nina Christesen, was likewise declined. (Later, the Russian-born Nina was mentioned adversely, with her husband — *Meanjin* editor Clem Christesen — in the notorious Petrov anti-Communist witchhunt.)

Preoccupied with war, the university's Committee passed up this opportunity to start a creative literature list as early as the 1940s. On the other hand, when the university was offered — over the telephone — a medical treatise euphemistically entitled 'The Nervous Soldier', its Committee did not hesitate, accepting also a small subsidy from the authors. Again, this was timely publishing, as many 'nervous' soldiers were then streaming back from the battle-front.

Such practical and scientific publishing continued right up until the late 1950s, with books and booklets on tropical fatigue, 'personality deviations' in pre-school children, calculus and trigonometry, fungi on algae, working class vocabulary, fluctuating sheep numbers, coral death, and dental caries in the albino rat.

As indicated in the Chronology that follows this Introduction, the Press's first Australian literary title was in 1959 — a celebration of Queensland writing for the state's centenary. Now, almost forty years on, the Press is distinguished by its literary list. As well as poetry, screenplays, literary fiction and non-fiction, UQP publishes several wide-ranging scholarly series and journals devoted to Australian Literature.

This volume celebrates — mainly with memoir and essay — UQP's fiftieth anniversary. It provides an opportunity to reflect on how a regional, university-based publisher has been able to survive and carve out such a distinctive identity in a few eventful decades.

From the 1960s UQP evolved well beyond its initial role as the university's publications arm, becoming a more culturally significant and innovative publisher on the national and even international stage. It is now firmly established as a leading Australian literary and scholarly house.

In the opening chapter, former manager Frank Thompson describes how this remarkable metamorphosis took place against a backdrop of Cold War conservatism. Even in the early 1970s, the first fiction titles were scrutinised by the university for explicit sexual content, with at least one highly talented young writer — Frank Moorhouse — taking his manuscript elsewhere.

As a cadet journalist I attended Frank Thompson's inspirational American Literature classes in 1971 and soon after began editing fiction for the Press. I was working not only with the Australian fiction of new writers Rodney Hall, David Malouf, Murray Bail and Peter Carey, but also with American 'buy-ins' like John Updike, Asian and Pacific fiction (brilliant Filipino Nick Joaquin was a favourite), and contemporary Russian writing in translation (featuring the exquisite work of Valentin Rasputin). Such editorially challenging variety came with the territory at this small, dynamic company.

To a largely desk-bound junior editor, it seemed that Frank Thompson was always travelling somewhere — either interstate for the Publishers' Association or overseas to book-fairs. He had become enthusiastic about the Russian series after an exploratory trip to Moscow. Such travel was indispensable to the evolution of UQP's often brilliant but always audaciously eclectic list.

Since the 1980s, and Frank's departure, UQP has become an 'Australian Studies' press, with a special focus on history as well as literature, and the opening up of two important areas: a quality children's list, and the ground-breaking

Indigenous list, supported by a range of Aboriginal writers and consultant editors such as Oodgeroo and Jack Davis.

The interview with Sandra Phillips in this collection outlines some of the issues confronting the editor of Indigenous writing, while another respected editor — Barbara Ker Wilson — writes of developing an award-winning young adult fiction list.

Among the other contributions, David Malouf and Martin Duwell discuss the genesis and evolution of UQP's incomparable poetry list, as does Roger McDonald who also strays into the tantalising, prehistoric world of audio-visual publishing ... when microfiche was whispered to be the coming thing.

Pearl Bowman writes of her remarkably effective distribution initiatives in North America and the pioneering efforts to introduce Australian authors and books to that vast but implacably parochial market.

Michael Wilding and D'Arcy Randall — both experienced editors and authors, as are many of the contributors to this volume — share their distinctively personal accounts of the hothouse atmosphere of fiction publishing from the masculinist seventies through the feminist eighties.

Historians Ray Evans and Denis Cryle assess UQP's scholarly publishing — past and present — as do literary scholars Laurie Hergenhan and Tony Hassall, themselves authors and general editors of key series. Anne Galligan brings to her overview chapter a background in librarianship and a measured assessment of the Press's progress, especially over the last three decades.

As the new millennium looms — with the Orwellian prospect of saturation electronic media — there is increased interest in the history of book-publishing enterprises in Europe, North America and Australia. Some see books joining the ever-lengthening list of endangered species, but publication has a very long history. The most venerable imprinted symbols in the world are still visible in this continent's ancient rock carvings.

By comparison, the book — or rather the hand-copied codex — is a mere two millennia old, while movable type has been around for only a few centuries. 'Hot metal' setting gave way to revolutionary 'cold type' as recently as the 1960s, and digital technology has further refined the process.

Smaller 'on-demand' photo-printers may one day enable the local bookshop to print instant books selected from an electronic database. And yet, despite all this ingenuity, it is still the codex book which remains the preferred 'delivery platform'. UQP has actively experimented with non-book publishing but, over time, books remain the familiar favourite — providing maintenance-free entertainment and engineered to last.

The Press has embraced and occasionally pioneered fashionable formats — large or small, paperback or hardback, sometimes both simultaneously — though its publishing philosophy has been remarkably consistent. Because of Frank Thompson's background — and that of his successor as general manager, Laurie Muller — the Press combines the traditions of a general publisher with the strong commitment to cultural and intellectual values found in the best North American university presses.

Laurie's own passion for politics, history and sport has encouraged the Press's further development of these areas, while his initiatives in children's publishing have resulted in an increasingly important new list.

Frequently in the public eye, the University of Queensland Press has never been afraid to publish adventurously and even courageously — especially during the darkest days of the Bjelke-Petersen regime. Politicians tend to dislike being immortalised in corruption-exposing accounts by fearless writers like Hugh Lunn, Ross Fitzgerald and Phil Dickie. It was such investigative reporting, along with that of the ABC's Chris Masters (son of novelist Olga Masters), which led to the revelations of the epoch-making Fitzgerald Inquiry.

Looking back from the sober if precarious vantage point of the late 1990s, it seems remarkable we ever survived the legal and literary minefields of those far-off days.

Accompanying Frank Thompson, Roger McDonald and sundry authors on their various escapades was always an education, the famous 1970s literary 'lunch' often extending deep into the evening.

Each new manuscript was also a journey of discovery. After blithely chopping up one novel's apparently meandering sentences, I was shocked at the author's irate reaction. I had failed to realise that such 'successive indirection' was actually a Henry Jamesian stylistic technique. So the long, languid sentences were duly reinstated.

Fiction editing is a tough assignment, but non-fiction means living with the ever-present danger of defamation. The term 'cunning as a shithouse rat', applied to a certain notorious Queensland Premier, was edited down to 'rat cunning' and finally emerged as 'animal cunning'. Our principal libel adviser Chris McKelvey once famously observed that, in any defamation suit, 'words are put in the same legal category as dangerous animals and explosives'.

While many professions lay claim to being the world's second-oldest, only publishing makes such a fuss over soliciting. As an editor and publisher it has been my professional duty to solicit manuscripts — often from complete strangers. On two memorable occasions I asked to see a collection after reading a single story. Neither author had published a book before and neither was personally known to me.

Each time it was like opening a literary time-bomb as I sat at my desk and unwrapped the parcel of manuscript. All I recall now was the intense thrill of discovery as I slowly began reading ... and reading. Story collections often have a few good pieces. But these were spectacular: the first collection was by Peter Carey (published as *The Fat Man in History*, 1974) and the second by Olga Masters (*The Home Girls*, 1982). For me, it was the beginning of literary friendships with authors whose careers became closely associated with the University of Queensland Press.

Such lasting friendships also developed with former journalists Hugh Lunn and Gerard Lee, authors of many entertaining works of fiction and non-fiction based on their experiences and travels. Gerard is now an award-winning film-maker while Hugh has specialised in memoir. His acclaimed Vietnam story grew out of his bestselling book on Bjelke-Petersen. While we worked together on that biography, Hugh told me many bizarre stories from his year as a Reuters correspondent in Vietnam at the height of the war. Over several years and countless cups of tea, those stories became *Vietnam: A Reporter's War* (1985). Hugh's next memoir, *Over the Top with Jim* (1989), tracing his Annerley Junction boyhood, became Australia's all-time bestselling childhood memoir following a popular ABC radio serialisation.

In championing the work of UQP's most prolific woman

novelist, Barbara Hanrahan, I was struck by her powerful vision and also by her artistic integrity. Uniquely, she was an acknowledged visual artist as well as a novelist, sometimes decorating her own fictional texts. With the publication of her sensational *Diaries* in 1998, Barbara's intensely confronting novels will undoubtedly be revalued in Australia; in Britain, where she lived for many years, her work has always been highly regarded. Like Olga Masters, Barbara died tragically in mid-career.

One of my enduring memories of Olga Masters is a scene from the Sydney book launch of *A Long Time Dying* (1985). Speaking after Tom Keneally, Olga tore strips off the local literati, including those present, for the unruly misbehaviour which had rendered that year's Premier's Awards dinner such a memorable fiasco. Publishers as well as authors had disgraced themselves, and Olga's tongue-lashing chastened us all.

Another shock awaited me, this time in Sydney's famed Marble Bar where I'd arranged to meet Barry Oakley. I had the cover proof of his autobiographical collection *Scribbling in the Dark* (1985) to show him. The design featured a specially commissioned caricature of Barry at his quizzical best — one eyebrow raised.

Staring at the proof, he raised both eyebrows and then his voice. 'I'll sue!' he exploded, somewhat theatrically. Barry is always amusing company, so I ordered him another drink, but on this occasion he proved impervious to bar-room bonhomie. He was adamant and, with the presses about to roll, another illustration had to be hastily substituted.

Because of the vast underworld of literary myth and legend, a comprehensive history of such a press as UQP would be impossible, even disregarding defamation. Yet a glance through the appendix — listing the two thousand books published by UQP since the 1940s — is most revealing. Every conceivable subject or genre is covered by authors from all over the globe. And the making of each of those books is a story in itself.

My successors as UQP fiction editor, D'Arcy Randall and Rosanne Fitzgibbon, have worked closely and creatively with many talented writers, as have Sue Abbey, poetry and Indigenous books editor, and children's editor Leonie Tyle. Such a team is indispensable, especially in literary publishing.

Over the years UQP has had numerous editors and editorial staff including freelance and consultant editors. Many have been influential in the Press's development. They include Ann Lahey, Shirley Hockings, Penny Rogers, Sue Pechey, Roger McDonald, Maria Nadalin, Merril Yule, Tom Shapcott, Tony Barker, Barbara Ker Wilson, Jacqui Katona, Helen Dash, Nicola Evans, Judy MacDonald,

Martin Duwell, Margaret Kennedy, Clare Forster, Bernadette Foley, Sandra Phillips and Felicity Shea.

Freelance cover designers include Cyrelle Birt, the prolific Christopher McVinish and Cynthia Breusch, Ted Poulter, Craig Glasson, Gregory Rogers (Kate Greenaway Medal winner), David Mackintosh, Michael Ward, Peter Evans and Kate Barry. Also Horsley Dawson (layout).

Current staff include Production Manager Terry Farley, with Paul Rendle and Karen Lennard, Sales Manager Robert Brown, with Rosemary Chay and Jeanette Mastenbroek, Editorial and Rights staff Eileen Sneath and Dinah Johnson, Finance Manager Keith McDonald, Chris Wall and Lydia Teo (Accounts), and Bookshop Manager Greg Spencer, with Christine Garrett, Nita Keig and Kathy Carlyon.

Chronology

[*Note:* Awards are cited under a book's year of publication. For a chronological list of all published books see Appendix I.]

1911–48: The University of Queensland was established in 1911. Its first published series, the Macrossan annual lectures, began in 1927 and the University Papers ten years later. In 1941, the year of Pearl Harbor, the university thoughtfully issued *Japanese for Beginners*.

Clockwise from top left:
Lane cover (1941); Naylor jacket (1948); Mathew cover (1961) featuring the university crest

1948: The University of Queensland Press was finally gazetted as a department on 13 March 1948, occupying a university demountable in George Street. The first manager was F. A. (Athol) Perkins (1897–1976), an entomologist and member of the university Publications Committee. During his term as part-time manager (1948–61), scientific titles comprised three-quarters of the Press's output. The first bestseller, however, was a study of Australian banking which stayed in print for decades. There were no full-time publishing staff until 1961.

1949: In January the Press opened its first bookshop in George Street. Another shop, at St Lucia, was built in the late 1950s on the Staff House Road site of the present Bookshop and Press.

1956: *A Study of the Oral Vocabulary of the [Australian Worker]*, by Fred (later Sir Fred) Schonell and others, was published jointly with the University of London Press. Schonell later became vice-chancellor (1960–69).

1958: The first literary critical title, on Thomas Mann, was by the German Department's Keith Leopold.

1959: The first Australian literary title, on Queensland writers (for the state's centenary), was by the English Department's pioneering Cecil Hadgraft.

1960: A study of Queensland Aboriginal children, at school and at home, was by the indefatigible Fred Schonell and others including Betty Watts.

1961: Frank W. Thompson became manager, Press and Bookshop (1961–83). With a US scholarly press background and literary interests, he transformed UQP into the country's largest, most innovative university press. In 1961 he published UQP's first original literary work, a play by Ray Mathew, launching the Contemporary Australian Plays series — the first of many literary series. Ann Lahey was appointed UQP's first editor (1961–77).

1962: Retaining its strong links with Queensland scholars, the Press began to attract new authors from the wider Australian community and from overseas.

1963: R.D. Lumb's text on Australian constitutional law appeared in the first of many editions. D. P. Singhal's *India and Afghanistan: A Study in Diplomatic Relations* was republished by Michigan State University Press (Frank Thompson's alma mater). A pioneering US rights sale, it was followed later by many more co-editions with a range of North American scholarly publishers.

1964: *Image in the Clay*, the first book by David Ireland (later an acclaimed novelist), was added to the UQP plays series. The original, 1829 edition of *The Hermit in Van Diemen's Land* by convict Henry Savery, Australia's first essayist and novelist, had cost its publisher 80 pounds in a libel suit. The new UQP edition was not so controversial. John Springhall's enduring classic *Elements of Horseshoeing* (still in print after 34 years) made its first appearance.

1965: Renowned Bribie Island artist Ian Fairweather translated and illustrated a popular early Chinese text, *The Drunken Buddha*, now highly prized by collectors. Cyrelle Birt was appointed first Production Manager (1965–80).

1966: Scientific titles dominated the UQP list for the last time. Larry Chapman was appointed first Sales Manager.

1967: The large-format Artists in Queensland series was launched, featuring writers and artists such as Judith Wright and Charles Blackman.

1968: In this memorable year UQP released its first Australian poetry anthology (edited by Rodney Hall and Tom Shapcott) along with its first volume of original verse, *Citizens of Mist* by

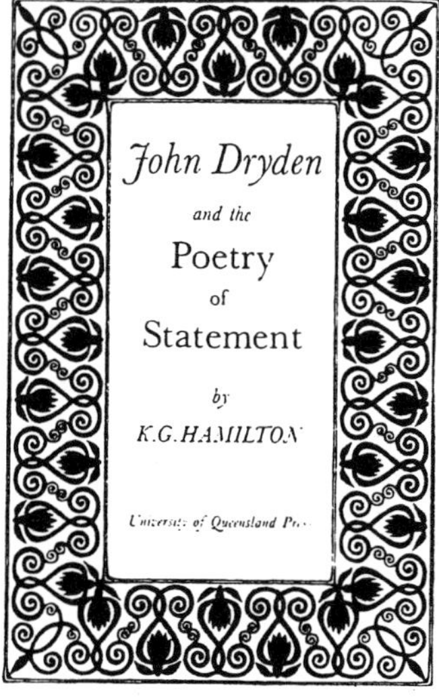

JAMES
BRUNTON
STEPHENS

CECIL HADGRAFT

UNIVERSITY OF QUEENSLAND
PRESS

Clockwise from top left: Hamilton jacket (1967); McDonald jacket (1968); Hadgraft title page (1969) featuring the Press's sunburst logo designed by Rick Ressom about 1964

(For designers of covers featured, see page 33)

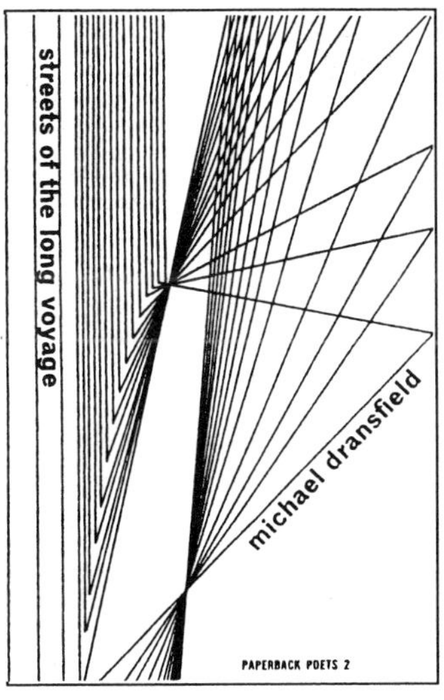

Strikingly graphic covers of the first three titles in the Paperback Poets series (1970)

Roger McDonald, who soon after became inaugural Poetry Editor (1969–76). In a more rustic vein, UQP began to republish Steele Rudd's many works. (Twenty years later, the four-volume hardback boxed set, with an introduction by the stalwart Cecil Hadgraft, was an unexpected bestseller.) Another 1968 initiative was microfilm publishing of theses, rare books and newspapers. The micro 'bestseller' was Richard Walsh's provocatively diverting *Nation Review*, closely followed by a rare archive of PNG newspapers.

1969: Cecil Hadgraft's study of early Queensland poet James Brunton Stephens was the Press's first major biography. The UQP Audio-Visual Division was established to produce a range of non-book teaching/reference materials and later audio-cassette series (including interviews with writers).

1970: The first three slim, dollar-a-copy Paperback Poets were published, featuring David Malouf, Michael Dransfield and Rodney Hall. The innovative Poets on Record series also began that year — each hardcover with a 45 rpm recording by its author.

1971: New poets, such as Andrew Taylor and J.S. (Jan) Harry, were again featured as well as recordings by Douglas Stewart and R.D. FitzGerald. John Manifold's 1960s poems were collected together, and a lavish, leather-bound edition of Alvarez poems was illustrated with Blackman gouaches.

1972: The first original UQP fiction was launched (in hardback and paperback editions): Michael Wilding's story collection *Aspects of the Dying Process* and Rodney Hall's satirical novel *The Ship on the Coin.* The first non-Australian literature series — Asian and Pacific Writing — began under the general editorship of Michael Wilding (later joined by Harry Aveling). As well as Indonesian fiction, the first list featured Filipino writer Nick Joaquin's powerful collection *Tropical Gothic.* This eclectic series drew authors

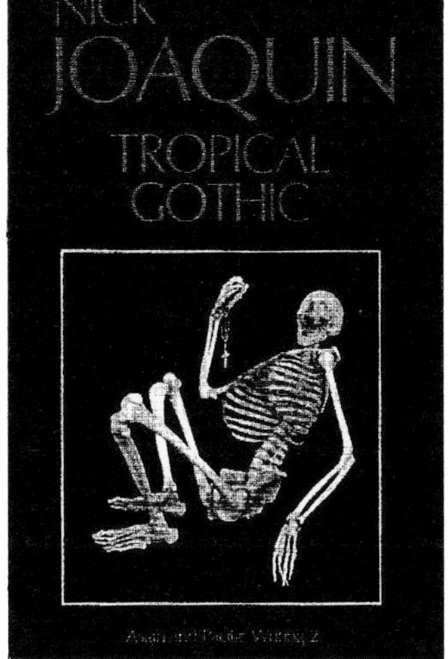

Dawe (1971) and Wright (1973) covers; the jacket for Joaquin's *Tropical Gothic*, launching the Asian and Pacific Writing series (1972)

from Fiji, Papua New Guinea, Korea, Bangladesh, China and Japan, and published the first English translation of a Thai novel. Six more Paperback Poets were released, including work by Rhyll McMaster (drawing Patrick White's rare praise) and Tom Shapcott.

1973: As well as production and sales staff, there were now several editors — covering fiction, poetry, scholarly books and audio-visual. Rodney Hall's *A Soapbox Omnibus* (one of the first books assisted by the new Literature Board) won the Grace Leven Poetry Prize.

1974: David Malouf's *Neighbours in a Thicket* won several awards including the Australian Literature Society's Gold Medal and the Grace Leven Poetry Prize. *The First Paperback Poets Anthology*, edited by Roger McDonald, showcased this burgeoning list. Michael Wilding's comic novel *Living Together* was published with a collection of short stories, *The Fat Man in History*, by a young unknown writer — Peter Carey.

1975: David Malouf's autobiographical novel *Johnno* launched his spectacular career in literary fiction. In political scholarship, Denis Murphy's landmark biography of early Labor Premier T. J. Ryan won the Colin Roderick Award.

1976: UQP's Portable Australian Authors series of teaching texts, under Laurie Hergenhan's general editorship, began with editions of Henry Lawson and Marcus Clarke. UQP's most successful text, *What Is This Thing Called Science?* by Alan Chalmers, was followed by numerous overseas editions and translations.

1977: More than 60 new titles covered education, sociology, sport, history, politics, economics, ecology and the environment, natural history, literature and biography.

1978: In the era of strongman Bjelke-Petersen, Hugh Lunn's controversial unauthorised biography set a UQP hardback sales

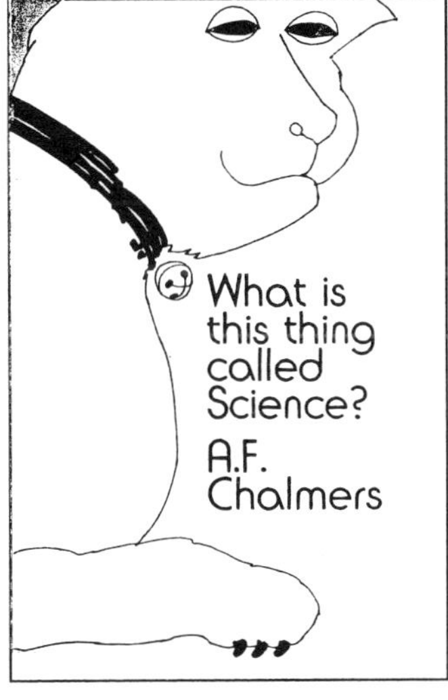

Covers of Lawson and Chalmers (1976), and the *1915* jacket (1979)

record. The Press's first book by an Aboriginal author was Kevin Gilbert's confronting poetry collection *People Are Legends*.

1979: Roger McDonald's bestselling Gallipoli novel *1915* won the *Age* Book of the Year and was successfully adapted as a television series. Peter Carey's second collection, *War Crimes*, confirmed his early reputation and led to international publication. The ambitious Contemporary Russian Writing series began, with translated fiction by Sergei Zalygin and Valentin Rasputin. Russian poetry also appeared on UQP's list, and non-Australian authors now featured across the catalogue.

1981: Peter Carey's first novel, *Bliss*, won not only the Miles Franklin Award but also the NBC Banjo Award and the Christina Stead Prize. Published extensively overseas, it was made into an award-winning feature film (the screenplay for which launched UQP's film series in 1986). UQP began the mammoth task of reprinting the dozen volumes of Bean's Official History of Australia in World War I and later published many war memoirs and histories, covering both world wars, Korea and Vietnam.

1982: A first story collection, *The Home Girls*, by Olga Masters won the coveted NBC Award. Greek-Australian poet Dimitris Tsaloumas also won this award in 1983 (for his dual-text volume *The Observatory*), a credit to translator Philip Grundy and also to poetry editor Tom Shapcott. Fay Zwicky's *Kaddish and Other Poems* won the Kenneth Slessor Prize, and Bob Endean's four-colour large-format study of the Great Barrier Reef sold well, especially in the US.

1983: The list ranged from Elizabeth Jolley's novel *Miss Peabody's Inheritance* to a study of Patrick White's fiction, two works on convictism, and a ballet memoir. Asia also featured, with a history of modern Thailand, a book on Papua New Guinean independence, and Ninotchka Rosca's Filipino stories. Linguist Bob

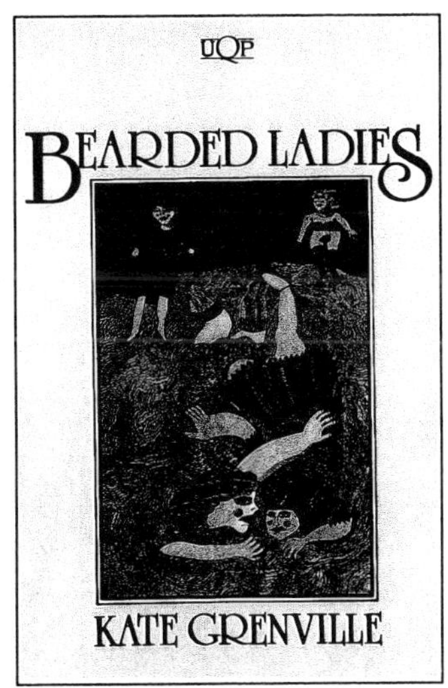

Three fiction jackets: for Carey (1981), Grenville (1984) and Masters (1984)

Dixon published his memoir *Searching for Aboriginal Languages*, about the tragic erosion of language and culture. Such variety was a fitting tribute to Frank Thompson, who left to become Rigby's publisher in Adelaide. He was succeeded as General Manager (Press & Bookshop) by Laurie Muller, Lansdowne's former chief executive.

1984: Penguin Books in Melbourne, with its own expanding Australian list, began to distribute UQP's new trade paperback imprint along with backlist titles. Olga Masters' first novel, *Loving Daughters*, shared the spotlight with *Bearded Ladies*, a story collection by new writer Kate Grenville, later a Vogel Award winning novelist. Olga Masters completed several books before her untimely death in 1986.

Ross Fitzgerald's controversial Queensland history had to be temporarily withdrawn from sale. In both original and reissued forms it contained matters of much interest to corruption Commissioner Tony Fitzgerald. Political life from an earlier era was dissected in Roger Joyce's landmark biography of Samuel Walker Griffith, state premier and founding father of the Australian Constitution.

1985: Prizewinners included Hugh Lunn's battlefront memoir, *Vietnam: A Reporter's War* (*Age* Book of the Year), Peter Carey's picaresque novel *Illywhacker* (four awards and a Booker Prize shortlisting), Victor Kelleher's futurescape novel *Beast of Heaven* (Ditmar Award), and John Gunn's inter-war history of Qantas, *The Defeat of Distance* (Colin Roderick Award).

1986: UQP's Young Adult Fiction list began, under the guidance of Barbara Ker Wilson (1997 Pixie O'Harris Award winner for distinguished service to children's books). *Blue Days* by Donna Sharp was shortlisted in the CBC awards, and Maureen Pople's

Jacket for Carey (1985), covers for Sharp (1986) and Dransfield (1987), all featuring the new UQP logo designed in the mid-1980s by Christopher McVinish

The Other Side of the Family was chosen *American School Library Journal* Best Book of the Year.

John A. Scott's *St Clair* won the C. J. Dennis Prize for Poetry, and Tom Boland's exemplary biography of Archbishop James Duhig took out both the Colin Roderick and Herb Thomas awards and later the prestigious Bicentennial Biography Prize. University Bursar Jim Tolhurst succeeded Deputy Vice-Chancellor Jim Ritchie as Chairman of the Press Board of Management.

1987: An 'Australian Studies' publishing policy confirmed UQP's strengths in history, literature and linguistics, including Aboriginal Studies. (*Aboriginal Music* by Catherine Ellis and *Religion in Aboriginal Australia* edited by Max Charlesworth and others had recently appeared.) The *Michael Dransfield Collected Poems* (edited by Rodney Hall) began a new collected series featuring, among others, Anthony Lawrence, Robert Adamson, Judith Rodriguez, David Malouf, Bruce Beaver, Andrew Taylor, Thomas Shapcott and Jennifer Rankin. Janette Turner Hospital won the FAW Australian Literature Award for her story collection *Dislocations*, while *King Wally*, Adrian McGregor's bestselling biography of Wally Lewis, set a new standard for rugby league books.

1988: Peter Carey's novel *Oscar and Lucinda* sold half a million copies worldwide after winning the Booker Prize, the Miles Franklin and many other major awards. Janette Turner Hospital's highly praised novel *Charades* was shortlisted for many key awards. John Tranter's *Under Berlin* won the Kenneth Slessor and Grace Leven poetry prizes, while Marion Halligan's story volume *The Living Hothouse* won the Steele Rudd award. Investigative journalist Phil Dickie's corruption-busting *Road to Fitzgerald* was published after rigorous legal scrutiny.

1989: Hugh Lunn's memoir of a well-spent boyhood, *Over the Top* *with Jim*, was serialised on radio and broke all sales records for such a story. (The sequel, *Head over Heels*, was also a bestseller.)

First titles in the new Studies in Australian Literature series (general editor Tony Hassall) were *Literature and the Aborigine* by J. J. Healy and *Black Words, White Page* by Adam Shoemaker. The latter won the Walter McCrae Russell Award for Literary Scholarship — an award UQP writers won six times in seven years, for studies of Joseph Furphy, Shaw Neilson, Brian Penton and Steele Rudd; also for Peter Kirkpatrick's *Sea Coast of Bohemia*. Leading prehistorian John Mulvaney looked at Aborigines and outsiders in *Encounters in Place*, and Jennifer Isaacs's *Aboriginality* introduced many to the masterpieces of contemporary Aboriginal art.

UQP initiated the national David Unaipon Award for Aboriginal and Torres Strait Islander writers. Inaugural judges were playwright Jack Davis, poet Oodgeroo and novelist Mudrooroo. The new Black Australian Writers series published award-winner Graeme Dixon's *Holocaust Island* collection and the first comprehensive anthology of Black writing, *Paperbark*. Among the writers introduced by the series were Wayne Coolwell, novelist Doris Pilkington (Nugi Garimara), and former drover Herb Wharton, now a novelist and storyteller.

1990: R.M.W. Dixon and Martin Duwell edited *The honey-ant men's love song and other Aboriginal song poems*, as performed by a range of singers from northern and central Australia. The unique 'triple' text layout was also used in their sequel collection, *Little Eva at Moonlight Creek* (1994).

1991: UQP published the Australian edition of Maori novelist Alan Duff's *Once Were Warriors* (later a powerful film). Joan Dugdale's novel *Struggle of Memory* won the Colin Roderick Award, and Gary Catalano's *The Empire of Grass* won the Grace Leven Poetry Prize. Gerard Lee and Jane Campion won the NSW

Covers for Dickie (1988), Lunn (1989) and *Sweetie* (1991)

Covers for two 1990 Aboriginal collections and Alan Duff's Maori novel *Once Were Warriors* (1991)

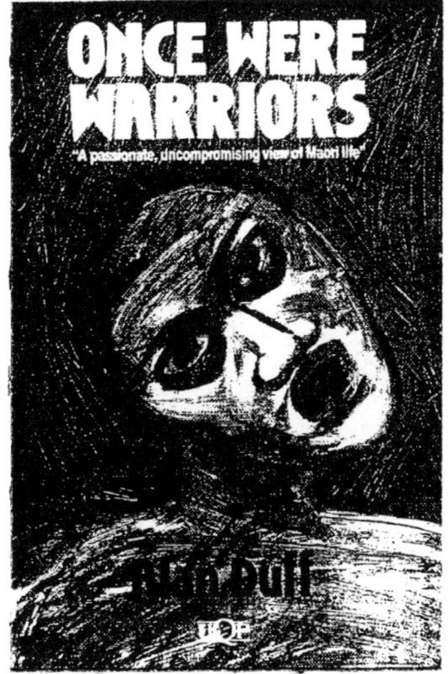

Premier's Award for Scriptwriting for *Sweetie* (UQP screenplay series).

1992: James Moloney's teenage novel *Crossfire* won the Family Award for Children's Literature (which he won again in 1993 and 1996). For her wryly funny story collection *What God Wants* Lily Brett received the Steele Rudd Award. Film writer-director Jocelyn Moorhouse took the Louis Esson Prize for her screenplay *Proof*.

1993: A new children's list — the Storybridge series — was launched to bridge the gap between younger books and teenage fiction. Michael Gordon's biography of Prime Minister Paul Keating shared the list with Richard Walsh's *Ferretabilia* (selections from *Nation Review*). Liam Davison won the NBC Banjo Award for his novel *Soundings*, while hoax-hunter Michael Heyward won the FAW Australian Literature Award and the A. A. Phillips Prize for unravelling *The Ern Malley Affair*. Laurie Muller received an NBC Gold Medal for services to publishing.

1994: UQP combined forces with picture-book publisher Jam Roll Press. Children's books contributed almost half the published output, now totalling up to 70 titles per year. On the local front, Wordsmiths: the Writers Cafe opened at the St Lucia Bookshop, with regular readings and launches.

Patrick Buckridge won the Colin Roderick Award (as well as the McCrae Russell) for his biography *The Scandalous Penton*, and UQP poet Dimitris Tsaloumas was honoured with the Patrick White Award. Bruce Beaver won the C. J. Dennis Prize for *Anima and Other Poems*. The Collected Stories list was launched with a Peter Carey volume, later augmented by volumes from Janette Turner Hospital, Olga Masters, Beverley Farmer, Thea Astley, Gillian Mears and Marion Halligan. Harry Gordon's definitive

Australia and the Olympic Games was an official publication for the Olympic movement.

1995: James Moloney's *Swashbuckler* (Storybridge series) was chosen CBCA Book of the Year for Younger Readers, while Brian Caswell's novel *Deucalion* won the Children's Peace Literature Award. The screenplay series published an episode from the multi-award-winning *Brides of Christ* TV series, scripted by John Alsop and Sue Smith (and produced by Sue Masters, daughter of Olga). Other key titles included a tribute to Oodgeroo, Hugh Lunn's China-watching memoir *Spies Like Us*, and Frank Brennan's *One Land, One Nation* on Mabo and native title.

1996: *A Bridge to Wiseman's Cove*, James Moloney's new teenage novel, was chosen as CBCA Book of the Year for Older Readers and also won the Children's Peace Literature Prize. Nick Earls' novel *After January* won the 3M Young People's Talking Book Award, and Anthony Lawrence won the Kenneth Slessor Poetry Prize for *The Viewfinder*. Eric Rolls' *Citizens* (on the Chinese and Australia) was published along with Sang Ye's oral history *The Year the Dragon Came*, Noel Loos's *Edward Koiki Mabo* and Cassandra Pybus's *The White Rajah*. Judith Beveridge's long-awaited new poetry volume *Accidental Grace* appeared, as did a collection of essays presented to Professor Laurie Hergenhan on his retirement.

The first volume in the new Academy Editions of Australian Literature series was a scholarly edition of Henry Kingsley's classic novel *Geoffry Hamlyn*. Other works of textual scholarship in the series include novels by Henry Handel Richardson and Marcus Clarke, and the lively *Journal of Annie Baxter Dawbin, 1858–68*.

1997: Peter Carey's teasingly Dickensian novel *Jack Maggs* shared the bestseller lists with Gough Whitlam's *Abiding Interests*. *Jack Maggs* won the *Age* Book of the Year for Fiction and went on to win the Commonwealth Writers Prize and the Miles Franklin

Award. First novels by Aboriginal authors Alexis Wright (*Plains of Promise*) and Melissa Lucashenko (*Steam Pigs*) were both shortlisted for the Commonwealth Writers Prize (Asia-Pacific region) as well as other major awards. *Steam Pigs* won the 1998 Dobbie Award. Anne Whitehead's rich tapestry of history and travel, *Paradise Mislaid*, won the 1998 NSW Premier's History Prize. The historic collection *Our Land Is Our Life: Land Rights — Past, Present and Future* was edited by Galarrwuy Yunupingu. Rosalind Kidd's compelling indictment of government maladministration of Aboriginal Affairs, *The Way We Civilise*, was reprinted before publication. Rosamond Siemon's *The Mayne Inheritance* provocatively laid bare not just Brisbane's scandalous early history but also a skeleton in the university's closet.

Kim Toft's environmental children's picture book, *One Less Fish*, set a UQP first-printing record, with large orders from a US co-publisher and from book clubs. (At the time of going to press, it was also shortlisted for the CBCA's Eve Pownall Award for information books.)

1998: Celebratory publishing includes this 50th anniversary History along with anthologies of the best UQP short stories and poetry. Selected UQP classic reissues incorporate a specially designed UQP symbol (also used on the jacket of this History). Other highlights are memoirs by Michael Wilding (*Wildest Dreams: A Selective Memoir*), Dulcie Deamer (*Queen of Bohemia*), Alex Saranin (*Child of the Kulaks*) and Cassandra Pybus (*Till Apples Grow on an Orange Tree*), the first major biography of Xavier Herbert (by Frances de Groen), and the controversial diaries of writer and artist Barbara Hanrahan (1939–91), edited by Elaine Lindsay. Eric Rolls's *Celebration of Food & Wine* is now available in a single-volume edition. The film tie-in edition of UQP's all-time bestseller, Peter Carey's *Oscar and Lucinda*, appeared alongside Laura Jones's screenplay adaptation.

UQP's web site is now available at
http://www.uq.edu.au/austsc/UQP/

The paperback covers and hardback jackets reproduced in this Chronology were designed by:

Cyrelle Birt (*John Dryden* and *Citizens of Mist*, p. 16; p. 17 all; *Dawe* and *Wright*, p. 19)

Norman Birrell (*Tropical Gothic*, p. 19)

Ted Poulter (*Lawson* and Chalmers, p. 21)

Christopher McVinish (*1915*, p. 21; Grenville and Masters, p. 23; *Illywhacker*, p. 25)

Cynthia Breusch (*Loving Daughters*, p. 23; *Blue Days*, p. 25)

Gregory Rogers (Dransfield, p. 25; Dixon & Duwell, p. 29)

Craig Glasson (*Sweetie*, p. 28; *Once Were Warriors*, p. 29)

Kirsty-Ann Allen (*Road to Fitzgerald* and *Over the Top with Jim*, p. 28)

Peter Evans (*Paperbark*, p. 29)

Contributors

Pearl Bowman has had a long career in book publishing and is now an administrator at the Graduate School of the City University of New York in Manhattan. She has recently represented a number of smaller British publishers in the US and writes reviews for the literary journal *Antipodes.*

Denis Cryle is a Senior Lecturer at Central Queensland University. His publications include *The Press in Colonial Queensland: 1845–1875* (UQP, 1989) and, with Dimity Dornan, *The Petrie Family: Building Colonial Brisbane* (UQP, 1992). He is currently working on a history of Queensland Literature.

Martin Duwell is a Lecturer in English at the University of Queensland. He was an editor of *The Penguin New Literary History of Australia* (1988) and author of *A Possible Contemporary Poetry* (Makar Press, 1982). He co-edited, with R.M.W. Dixon, two volumes of Aboriginal song poems. Prior to working on the UQP poetry list, he edited the literary journal *Makar.*

Raymond Evans is an Associate Professor with the University of Queensland Department of History. He has published widely on the history of Australian race relations, gender relations, popular culture and wartime homefront relations. His latest book is *1901: Our Future's Past. Documenting Australia's Federation* (1997).

Anne Galligan is a tutor and doctoral student at the University of Southern Queensland. Her M.Phil. thesis 'The Australian Author in a Web of Change: Authorship and Publishing 1972–1997', which was completed in 1997, included a study of UQP. She is currently continuing her research on the culture of contemporary publishing in Australia.

Anthony Hassall is Professor of English Literature at James Cook University and founding general editor of the UQP Studies in Australian Literature series. He has published extensively on Australian Literature and eighteenth-century English Literature. His most recent book is a revised edition of *Dancing on Hot Macadam: Peter Carey's Fiction* (UQP, 3rd edition 1998).

Laurie Hergenhan is Professor Emeritus of Australian Literature at the University of Queensland. He edits the journal he founded in 1963, *Australian Literary Studies*, and is general editor of UQP's Australian Authors series. His study of convict fiction, *Unnatural Lives*, was reissued in 1993, and his study of Hartley Grattan, *No Casual Traveller*, was published by UQP in 1995.

Barbara Ker Wilson has enjoyed a long career in publishing in both England and Australia. She has edited mainly work for young readers and has written some thirty books including picture books, teenage novels and two adult novels. A consulting editor for UQP, she won the 1997 Pixie O'Harris Award for distinguished service to children's books.

Roger McDonald has worked as an editor and ABC producer. After leaving UQP in 1977, he lived for some years at Braidwood and now divides his time between there and Sydney. Author of six novels, two books of poetry and various other titles, he has also written for television, including an adaptation of his award-winning novel *1915* (UQP, 1979). His non-fiction work *Shearer's Motel* won the 1993 Banjo Award. *Mr Darwin's Shooter* (1998) is his most recent novel.

David Malouf's novels include *Johnno* (UQP, 1975), *An Imaginary Life* and *The Great World* which won the 1991 Commonwealth Writers Prize. His novels have won many major national and international awards. UQP has published five collections of his award-winning poetry, and he has also written several opera libretti.

Sandra Phillips is a University of Queensland graduate and has taught at the University of Technology Sydney, the Sydney University Koori Centre and Tranby Aboriginal College. In Sydney she co-edited *Racism, Representation and Photography* (1994). She worked as an editor at Magabala Books in Broome and as Indigenous editor for UQP before moving to the Australia Council as a program manager.

D'Arcy Randall, formerly UQP fiction editor, has had her poetry, articles and reviews published in Australian, Canadian and US journals and newspapers. She co-founded the journal *Borderlands: Texas Poetry Review* and is now a doctoral candidate at the University of Texas at Austin.

Frank Thompson has spent virtually all his working life in book publishing. From Michigan State University Press, he migrated to Australia and was production manager at Angus & Robertson, a marketing representative for Prentice-Hall International, manager at UQP, general manager of Rigby Publishers, publishing manager at the Institute of Aboriginal and Torres Strait Islander Studies, and, before his retirement, director of publishing and marketing at the Australian Government Publishing Service.

Michael Wilding is the author of a dozen volumes of fiction including four UQP titles: *Aspects of the Dying Process* (1972), *Living Together* (1974), *The West Midland Underground* (1975) and *Wildest Dreams: A Selective Memoir* (1998). His other titles include *Pacific Highway, The Paraguayan Experi-*

ment, *This Is for You*, and *Somewhere New: New & Selected Stories*. He holds a personal chair in English and Australian Literature at Sydney University and is a Fellow of the Australian Academy of the Humanities.

Creating a Press of National Value

FRANK W. THOMPSON

MY FAMILY ON BOTH SIDES has its roots in the United States dating back to the eighteenth century and perhaps earlier. They formed part of the great westward expansion in the nineteenth century until they were stopped by the Pacific Ocean. I was born in Long Beach and grew up in Los Angeles. Later, I was to pick up where my grandfathers had left off and continue moving west to Australia.

I received my tertiary education at Michigan State University, where I studied Literature and Economics and earned a BA and an MA. Although my studies and my involvement in student writing as fiction editor of the university magazine were ideal for a career in publishing, it was my intention to become an academic. While in graduate school, however, I began working part-time for the Michigan State University Press in the warehouse packing books. The Director of the Press, Lyle Blair, was an Australian who had come to the Press a few years earlier after a short but distinguished publishing career in London with Jonathan Cape immediately after the war.

To my profound amazement, after a rather lengthy drinking session at a local bar, during which Blair had described life in academia as an exercise in taking in each other's laundry, he offered me a publishing job at Michigan State University Press. Thus began my career as Assistant to the Director and four turbulent years of hard-edged training in all aspects of publishing. These years were so intense, so frustrating and so fraught that even today, forty-five years later, I remember them with a combination of terror and pleasure.

I owe Lyle Blair an enormous debt of gratitude. Not only did he give me the training to ply my trade professionally and confidently but it was at his suggestion and with his blessing that I climbed aboard a Qantas Constellation in September 1958, a couple of days after my twenty-sixth birthday, to start a new life in Australia.

Aside from a short stint teaching at Manly Boys High School, my first Australian job was as a shop assistant at Angus & Robertson. I didn't like it much and as I banged books together, wielded the feather duster and put the titles in alphabetical order I dreamt of going home. But I learned a lot about bookselling in spite of myself. After six months I was transferred to publishing. Through a combination of unlikely events, I found myself with John Ferguson running the entire production department. We were both rather ignorant about production technicalities, but with 150 titles pumping through a year we learned fast.

I was very happy but broke. Angus & Robertson had a certain Scottish Presbyterian reluctance to expose its staff to the temptations of wealth, and so in 1960 I left to become Prentice-Hall's first Australasian tertiary marketing representative. As a result of contacts made while visiting the University of Queensland, I was invited to apply for the position of Manager of the University of Queensland Press and Bookshop and I served in this capacity for the next twenty-two years.

I left UQP in 1983 to become General Manager of Rigby Publishers in Adelaide. Contingent on the sale of Rigby to Kevin Weldon and its transfer to Sydney, I left Adelaide in 1985 and moved to Canberra to become the Publishing Manager for the Institute of Aboriginal and Torres Strait Islander Studies. In 1986 I joined the Australian Government Publishing Service as Director of Publishing and Marketing, a position I held in one form or another until my retirement in 1993. In 1994 I was made an Honorary Life Member of the Australian Book Publishers Association for my contributions to literary publishing and to the Association, having been President in 1971/72 and a member of its Board for fifteen years.

My appointment to the Press in April 1961 was the direct result of a committee of inquiry into the operations of the Press and Bookshop which began in 1959 under the chairmanship of Reg Gynther, head of the Department of Accounting. The committee had concluded that most of the problems were confined to the Bookshop and were the result of a lack of professional management. Although I suspect the members of the selection committee were aware my real interest lay in publishing rather than bookselling, they felt my limited experience as a bookstore shop assistant and subsequent work as a tertiary textbook representative was sufficient to tackle the Bookshop problems.

In fact, those problems while severe were reasonably simple to solve. I culled the dead stock, opened the shop up to browsers and made it more user friendly, called on every academic I could find, making notes of their complaints, and created the position of Buyer and hired a professional bookseller to fill it. The first person in this position was Ron Dingley who had been my boss in the technical department at Angus & Robertson's bookshop. He was succeeded eighteen months later by Frank Sandison who came from a distinguished career at the Queensland Book Depot. From that time on, thanks to Ron's and Frank's superb professionalism, apart from the occasional hiccup now and then the Bookshop ceased to be a major problem.

The Press was a much bigger challenge. It was a very small operation in 1961. Prior to my arrival it was run part-time by the Reader in Entomology, Athol Perkins. Indeed, the entire staff consisted of Perkins and his departmental secretary and they ceased all connection with the Press on my arrival. In the preceding year only three books had been published and sales were well under $15 000. Most of the Press's publishing was confined to scientific papers and official publications, such as faculty handbooks and the university calendar. Perhaps because of its low profile there was a rather poor opinion of the Press among many academics, particularly within the senior ranks. This rather depressing attitude was even more widely held in the university's administration. Early strong advocates for the Press were scarce on the ground and in fact I can recall only three: Professor T. G. H. Jones from Chemistry, who was Chairman of the Publications Committee, Reg Gynther in Accounting, and perhaps most importantly Sir Fred Schonell, the Vice Chancellor.

It was also rather lonely professionally with only one other publishing house in the entire state. This was Jacaranda and its founder and driving force, Brian Clouston, became a lifelong mate. Without those long lunches with Brian where he dispensed advice and encouragement and without his willingness to lend valuable staff to assist in the inevitable early crises, I am certain my life and the future of UQP would have been much bleaker.

On my arrival I found not only did I literally have no staff, except Bookshop staff, but I had no place to put a desk and a chair. Furthermore, travel (essential in publishing) was not considered by the administration to be part of my job; the entire Press and Bookshop organisation was committee-ridden and little could be done without the permission of the Publications Committee which met infrequently; there was no publishing philosophy; and, worst of all, there were no manuscripts. I was still very excited about my new job but I was beginning to realise it was not going to be easy. It was at this point that I received the best advice I ever had. Reg Gynther said to me, 'Universities are run on precedent. You don't know yet what the precedents are. I suggest you start running as fast as you can until they stop you.'

I wrote to the Registrar, by hand, explaining that I needed somewhere to sit and a secretary. I was given the auditor's office but told I would have to vacate it when the auditor returned in a month's time. I wrote again, in a badly deteriorating hand, that I needed a secretary. Silence. The third memo was barely readable except for the word 'secretary' and my name. The Registrar rang me and said I was being difficult. I told him that if he gave me a secretary with a degree I would train that person to be an editor. To my profound joy they not only listened but transferred Ann Lahey to the Press. Ann possessed not just a degree but editorial experience with Readers Digest as well. Although she had to do some office duties until I managed to get an actual secretary, Ann became our first editor and one of our finest.

Before the auditor returned a small office was found for us in the General Purposes Hut. The students' weightlifting club was in the next room and Ann and I often found our concentration broken by grunts, oaths and assorted noises as well as the rich pong of sweat on steamy Brisbane summer afternoons.

Early on I had been encouraged by Sam Ure Smith to join the Australian Book Publishers Association and I made sure the Press became a member shortly after my arrival. I had noticed that if one said more than a few words at meetings, one ended up on a committee and committee members had their fares paid to attend meetings. So by the end of 1961 the travel problem had been solved.

The Publications Committee itself was a more difficult problem. It was used to having its way and the virtual running of the Press was firmly in its hands. After a couple of meetings it was clear I was going to have difficulty gaining control of the Press. I started with the selection of readers for manuscripts, a prerogative the Committee had always seen as its own. I pointed out that because the academic community leaked like a sieve, it was likely authors knew who were reviewing their manuscripts. Since readers could not be assured of anonymity, they were unlikely to submit reports which were unfavourable or, at least, strictly objective. My argument was reinforced by a rather heated feud which had broken out between a reader and an author not long before. I also told them that a well-known reader with a big reputation did not necessarily guarantee a useful and timely report. I suggested that since I had no vested interest other than the welfare of the Press the choice of readers for all manuscripts be mine and that, while the reports would be tabled at Committee meetings, the identity of the readers would be known only to me and the Chairman of the Committee. After a good deal of heated discussion, they bought it. (No doubt I was aided by the fact that I had taken the trouble to discuss the idea with the Chairman prior to the meeting.)

This was the first of many such battles and it took a number of years of incremental changes until the Publications Committee became, under the enlightened chairmanship of Deputy Vice-Chancellor Jim Ritchie, a Board of Directors with overall responsibility for policy formulation and financial monitoring, and I was given total freedom to make all publishing decisions. It was not easy and it meant putting my job on the line more than once. I was fortunate in that I could truthfully say I was hired as a professional publisher and I could not do my job without making everyday publishing decisions free from interference by people who were not professional publishers. During one heated exchange I told one of the professors of medicine I didn't tell him how to do brain surgery and in turn it was not his job to tell me what to publish or how to publish. It was perhaps not the smartest or most tactful remark I ever made, but to my eternal gratitude the university managed to tolerate my youthful brashness and I, in turn, came to respect and admire the university. Indeed, I believe the University of Queensland learned faster and understood better than its sister universities the value of a good press. This encouragement and support helped to ensure our success.

I was concerned neither the Press nor the Publications Committee had any clear-cut philosophy on what we should be publishing. It seemed to me that without such a philosophy (or what would be called these days a mission statement) I was vulnerable to the whims of the Committee which, like most university committees, frequently changed its composition. There were, of course, some givens in that we published scholarly books, official publications, some occasional papers and a number of journals. I discussed the problem with the Chairman and suggested to him that I formulate a statement which we could discuss at the next committee meeting.

My problem was I needed something which would satisfy the scholars within the academic community but which would also be broad enough to give me the freedom to move into other areas. As an American I had been accustomed to university presses publishing beyond the narrow confines of academia. Michigan State University Press, for example, had been the first American publisher of the distinguished Indian novelist R. K. Narayan. The argument I brought to the Committee was that all Australian universities were (at that time) funded by taxpayers and therefore had a wider community responsibility, that part of this responsibility lay in encouraging cultural initiatives, and that one way of doing this was to publish in cultural areas neglected by commercial publishers. A fairly broad and flexible philosophy was necessary because cultures were dynamic and such areas of neglect changed over time. To my relief the Committee endorsed my words which were (from memory): 'The University of Queensland Press is dedicated to publishing works of a scholarly nature as well as books of general cultural interest to the community at large.' This became our philosophical guideline during the whole time I was at UQP.

There was still one big problem. We had no manuscripts and no one was particularly interested in offering us their work because no one outside of the University of Queensland knew we existed. I decided to attack the problem on two fronts. On the scholarly side I knew from my time at Prentice-Hall that there was a reluctance on the part of academics to submit their work to their own Press for fear it would appear they couldn't get published anywhere else. I also knew, however, that most academics had a yellowing PhD thesis or an esoteric study mouldering in the bottom drawer of their filing cabinet which they would dearly love to see published. One of my first tasks, therefore, was to find out where the academics drank and socialised and to join them over a convivial glass or two. This turned out to be The Royal Exchange Hotel in Toowong, affectionately known in those days as The Grey Ghost. As a result of this networking, we soon had a few manuscripts on offer. I knew they wouldn't sell in great quantities, but I also knew if the content was good and I did a good editing, design and production job we would get favourable reviews in the scholarly journals which in turn would bring us to the attention of possible future authors. The first title was Nick

Tarling's *Anglo-Dutch Rivalry in the Malay World 1780–1824*. I hasten to point out that this was, in fact, an excellent book and not only was it reviewed widely and favourably, but we sold an edition to Cambridge University Press in the UK.

My second plan of attack was to push into those creative cultural areas I had persuaded the Publications Committee to accept. I had been very taken with Ray Lawler's *Summer of the Seventeenth Doll*, it being the first Australian play I had seen following my arrival in this country. I had also been told it signalled a revival of Australian drama, yet with the exception of a few plays rather grudgingly published by Angus & Robertson there appeared to be no effort to get new Australian plays in print and easily available. I thought unless something were done about the so-called Australian drama revival, it would not last long. We were extremely fortunate in having one of the great scholars of Australian drama in the English Department. Eunice Hanger was not just well versed in the scholarly study of Australian plays, she was also an enthusiastic champion of contemporary Australian theatre and very active in the Brisbane theatre scene. We teamed up and the series Contemporary Australian Plays was begun. Our first play, produced in a cheap, early-Penguin-style paperback format, was Ray Mathew's *A Spring Song* which was published towards the end of 1961 — my first year at the Press. It was a good play and is still going strong.

(My wife and I saw an excellent performance in Canberra in 1995.) This was followed by David Ireland's first published work, a play called *Image in the Clay*, which has been reprinted several times. Many more titles followed over the years until I tried to sign up David Williamson for one of his first successful plays, *Don's Party*, only to find that Katharine Brisbane from Currency Press had got in ahead of me. I reasoned that if a publishing house had emerged solely to publish drama it was probably time to move on to more neglected areas.

In the early 1960s few publishers were interested in doing art books, probably because of the high production costs involved. Sam Ure Smith was the only mainstream publisher working in that field and most of his resources were focused on his journal *Art and Australia*. My friendship with Sam and the informative discussions I had with him about Australian art led to my interest in the subject, and this was heightened through my close friendship with the then university architect, Jim Birrell. Jim had written a critical biography of the architect Walter Burley Griffin, and we worked closely together to produce in 1964 what I still think was one of UQP's most significant books. When we weren't working on the book, we were arguing about art, and I discovered not only did Jim know a lot about contemporary Australian art, he also personally knew many of its creators.

In 1965 we published Ian Fairweather's *The Drunken Buddha* which was his translation of an early Chinese fable illustrated with twelve magnificent paintings done especially for the book. Through Jim Birrell I had met Laurie Thomas who was then the Director of the Queensland Art Gallery. Laurie had given me great encouragement to push on with *The Drunken Buddha* despite its cost and its difficult author. In those days Fairweather was not as well known as he is now and the Sunday tabloids portrayed him as a loony hermit who lived in the bush on Bribie Island and thought he was an artist. I am very proud to have published *The Drunken Buddha* and I hope it assisted in its small way to encourage an appreciation of what a great artist Ian Fairweather was.

Jim also introduced me to another artist who became a lifelong friend, Charles Blackman. Charles and Barbara had arrived back from several years in London in early 1966 and were living in an old Queensland house not far from the university. In talking to Charlie it occurred to me that a number of artists had their start in Queensland, as he had, or had come from Queensland originally. Yet for the most part this was either not acknowledged or was passed over as unimportant. Out of this I developed the idea for a series on Artists in Queensland which we called our Focus series. Appropriately, in 1967 the first title to be published in the series was *Focus on Charles Blackman*, written on commission by another eminent Queenslander, Tom Shapcott. We followed with titles on Andrew Sibley, Milton Moon, Ray Crooke and, branching into poetry, Judith Wright and David Rowbotham. We continued to publish art books until I left the Press in the 1980s, but by that time it had become a crowded field.

The Artists in Queensland concept was in fact part of a larger view I had about the role of university presses, particularly those located away from the major publishing and population centres. The cultural life of any nation is greater than what takes place in its largest cities, but because of market size mainstream publishing tends to ignore regional interests. I felt one of the major contributions the University of Queensland Press could make to its immediate community was to publish books about Queensland. Although the Focus series was the only regional series, as such, we published, we actively sought and commissioned works of interest to the Queensland community. As a result, we produced a large number of Queensland-oriented titles over a very broad spectrum including the applied sciences, the social sciences, economics, biography and especially history.

Yet another good companion of those early days was a young ABC television producer working at the local Brisbane studio. His name was Roger McDonald and we used to meet often after work over a few pots at the Royal Exchange for heated arguments about writing. As we got to know each other better, Roger showed me some poems he had been working on. I had done a lot of work as a graduate student on F. Scott Fitzgerald and I was fascinated by the way Roger's imagination was triggered by his feel for Australian history just as Fitzgerald's had been by American history. Ashamed of my ignorance of Australian history, I had monitored Roger Joyce's Australian history course and had read extensively in the area, somewhat discouraged by how boring most of the then published material was. Roger McDonald's poetry excited me and showed me that Australian history was not so dull after all. It also rekindled my interest in poetry. I told Roger that if he could produce enough poetry to make a book, he had a publisher. It was to be several years before he had accumulated enough poems that passed his stringent standards of quality and we were able to publish our first poetry volume, *Citizens of Mist*, in 1968.

In fact 1968 was a banner year for us in poetry publishing because we also published Rodney Hall's and Tom Shapcott's anthology of contemporary poetry, *New Impulses in Australian Poetry*. It was a highly significant book because it heralded the renaissance of poetry in this country. Its success took us all by surprise. Both Hall and Shapcott had been extremely annoyed by the delay in publishing while we waited for a Commonwealth Literary Fund grant, no publisher in those days being willing to take a punt on poetry without a grant because the accepted wisdom was poetry did not sell. They were convinced the delay had ruined any sales we might make, because, they argued with some justification, the impulses were no longer new. But in fact the sales of *New Impulses* forced us into a reprint within a remarkably short time, and into a paperback reprint at that — an unheard of occurrence. Even *Citizens of Mist* sold out and we were launched on one of the major voyages of the University of Queensland Press.

Our entry into poetry publishing could not have been better timed. Few publishers were interested in handling poetry because of the difficult economics involved. Angus & Robertson had what little market there was and most of the well-known names. But almost all of these names belonged to an older generation which had come of age either before or during the war. Aside from our friendly rivals in the city, Jacaranda Press, very few publishers had attempted more than the occasional volume by a younger poet. There were good reasons for this. The poetry market was seen as small, and conventional wisdom dictated lavish design, paper and binding to help make the comparatively high retail price, necessitated by a small print run, more palatable. The few publishers chancing their arm with poetry (the Press included) also insisted on a Commonwealth Literary Fund grant as a hedge against the inevitable loss poetry incurred. There were, however, some real problems connected with CLF grants which in fact militated against their avowed purpose of encouraging cultural publishing. First, they were very slow in approving grants, which made it difficult to catch the wave of interest a young writer might be receiving, and a publisher ran the risk of either losing a good manuscript or losing a potential market opening. Second, the grants were made as a subsidy against loss which meant the book had to be priced at a level that allowed a return to the CLF should it sell sufficient quantities to break even. This encouraged the slim expensive volume mind-set and the self-fulfilling prophecy that poetry books did not sell.

Few realised the market had changed. In 1969 David Malouf came to see me with a poetry manuscript. I was very excited by it and really anxious to publish, but David was adamant that it had to be a paperback. I feared we would end up with an expensive paperback that would be rejected by a market used to paperbacks at very cheap prices. David remained stubbornly rock solid. What to do? It occurred to me we had several poetry manuscripts under consideration and we had recently purchased an IBM typesetting typewriter which was capable of passable imitations of conventional typefaces. I called in our production manager and asked her what the per-copy production cost would be if we set the manuscripts in-house ourselves and printed 1000 copies of four titles simultaneously. After some scribbling on the back of an envelope (in those pre-calculator days), she came up with 25 cents a copy. I told David we had a deal, and Paperback Poets were born at a retail price of $1.00. They were an instant success and sold in their thousands to a young market rebelling against the Vietnam War and eager to read and listen to the words of their peers rather than their elders.

By the end of the 1960s the Press had certainly grown beyond what the university at the beginning of the decade had envisaged. We were publishing close to forty book titles a year and we had a staff of fifteen. One of the most important additions to our staff in terms of impact on our reputation as a literary publisher was Roger McDonald. Before *Citizens of Mist* was published in 1968, Roger had been transferred to Hobart. He wrote to me and said he felt it was time to leave the ABC and would like very much to get into publishing. Did I know anyone in the business who would be willing to give him a go? I did and his name was Frank Thompson. It looked to me as if poetry could become a significant part of our list and Roger would make the perfect poetry editor. Unfortunately, the university was not as convinced as I was that poetry was important enough to justify an editor's salary. I knew if I put up the creation of a poetry editor position it would be knocked back. However, I also knew the university was keen on new technology and I could convince them that new ways of imparting information was an important next step for us. Who better to become the new audio-visual editor than the bright young ABC television producer in Hobart? Roger, in fact, filled both roles with distinction. Not only did we develop, largely through his efforts, the best poetry list in Australia, but we also became early and major players in non-book publishing.

In 1964 John Strugnell from the English Department asked me if I would be interested in helping him form a course in American Literature. Although my degrees were in English Literature, I had taken a large number of courses in American Literature at both undergraduate and graduate level. I also had some experience as a tutor in English at Michigan State University and as a teacher at Manly Boys High School. Given the direction I was trying to take the Press, it was a terrific opportunity and I jumped at it, although it meant increasing my workload by about 50 per cent in the early years. Together John and I decided which authors we each felt best qualified to teach and divided the lecturing load fairly evenly between us. The ten years or so I spent teaching American Literature turned out to be one of the most enjoyable experiences of my life. It meant I was in constant contact with my market, the young generation of readers and thinkers who were buying and reading the kinds of books I was publishing. As an added bonus the course attracted a large number of young writers — like Roger McDonald, Tom Shapcott, Rodney Hall, Craig Munro and others — which helped my networking no end and kept me intellectually in touch with what was going on in Australian letters.

Unfortunately, the course became so popular that coping with it and the main game of the Press became increasingly difficult. We started with only a small number of students and were able to run the lectures almost like tutorials with lots of give and take, but by the mid-1970s class numbers were huge and the lectures had become formal affairs with the same lecture being given several times a week in large lecture halls, with little student contact. I was also by then often travelling overseas for weeks at a time and John was constantly having to fill in for me. There were now people in the English Department better qualified to do what I had been doing and in the end I was not sorry to give it up.

The Press expanded so rapidly in the 1960s it was difficult to keep up with the volume of work being generated by such a wide-ranging and large list. When I started in 1961, trained staff (if one were allowed to hire them) were difficult to find because there were so few active publishers in Australia. To a large extent I trained the staff myself and most times it was the classical case of the pupil surpassing the master. At least I chose the raw candidates well! One student of mine who had impressed me with his quiet abilities and genuine feel for writing, perhaps partly due to his being a trained journalist, was Craig Munro. After Craig finished his degree in late 1971, I offered him a job in editorial which was feeling the strain in the literary area of having to cope without Roger McDonald who was away on a well-earned sabbatical in England. Craig became an excellent literary editor and continues to be one of the major figures at the Press.

Presentation involving good design and exacting production standards are very important in all publishing and essential in literary publishing where clever design can mask the economies necessary in low-print-run work. This was difficult to find in Brisbane in the 1960s. Many of our earlier books were designed in Melbourne by Rick Ressom and printed at Wilke's. Occasionally we used designers from Jacaranda, but it became increasingly obvious we would have to do something ourselves. Production and design are demanding disciplines and require more time than I was able to give them. One of our young shop assistants, Cyrelle Birt, was an artist who drew and painted in her spare time. I offered her a job in publishing as a production assistant and trained her myself in production and book design. I also arranged for her to spend several weeks with Wilke Printers in Melbourne and Halstead in Sydney. She became in time our production manager and chief designer. She proved to be a much better designer than her teacher, went on to win a number of design awards, and was certainly one of the leading members of the team which made the Press the distinguished publishing house it has become.

Another vital element in any successful publishing organisation is marketing and sales. I had had some marketing training at Michigan State University Press but my really intensive training was with Prentice-Hall. This had left me with no illusions about the importance of effective marketing. As we began to grow, our lack of any coherent marketing was becoming more and more obvious. We were not large enough to justify sales staff outside of order processing, so I arranged a deal whereby our marketing was done by Ure Smith. Our list, on the whole, fitted nicely with theirs in that it didn't directly compete but filled gaps which enabled their sales people to present a well-rounded package to the trade. Eventually in the mid-1960s we reached a stage where our publishing was large enough to require the talents of a full-time sales manager, and we were successful in persuading Larry Chapman, Ure Smith's New South Wales sales representative, to join us. Larry and I had been close friends since my first day at Angus & Robertson in 1959 where he had been a bookseller under the great Hedley Jefferies, and we made a good marketing team at the Press.

Because of my interests as a university student and my subsequent stint lecturing in American literature, it had always been a dream of mine that we would someday publish serious fiction. Our success with Paperback Poets had led me to think we might be able to do something similar with prose fiction. I had met Michael Wilding sometime before at the Newcastle in George Street where I often drank when I was in Sydney. Michael had introduced me to Frank Moorhouse and I knew they were both writing short stories and publishing them in 'men's' magazines such as *Chance*. In fact, through knowing them I was acutely conscious of how difficult it was to get short fiction published. It seemed to me that if *Chance* was prepared to take them on there must be some kind of market out there for serious young fiction, and I thought we might be able to do something akin to Paperback Poets in production terms to make it affordable for that market.

A more difficult problem was the political situation in the university. The anti-Vietnam War demonstrations were reaching their peak and students were rebelling on campuses all over Australia. The Queensland government was also particularly exercised by its perception of what constituted pornography and tended to see it everywhere. Cyrelle had been threatened in 1970 with legal action over a poster she had designed for a student performance of *Lysistrata* in which she had used an Aubrey Beardsley drawing. The police had arrested the cast of Alex Buzo's play *Norm and Ahmed* for obscenity on the strength of one four-letter word. Michael Wilding's and Frank Moorhouse's work exploring explicit sex and drug taking was not going to be easy to sell to a university administration shell-shocked by attacks from left-wing students and right-wing governments who held the purse strings. I was determined to push on with my plan to publish contemporary fiction, but in the end it was made clear to me, to my everlasting regret, that if I were to persist with Moorhouse's *The Americans, Baby* it would be the last fiction we would publish. Our first two titles in the new Paperback Prose series published in 1972 were, therefore, Michael Wilding's *Aspects of the Dying Process* and Rodney Hall's *The Ship on the Coin*. They were both good books and I am proud of them, but I shall always regret that the brilliant Frank Moorhouse never became a UQP author.

This was also about the time we began to publish hardback fiction. David Malouf and I over a dinner to celebrate the publication of *Bicycle and Other Poems* in the inaugural Paperback Poets series began talking about the poems in the book. I told him how much I liked a poem entitled 'The Year of the Foxes' and he pointed out it was a poem about his mother wearing a fox fur, a style much in vogue during the war years. This led us into a discussion about the Brisbane of David's youth, and I was absolutely enthralled by his vivid descriptions of life in what seemed a far off but fascinating time. I particularly remember him describing the prostitutes sitting on the verandahs in the sultry summer evenings with Rita Hayworth hair styles and the smell of frangipani pervading the night air. I suggested we do a Brisbane book based on his recollections. He would supply the text and we would do the picture research. We parted still excitedly discussing this new project.

A few months later I was at Sydney University seeing Michael Wilding in the English Department where David was a tutor. We encountered each other in the hall and David said, 'Oh, by the way, that Brisbane book has turned into a novel.' I must confess my heart sank. I thought, 'Oh, God, another poet who thinks he can write prose fiction!' Hopefully, David never saw my disappointment as I smiled and made as many encouraging remarks as I could. Of course, the novel turned out to be *Johnno*, surely the best novel ever written about Brisbane and the first novel by one of Australia's greatest living writers. It was also our first fiction title published initially only as a hardback.

Because Australian fiction writers had been starved of publishing outlets for so long, there were actually not many young talented writers looking for publishers. With the success of Paperback Prose and our hardback fiction well launched, we needed quality manuscripts to keep up the momentum we had created in the marketplace. Michael Wilding suggested looking further afield than Australia and after some discussion we agreed to form a series devoted to Asian and Pacific writing. Like me, Michael did not have any Asian languages and what he had read came from translations which were often hard to find. Later he suggested we enlist Harry Aveling who was fluent in Indonesian, a good judge of writing and most importantly had Asian connections. Eventually the Asian and Pacific Writing series was co-edited by Wilding and Aveling. This series later led to another under the general editorship of Kevin Windle called Contemporary Russian Writing.

These later series reflected a change in our marketing emphasis. Towards the end of the 1960s Ure Smith had merged its marketing operation with Horwitz. The Horwitz list with its emphasis on school texts and mass market paperbacks was not very compatible with ours. We were also rapidly reaching a difficult position in that we had achieved all the market penetration possible through using agents. If we were to expand penetration, we would need to do it ourselves. Furthermore, I realised it would be difficult to retain literary authors if we did not have international marketing. It seemed to me the best plan would be to establish a national marketing operation on our own and form an alliance with a multinational publisher to represent us overseas. Up until this point I had served as the front person making policy and as the contact for our marketing agents, with Larry Chapman doing the really hard work of making sure it all came together as well as covering Queensland as a sales representative. It took some time to put all the elements of a new marketing operation together, but eventually I believe we found the right mix.

The key to our international thrust was Prentice-Hall who agreed to act as our marketing agent throughout the world excluding North America. Although our list was not completely compatible with Prentice-Hall's (theirs being oriented mainly towards tertiary-level textbooks), there were enough synergies to ensure we were well represented and sales while not spectacular were satisfactory. It had the added advantage that I personally knew many of the overseas representatives through my time at Prentice-Hall.

The United States remained a problem. We just could not afford to do nothing in New York and expect to retain our authors. As President of the ABPA I had represented Australia in Paris at UNESCO's Year of the Book in 1972 and while there had met Ted Crane, the former President and owner of Van Nostrand. Ted had recently sold Van Nostrand and had formed a publishing/consulting company, Crane Russak, in New York. I had some preliminary talks with him following our Paris meeting about North American representation, and I was able to follow these up in New York later in the year after a meeting in Toronto in September which founded the International Association of Scholarly Presses. Ted convinced me that we could do nothing in the United States without an agent working on our behalf. This was a fairly expensive option for us at the time, but I felt it was a case of investing for the future. Our first agent was Penny Warren and she did much of the early groundwork before leaving us to join Pitman. Together she and I found a replacement in Pearl Bowman who proved to be a real winner. Pearl helped put in place a distribution operation working out of Massachusetts and through her championing of Australian literature became one of the most respected American sources for information on contemporary Australian writing. Although Pearl herself was not enthusiastic about selling rights, her efforts in finding the best rights contacts for me on my periodic visits to New York enabled us to sell North American rights to US publishers and heightened our credibility with our authors. Pearl also became a point of contact for our authors visiting the US and she acted as a benevolent Godmother to many Australians encountering the Big Apple for the first time.

In writing of Pearl it reminds me that UQP's success and personality are the work of many hands, and I am sorry I cannot mention them all in a chapter primarily devoted to setting the scene. It was my privilege to work with a number of very dedicated and talented people who were the real creators of this wonderful publishing house. It was an exciting place to be and a lot of fun. It was also a lot of hard work and there were times when we all suffered from burn out. I left in 1983 to take on new publishing challenges. I left with considerable regret and I shall always be rather sorry I did, but it was time someone else took the Press into fresh fields. I had the privilege of leading it for twenty-two years, and this has been a small and rather selective account of those years.

Poets in Paperback

David Malouf

WHEN I CAME BACK to Australia in August 1968 I had, tucked away in a knapsack, the thirty or so poems I had been working on since *Four Poets*. Out of diffidence, or laziness, or simply because I was so far from home, I had made no attempt to get them into print. Six years is a long time to be off the scene, so I was surprised when Douglas Stewart included me in his two-volume *Anthology of Australian Poetry*, even more when Thomas Shapcott and Rodney Hall, in *New Impulses in Australian Poetry*, simply took it for granted that I was part of what was happening that was new. I'd better get going, I thought (I was already over thirty), and produce a book. These recognitions can be decisive. So is timing.

Poetry in the late sixties had suddenly become the liveliest and most visible of the literary arts. Almost any night of the week in Sydney there was a reading, either formal or informal — a good many of them, in those days of intense political activity, protest readings against the war in Vietnam.

Each week the Saturday *Australian* and the Saturday *Age* published a poem, the first chosen by Rodney Hall, the second by R. A. Simpson, and it was an appearance here, in the popular medium of the press rather than in one of the established literary magazines, that now constituted the arrival of a new voice.

As for the magazines that were devoted exclusively to poetry, *Poetry Australia* and *(New) Poetry*, they had been, only a short time ago, very amateur affairs. Now, when I looked into them, they were full of poetry of an exciting dash and interest and included critical articles, the best of them by an old friend from university days in Queensland, Jim Tulip, that were wide-ranging, authoritative, and dealt with local work as if it had the same claim to seriousness as the best of Berryman and Lowell.

A new generation of poets had emerged that was well-read in international poetry, European as well as American, and chose its models from there rather than from earlier Australian practitioners. Bruce Beaver had just published *Letters to Live Poets*, which still seems to me to be the most original and impressive book of the sixties, and John Tranter was writing the poems that would go into *Parallax*. Beaver and Tranter, along with Craig Powell and Norman Talbot, were the house poets of *Poetry Australia*, which also published new work by A. D. Hope, Gwen Harwood, Geoffrey

Lehmann, some of the poems that would go into Les Murray's *The Weatherboard Cathedral*, and later Vincent Buckley's 'Golden Builders', James McAuley's 'On the Western Line' and David Campbell's 'Deaths and Pretty Cousins' — all major achievements of the period. At *New Poetry* the poems of Robert Adamson and Charles Buckmaster had begun to appear beside the work of older poets like Roland Robinson and William Hart Smith, and were followed soon afterwards by the first poems of Michael Dransfield, J. S. Harry and Jennifer Maiden. I found myself, by accident, at the centre of all this.

The circle of poetry activists at Sydney University, where I went to teach, included James Tulip, whose extended articles on poetry I had admired in *Poetry Australia*, Phil Roberts, a Canadian poet then working in Sydney, who would go on to become an important small-press publisher, and Greg Curtois and Carl Harrison Ford, two of the three 'young turks' who in 1969 wrested *The Poetry Magazine* out of the hands of an older generation, called it *New Poetry*, and set it on a new course. Under the influence of so much excitement and interest I produced another dozen poems and decided I had enough to make a book.

Poetry publication in those days was a slow business and the appearance of a new collection of poetry a heavy affair. With subsidies from the Commonwealth Literature Fund, seven or eight volumes appeared each year but had to wait, sometimes for many months, on the Fund's deliberations. What I wanted, in the new situation as I saw it, was something lighter: a form of publication that would take account of the new popular audience and be cheap, quick to produce and free of the rather top-heavy decisions and bureaucratic delays of the Fund. What I had in mind was a full-length, original paperback — a common enough phenomenon in Britain and the United States, but unknown at that date in Australia.

I took the idea first to Grace Perry, who had already published a group of my poems in *Poetry Australia*. But her South Head Press had by then come up with its own solution — John Tranter's first collection, *Parallax*, was to appear as a complete issue of the magazine; a good move, I thought, but not what I had in mind. I let my notion lapse. Then, on a visit to Brisbane in the second half of 1969, I went to talk to Frank Thompson at the University of Queensland Press about a quite different project, which I had dreamed up in collaboration with another old friend, the theatre director Rex Cramphorne. This was for a book on Australian suburban and country picture-houses, a book we saw, quite rightly as it turned out, as a race against time, since almost weekly these old palaces of popular culture were being knocked down. The book would be illustrated and would be partly a record of decorative styles, from mock Egyptian through neo-Rococo and fake-Oriental to Art Deco, and partly an investigation of the anthropology, the mythology, of picture-going. Frank was interested, but for some reason the book never got written. (I used a litany of Brisbane theatre names in *Johnno* — the Elite at Toowong, the Savoy at Clayfield, the Greenslopes Hollywood, the Alhambra at Stones Corner — and the mythology of picture-going went into three or four paragraphs in the Pier Pictures section of *Harland's Half Acre.*) But in the course of our talk Frank asked if I had a book of poems — the Press had recently published its first poetry collection in Roger McDonald's *Citizens of Mist*, and already had a second in production, Tom Shapcott's *Inwards to the Sun*. I told him I did have a book but that I also had a firm idea of the kind of publication I wanted: a paperback of 64 pages that would sell for a dollar. Frank astonished me by saying — it was, as I was to discover later, a wonderful example of his daring and impulsive style — that if his people told him it was financially viable he would do it. He picked up the phone, called in two or three of his production crew (one was Cyrelle Birt), and after a quarter of an hour of argument and calculations they came up with a unit cost of, I think, twenty-three cents. 'Okay, mate,' Frank told me, 'you're on.' I left with a firm undertaking and a deadline for delivery of the manuscript.

When *Bicycle and other poems* finally appeared, in March 1970, it was volume one in a series of three (with Rodney Hall's *Heaven in a Way* and Michael Dransfield's first collection, *Streets of the Long Voyage*), available either individually or as a boxed set. One of the most brilliant publishing initiatives of the decade, this format was the joint brainchild, I should imagine, of Frank himself and of Roger McDonald, who had recently joined the staff of the Press and became the editor of the first long series, then of a second, then of an anthology drawn from both.

Imbibing Culture at the Royal Exchange

ROGER McDONALD

I WAS IN MY EARLY twenties and working for the ABC when I first met Frank Thompson at the bar of the Royal Exchange Hotel at Toowong. There was no university staff club in 1965 (though Frank was leading the push to start one) and so the Royal Exchange served as an academics watering hole. The ABC TV studios were nearby. There was no food at the pub except for hot pies, cabana sausage and Kingaroy roasted peanuts. Among jugs of Fourex in the beer garden, the genial, intelligent and somewhat Machiavellian Frank was found from late afternoon onwards. I did not know it quite yet, but the scene at the Exchange was the blacksmith's forge of an Australian publishing house that took its willing, eclectic and innovative style from the style of Frank himself. Anyone with an idea to spark gravitated to Frank's table and spouted an idea for a book.

My first book (and UQP's first poetry title), *Citizens of*

Mist, was published in 1968. A year later, when I wrote to Frank from Hobart asking for advice about working in publishing — under the somewhat romantic delusion that publishing and writing were out of the same cradle — he responded almost instantly by giving me a job. He remains a valued friend twenty-two years after I tucked my farewell present under my arm (the two-volume *Concise Oxford Dictionary*) and said goodbye to a career in publishing to try my luck as a novelist.

My memories of when I worked at UQP (1969–76) are coloured by Frank's way of doing things. A Californian from the long-established American university press tradition, he brought a flexible, barrier-busting attitude to the job, handling sometimes hostile university authorities with brilliant tactics and creative cunning. Without him there would have been no Press worth the name. UQP existed before Frank Thompson, but effectively he was its true founder, transforming a part-time university publications office into a national institution.

In the wider context of how things were done in the book world, Frank dissolved a number of British-Australian publishing inhibitions. Cheap, widely available current literary titles gave UQP an identity among opinion makers, but they were just one aspect of the list under Frank's management. He was always interested in artists and writers (Fairweathers,

Blackmans and Godfrey Millers hung on the office walls). Yet he was equally interested in a wide range of other creators who fed work into the publishing program: architects, zoologists, anthropologists, lawyers, biochemists and historians.

There was a brief period at the start — when he presented me with Sir Stanley Unwin's *The Truth About Publishing* and a new edition of the *Chicago Manual of Style* — when Frank expressed the fond hope that I would become a publishing executive in proper grown-up fashion and perhaps even his successor. I always knew I was ultimately going to disappoint him — although hopefully not as a writer. Long after I left that hot, flat-roofed and always hectic workplace on Circular Drive, Frank appeared in my dreams, urging me to do better, try harder, fly higher — to make the grade. He wasn't all that much older than me, but he remained a father figure.

I had taken a big salary drop to move from the southern states to what Max Harris called the sweaty arm-pittery of Queensland. In exchange Frank offered a title on the door (Audio Visual and Poetry Editor) and a few other non-financial enticements as well — principally the opportunity to carve out a publications list in the uncharted territory of early 70s new writing. This led to Brisbane becoming, for a while, the destination of every would-be young hopeful with a manuscript of poems or stories. The audio-visual side of my work consisted of a certain amount of literary material, *Poets on Record* (under the general editorship of Tom Shapcott) and *Poets on Tape* — a project that involved me travelling around recording almost everyone writing literary verse in eastern Australia.

Otherwise I focused on the remoter reaches of clinical diagnosis, working with the dynamic Reader in Radiology, Dr Jim Hood, who known only to himself was dying of a rare radiation-induced leukemia. He had invented a metal teaching machine about the size of a library carrel for instruction in recognising everything from malignant melanomas to lesions on the lung. We sorted slides and edited scripts. I employed Rodney Hall to read the scripts, and for a while we were self-appointed diagnosticians, amateur surgeons able to judge at a glance the prognosis of a mole. For several years cabinets around the Press held cascading boxes of slides and innumerable micro-cassettes. Undoubtedly computer imaging has now achieved what was clumsily attempted. Frank's hopes that I would usher in a Marshall McLuhanesque non-book publishing era languished.

The social revolution aspect of the 1960s and 1970s can be overemphasised — most of us had our heads down carving careers, even if some soon went bung. But it remains true that the gold-topped mushroom trail led north to Nimbin, Byron Bay, the Gold Coast hinterland, thence to St

Lucia along a muddy curve of the Brisbane River, and up Circular Drive to UQP. The Press accountant, John Vanderbyl, once encountered an unconscious figure on the front steps, and I warned him, before he took drastic action with the law, that this was an author. I still remember the rictus of John's Dutchman's smile, which implied he might have known it. Regular readings had started, featuring UQP poets, and Frank had been scaring Accounts (and himself) with worries about poets shooting-up onstage, on university property. The accountant's other main contact with authors was through me, when I came begging on their behalf for advances on royalties — usually desperately needed sums of fifty dollars or less.

On my first day of work Frank had introduced me to two women behind the scenes who had never been part of the mostly male Royal Exchange crowd — Ann Lahey and Shirley Hocking, two of Australia's best academic editors. Ann and Shirley, along with their editorial protege Penny Rogers, valued accuracy and guarded the Press's future reputation in the face of the pressure from Frank's growing list. (Another young editor, Rosanne Fitzgibbon, left in the early 1970s to have twins. Craig Munro also joined the Press at this time.)

Ann and Shirley worked in an atmosphere of efficiency, devotion, exasperation and feverish deadline-chasing. On my first day Ann had given me manuscript and galley proofs of a botanical tour de force, and advised me to read them backwards with one finger on the manuscript and one on the galleys if I wanted to do a proper job. This was when I was hit by the reality of what working in publishing really meant. It wasn't all hectic shouting matches and excited blokey cultural contests over jugs of Fourex in a postgraduate atmosphere. It was a business, a trade, a craft where copy editing and proofreading were the equivalent of weeding to the gardener. (Another aspect of this was the sight of Frank packing books with Mal Moffatt, the warehouseman, or going on the road with Larry Chapman, the sales manager.) I firmly believed that Ann could pick a flyspeck on the moon, a metaphor put to the test on the day in 1969 when we all crammed into Frank's old office (before he got his new, air-conditioned Cinemascope-sized office, with the largest board table on the campus, milled from native silky oak, to the Registrar's chagrin) and watched the fuzzy moonwalk. Ann stayed watching just long enough to confirm the historic moment, and then returned to her desk. The day Frank decreed that authors would henceforward be responsible for their own proofreading was a dark day in the annals of Ann and Shirley's astronomically high standards.

Australia's traditional writers' press, Angus & Robertson, had been unable to cope with the flood of writing that burst around 1970. Under the literary editorship of Douglas Stewart, A & R tightened rather than loosened their lists, and so the gap in the cultural landscape demanded filling. I remember sessions with Frank over what he liked to call a glass of the nut-brown foaming ale (a phrase he elucidated in his unreconstructed Los Angeles accent) about how we might do the job without bleeding the Press finances dry. Tom Shapcott and Rodney Hall, having already published *New Impulses in Australian Poetry* with the Press, had plenty of ideas too. But it was the persuasive David Malouf who pushed for *Bicycle*, his first book of poems, to go straight into paperback at an affordable price. Frank had the Contemporary Australian Plays format in mind (first published in 1961 in a Penguin-style format) and had developed the production expertise to produce a paperback series cheaply. The idea clicked, so it was thanks to David, in a sense, that I found myself editing a big chunk of Australian poetry through those years. A few years later David gave me the manuscript of 'Johnno' to read at home — the gesture of a friend — and I went to work the next morning urging Frank to ignore David's diffidence over whether it should be published in his home state and put the book under contract, which he did. (When I started at the Press there were no contracts issued at all. Frank operated on the principle that a publisher's word was his bond.) In fact, 'Johnno' came out of a book that David and Frank had planned on Brisbane in the war years. Frank would have been surprised if it had not come to us.

Poetry editing was a job that came close to fulfilling my largely fallacious fantasy about publishing — that it was closely allied to the writing process — while also demanding the skills of a diplomat in a war zone. The word went round very fast indeed that Queensland was where the books were materialising. There were many times when I sat down to a stack of around one hundred manuscripts, and gave attention to the heaving tide of human aspirations that poetry, both good and bad, represented. It was, interestingly, almost as satisfying dealing with the worst as with the best. Or rather with the best of the worst — and so I became a de facto correspondence writing teacher at a time when there were no workshops and state writers' centres to soak up people's need for response to the written page. When Craig Munro joined the Press in 1972 he found the same thing — we each had our regular stable of would-be writers to encourage, counsel and nudge. These were the ones who rarely reached publication and they weren't always grateful, either. Meantime, at the other end of the scale, Tom Shapcott, working at Ipswich in his family's printing and accounting business, was my closest literary friend and a regular breaster of the Staff Club bar when Frank called for an end to the day's labours, as he frequently did around four in the afternoon, by leaning on the door jamb of my office and proposing a glass or two of the nut-brown foaming ale. Tom's valuing of me as an editor and Frank's delivering of opportunities to do the job as best I could went a long way towards giving me confidence to guide others at a time when I was just a beginning writer myself.

Adventurous Spirits

MICHAEL WILDING

FOR SERIOUS WRITERS in Australia, the early 1970s were much like now. Publishing was dominated by foreign interests — not as large and powerful as the current transnationals, but no less greedy and accountant driven. What local publishing had sprung up in the 1950s and 1960s had pretty well all succumbed to foreign takeovers. And the beginning of the takeover of independent distribution by overseas publishing groups was under way. Globalisation was in process. It was a bleak scene for local writing.

The origins of UQP's fiction list are somewhat hazy, though no less so than is the continuation and development. It must have involved meeting Frank Thompson over a drink or two, but whether in Brisbane or Sydney I don't remember. Memory has tended to blur it into one long continuous drink or two. It was Peter Edwards, with whom I had worked at Sydney University before he took up the chair of English at Queensland, who introduced my fiction to Frank. UQP had begun publishing poetry and their Paperback Poetry series was making an impact, certainly among the poets who in those days were nothing if not vocal. So the obvious thing to suggest to Frank was, if there was a Paperback Poetry series, why not a Paperback Prose series?

The argument went something like this. Since poetry was perceived as unprofitable by commercial publishers, a number of academic presses in the United States had begun to publish it in order to preserve the tradition. Wesleyan was the example always cited. But fiction, especially short stories, was also being perceived as non-commercial. Literary fiction was in as vulnerable a situation as poetry, and needed a visionary publisher.

Frank rose to the occasion. He didn't really have to be persuaded. Even as I was arguing the case he had already seen it. What was exciting about working with him in those days was his intuitive response and his adventurous spirit. He could see the need, see the opportunity, and he did it. Of course, it all took a bit longer than that. There were press boards and vice-chancellors and distributors who needed to be given a solid case. But he made it.

For some reason a series was decided on. Maybe those were the days of series. Maybe it was a matter of containment. Anyway, a series was decided on, I sent up my manuscript, and the next thing that happened was I was sent down the manuscript of Rodney Hall's *The Ship on the Coin.*

Rodney was the first of the poets who was switching to fiction: David Malouf and Tom Shapcott later followed him. I took a dim view of this, believing poets should stick in their own ghetto. They tended to turn to fiction with no sense of the constraints and disciplines and traditions, seemingly writing it off the top of their heads and consequently doing quite well at it. But even in those days I was shrewd enough to realise that if there was to be a series it needed titles, and if titles were not recommended there would be no series and I would be without a publisher. And so it happened that the first two UQP Paperback Prose volumes were my *Aspects of the Dying Process* and Rodney's *Ship on the Coin*. We launched them at Jim Thorburn's Pocket Bookshop in Sydney. The reporter from *Vogue* couldn't get her mind round it. 'So tell me, is this academic fiction? Are these university novels?' Brian Kiernan in the *Australian* wrote about the series as a workshop for new fiction. 'It promises to fulfil a valuable role that the underground poetry press and the theatre workshops have already performed for younger poets and playwrights.' I remember being rather offended by this and I was provoked to develop the less than positive idea of the sheltered workshop for new fiction in *The Short Story Embassy*. I viewed the UQP titles as fully finished, professional books with real commercial potential, and they didn't need to be put in any special category. It was hard not to feel embattled. A reading was arranged at the University of New South Wales to promote the first two titles. Rodney Hall and I turned up. But there was not one person in the audience, just the student organiser. She has since gone on to big things. Well, so has Rodney. But on this occasion the future didn't look so rosy.

And it hadn't been as simple as that either. These were the days of change. Australia had been living in a very protected, repressive environment of official censorship under the old Liberal–Country party coalition. The list of banned books contained titles by Henry Miller, D. H. Lawrence, Leonard Cohen, Vladimir Nabokov, Philip Roth, James Joyce and many more. It was a grotesque situation and it put Australia in the category of Ireland and South Africa and Franco's Spain. But that was the dominant environment.

For those of us beginning our writing careers then, these restraints were idiotic. Lawrence and Joyce had been writing forty years ago. Copies of most of the banned books circulated. In our own practice we disregarded the taboos on four-letter words and sexual incidents. It meant, of course, that there were constant skirmishes with printers, publishers, editors, magistrates and such like. Frank, taking another look at my manuscript, decided it was tricky enough publishing fiction with a university press without being impaled for pornography as well. The climate in Queensland at the time was less than progressive. He decided to show the manuscript to the vice-chancellor to ensure that he had support before going ahead.

I can see why Frank did it, though the consequences annoyed me at the time. The then vice-chancellor, Zelman Cowen, took a dim view of the book. Two stories he particularly objected to: 'The Phallic Forest' (which Peter Carey always insisted was the best thing I'd written) and 'The Image of a Sort of Death'.

I remember sitting lugubriously with Frank in the University of Sydney club as he, with some obvious anxiety, delivered the message. It was probably the time the manager came up to me and told me I was no longer a financial member and was not entitled to be there, having been on leave and forgotten to renew my subscription. It just added to the general sense of being outside the law. The Queensland vice-chancellor had been some sort of legal academic.

The message, briefly, was to cut out the offending material from the stories. I was outraged, of course. I often was in those days. My deathless prose to be mutilated! It was unthinkable, unacceptable. How could writing still be treated like this in the 1970s? This was the sort of thing that had driven Lawrence into exile fifty years earlier. I already was in exile. The whole splendid enterprise seemed to be thwarted before it had even begun. It was one of those long beery evenings with Frank of which I have no clear recollection. Indeed, no recollection at all. He was amazing in that he would always put up with long difficult sessions with his authors. Especially over a drink. In the end he made me see reason. I didn't withdraw the book. Where after all would I have withdrawn it to? Rather than rewrite and amputate and otherwise deface and dismember the two stories, I took them out altogether. The book went ahead. Frank swore me to silence, since he didn't want the series jeopardised by scandalous rumours of interference and compromise. Some years later I mentioned what had happened to Elizabeth Wynhausen and she ran the story in the press. But by then the censorship days were over, for a while.

The series established, Frank and his fiction editor Craig Munro began scouting around for further titles. The same censorship problem had come up with Frank Moorhouse. Moorhouse and I were closely linked in literary terms in those days, and Frank Thompson could see very good reasons for getting Moorhouse onto the list. Moorhouse offered him the stories that later provided the basis for the Dusan Makevejev movie *The Coca-Cola Kid*. But once again the vice-chancellor demurred, and the project came to nothing. It was a pity. UQP was attempting an innovative list and was in a position to have cornered the best new talent around. But, as always, the creative are thwarted by the uncreative.

There were endless battles in the early seventies over four-letter words and sexual content. Looking back on it all now, this issue seems to have been pretty much a diversion. The libertarians focused on taboo words, while substantive issues of political and economic change were displaced from attention. The censorship battles were a smokescreen behind which late industrial capitalism globalised. At the time, however, I was swept along in the anti-censorship struggle along with many others. Having had our fiction rejected as disgusting and unacceptable, we decided to try to promote it under just those labels. I assembled a collection of so-called Disgusting and Unacceptable Stories at the invitation of Ron Smith of Horwitz. Needless to say they didn't publish it. But when Craig Munro phoned me to say UQP had a spare subsidy or spare slot or spare something for another title in the Paperback Prose list and did I have any ideas, I sent up the collection. It contained stories by Moorhouse, Vicki Viidikas, myself and Peter Carey, who had written 'Life and Death on South Side Pavilion' especially for the volume, or so he said. Craig, too, decided against the anthology but leapt on the Peter Carey stories with acuity and avidity and ended up securing a volume of them for the series. At that stage Carey was unknown. Moorhouse and I had been publishing his early work in *Tabloid Story* (where Craig first read him) and I'd been publishing him in Jon Silkin's UK journal *Stand*, for which I was Australian editor. I thought his stories were marvellous, though the blurb that appeared over my name on his second book, *War Crimes*, was written by Peter himself and read out to me over the phone for my approval late one night. I never felt it caught my idiom, but as Peter disarmingly put it to me once, his skills were not verbal. But he seemed like a talent worth encouraging. 'You'll regret it,' said Moorhouse darkly. Peter's stories appeared as *The Fat Man in History*, together with my novel *Living Together*. A year later Murray Bail's *Contemporary Portraits* was published, along with David Malouf's first novel, *Johnno*. The reviews were all good, the sales were all good, the series was established.

Writing in Australia in the late 1960s, there were two major problems. First was getting into print, given the paucity and unsatisfactoriness of local publishing and the lack of much connection with the English-language publishing centres of London and New York. The other was getting your work noticed once it was in print, the problem of how to showcase it. Apart from a reputation for cheap fortified wines, Australia was primarily perceived as a land of sport, a suitable place for the Olympic games. The UQP series Asian and Pacific Writing grew out of a venture I had worked on with Frank Moorhouse that had come to nothing. We had conceived of a southern-hemisphere, English-language literary magazine. We would challenge *Paris Review* and *London Magazine* on their own terms, by producing a world-quality magazine from the south. The models we had in mind were *el corno emplumado*, an avant-garde literary review that came out of Mexico City, and the US *New American Review*, that sold as a paperback. We tried various backers without success. But I had done a lot of research on English-language writers and translators in the region. In large part the project had been influenced by a visit I had made to the Philippines in 1966 with a Sydney colleague, Peter King. I had encountered a wealth of English-language writing and publishing unknown to readers in Australia, Britain or the US, much of it in Frankie José's marvellous Solidaridad bookshop in Manila. Frankie's enthusiasm, lively conversation and range of contacts was a major inspiration.

So when Frank Thompson asked, having settled the Paperback Prose proposal, whether I had any other ideas, I revived and adapted this one. A magazine no longer seemed the best way to run. Magazines were not in UQP's sights at that time. But what about a series of books drawing on contemporary writing in the region — Asia and the Pacific? My argument was that there were amazing and exciting things there. The stories of the Filipino writer Nick Joaquin were every bit as striking and original and magical as the Latin American writings of Borges, Cortazar, Fuentes and Carpentier that were currently in vogue. Here were new and invigorating approaches that would vitalise and cross-fertilise new Australian writing. My focus on all this was that of a writer in Australia — this could be the next avant-garde, the next new wave. My interests were literary, not anthropological or political or economic or geographical. These other interests could be served by the series; they would provide an additional market to the ubiquitous and never especially convincing 'general reader'. But they would be a bonus. They were not areas in which I could claim any expertise. It was my basic conviction that there was exciting work coming out of the region that anyone with an interest in contemporary writing would want to read.

The political agenda of Australia as part of Asia had yet to be vocalised. In that regard the series was ahead of its time, and that meant being ahead of the market. I had great visions for the series, international co-publishing and such like. Some of it indeed eventuated. A number of the titles were accepted into the UNESCO translations series. A number were sold internationally — *Modern Japanese Poetry* (translated by James Kirkup) became an Open University set text in the UK. Kiran Nagarkar was published in the US. Antonio Enriquez won a prize for his volume of stories in the

Philippines. *Padma River Boatman* has been made into a feature film. Ninotchka Rosca went on to write a biography of Marcos for a US publisher.

Asian and Pacific Writing was always hard to administer, though probably not especially more so than any other publishing list. Translators and editors were endlessly delayed, deadlines had continually to be revised. There was not much of a tradition of literary translation in Australia, and not much at all from Asian languages. Many of the translations were by people who knew the original languages well but who were not especially literary in orientation themselves — many were anthropologists, academics, political advisers, journalists. Consequently a lot of detailed work on the texts was necessary. Some titles took years to develop. Some projects came to nothing, despite endless correspondence, discussions and meetings.

The first two volumes were a collection of Nick Joaquin's stories, which he called *Tropical Gothic*, and an Indonesian novel, *Atheis* by Achdiat Kata Mihardja, translated by R. J. Maguire, a sub-editor on the *Australian*. Joaquin's stories I had discovered in Frankie José's bookshop on my visit to the Philippines. The Achdiat novel had come to UQP independently, but was obviously appropriate for the series. And this was how the series progressed; some titles I sought out, others came through UQP's own network. Once the series was established and the first titles were published, it attracted material from throughout the region. It made a considerable impact among writers in Asia, and I continue to meet people who remember it enthusiastically.

One of the virtues of the series was that it was eclectic. Its only agenda was that of finding good writing, and we found it in all sorts of areas. Ulli Beier was a German writer and academic, internationally famous for the work he did in developing writing in English in Nigeria. His work there, and that of the writers he had encouraged, was widely published, but his later work in Papua New Guinea, where he had moved in the 1970s, was scarcely known. I wrote asking if he would do a book for us, and the resulting *Black Writing from New Guinea* was one of our great successes. The English poet James Kirkup's translations of contemporary Japanese poets had been appearing in literary journals, notably in Grace Perry's *Poetry Australia*, so I wrote to him for a volume. He was eager to provide the translations, but diffident about writing a contextualising introduction and suggested finding an academic in the area to cooperate with him. A. R. ('Bertie') Davis was professor of Chinese and Japanese at the University of Sydney. He had edited a comparable volume of modern Chinese poetry for Penguin, working with the translators. He undertook the Kirkup collaboration with vigour and enthusiasm, immersing himself in contemporary Japanese poetry and engaging in a massive editorial and research project. It took a long time but the resulting volume was well worth it. Bonnie McDougall's splendid anthology of the work of the Chinese writer Ho Ch'i-fang was based on a doctoral thesis she had recently completed in Bertie's department. She is now professor of Chinese at the University of Edinburgh.

Harry Aveling sent in a volume of *Contemporary Indonesian Poetry* and a collection of stories by Pramoedya Ananta Toer. Pramoedya had been in gaol in Indonesia for years as a political prisoner. His case was hardly known in the West at that time. We published one of the stories in *Tabloid Story* and Frank Moorhouse and I wrote a letter to the *Australian* about his treatment. Harry's translations marked the beginning of the public recognition of Pramoedya's situation. Later, after the series had closed down, Penguin published a trilogy of Pramoedya's novels in a translation by Max Lane. Another lively Indonesian writer we published was W. S. Rendra: Harry translated some of his poems for the *Contemporary Indonesian Poetry* volume, and Max Lane translated his play, *The Struggle of the Naga Tribe*, for the series.

Harry Aveling was a prolific and enthusiastic translator from Indonesian and Malay. I suggested he should join me as co-editor of the series and he readily agreed. From then on we shared the load of reading the manuscripts that came in, and searching out new titles. At some point Harry became a follower of Rajnish, changed his name to Aridas Anand, and started wearing orange robes. We had one editorial lunch in a Brisbane restaurant, but after Harry's arrival in resplendent saffron I think Frank Thompson decided never to take us out in public again. He could disregard the name change, refuse to put it in the books and still write to Aridas as Harry, but he couldn't ignore the yellow robes across the table unless he closed his eyes or kept them fixed on a jar of amber fluid. I think he chose the latter.

The series ran for ten years and twenty volumes. The problems came when UQP decided to cut back to one title a year. I felt it wasn't enough to maintain the presence of the series. Worse, it meant either building up a lengthy backlog of titles waiting to appear, or rejecting manuscripts that were appealing but that would have had to wait two, three, four years for publication. The amount of reading for the series was becoming huge — and with only one title a year, frustrating. Overloaded with other commitments — by now I was running my own press, Wild & Woolley, with Pat Woolley — I regretfully resigned from the series. Frank left UQP not long afterwards, and in the reorganising the series was closed down. But it was marvellous while it lasted. I would do it again. Once in a while I meet Harry in Singapore or Canberra and we talk about reviving it.

They were exciting years in Australian publishing, the early seventies. Much of the writing had been done in the bottled-up years of the late sixties. I am not sure that the so-called Whitlam years were that creative. Certainly, the increased Australia Council funding and the more liberal climate meant things appeared that could not appear earlier. But even here the policies were ambiguous. Consistently the Literature Board refused to do anything about distribution. At a point when independent distributors were being absorbed by transnational publishers and when new small and independent presses could find no access to efficient distribution, the Literature Board did nothing. Publication subsidies were dispensed, publicity money splashed around, but a national distribution policy for all that funded writing was never drawn up. The Literature Board also always insisted on giving money readily to transnational publishers — unlike the Canada Council which restricted funds to Canadian-owned companies. In this as in so much else Australian governmental policy seemed to be in the pockets of the transnationals rather than trying to confront or mitigate their destructive effects.

UQP established itself valiantly in this hostile commercial climate. When it began its literary and Asian lists, it was perceived as a marginal, eccentric organisation. How could you have a publisher in Brisbane, publishers were all in

Melbourne? But UQP showed the way. Soon its literary list began to take the centre ground, and small presses like Wild & Woolley and Outback set up as publishers of the alternative and the avant-garde. There was room for all of us, though I felt that Frank always looked askance at my involvement in Wild & Woolley. But we never saw ourselves in opposition or competition. The reality was that there was all this amazing, exciting, new Australian writing, and no one but UQP and the small presses was publishing it.

And even if distribution was a nightmare and sales a problem, the media responded. The media recognition of the new writing, the way it welcomed the new initiatives, showed that there was an interest in what was being done. That readers wanted to know about the material, even wanted to buy it. Effectively the transnationals were shamed into having to publish Australian writing, easier as it would have been just to keep on importing the overseas product and monopolising distribution channels. But it was only after UQP and the small presses showed the way that the transnationals developed their local literary lists in the 1980s. And that development was not in response to specifically Australian conditions, needless to say. They were doing the same in Canada, New Zealand, India, keeping the natives quiet, making it look like they were giving writers access to international markets, but in fact just providing a local reservation. But that is to move to the unsatisfactory decade, the eighties. I prefer to end with remembering those happy days in the seventies, sitting in the twilight on the verandah of the university staff club at St Lucia, cane toads hopping around at my feet, clambering up my legs, the endless flights of flying foxes slowly flapping down the Brisbane River. Those were magical times. Frank's personal life by then was achieving a complexity of a rather Gothic or Baroque or Rococo flamboyance, one of those terms, anyway. But this was the seventies and that was what personal lives were all about in the seventies, it seemed. We would commiserate on the way in which things seemed to be lurching out of control and have another drink and watch another thousand flying foxes waft slowly past, and it seemed like it would all go on for ever.

West 85th Street, New York

Pearl Bowman

Back in the late 1970s, after a series of jobs in publishing, mostly in marketing, but also in book design and production with a bit of editing thrown in, I set out as a freelance. Along with most others of this ilk, I studied the 'positions open' columns of *Publishers Weekly* assiduously. One week an ad piqued my curiosity. 'Small overseas publisher seeks US marketing representative. Sense of humor helpful.'

The ad had been placed by the incumbent representative, who was going on, as she phrased it, to a real job in the real world. And, it was soon apparent, I was headed for the Land of Oz, at least figuratively. I recall meeting Frank Thompson, then Manager of the University of Queensland Press, at his favourite New York digs, the old Roosevelt Hotel on Madison Avenue. Charmed by the amiable Mr T., I soon became his American branch. I had already worked for two university presses — New York University Press and Cambridge University Press (in the New York office), and had other relevant experience. How different could Australia be, after all?

At that time, although I considered myself a literate, widely read and well-informed person, my knowledge of Australia was similar to that of most other Americans — a vision of a big island in the South Seas, a colony of England and a place with exotic fauna. I had read a book by Nevil Shute, one by Shirley Hazzard and one by Morris West. I had seen a kangaroo at a zoo somewhere and had actually met a real Australian while on a trip to Europe. He didn't talk much about his country, having desired greatly to get away and see the world, a common aspiration among his countrymen and women, I would soon learn.

As UQP's New York-based representative, I had a budget (modest), an objective (to sell my publisher's books) and an upbeat attitude. After all, I was starting at ground zero. As far as I could determine, at that juncture nobody was promoting Australian books or authors in the US. Peter Carey was the only UQP author with an American publisher. The Traditional Market Agreement still operated, so that Australian books were considered the property of the British publishers who controlled Commonwealth rights. A few years later Lansdowne-Rigby would open a US office, but when I started I had the field to myself. After a few more years the then head of Lansdowne-Rigby, Laurie Muller, took over as director of UQP, beginning a new era for the Press.

One of the first things I did was to set up my little, home-based operation as the American branch. In this way I was able to get the UQP books into the US Library of Congress cataloguing system, so that the US cataloguing data could be printed in the books and they would thereby gain greater acceptance in the American market. In time the Library of Congress baulked at this arrangement and refused to continue the practice. But while it worked, the UQP books were in the US system and on recommended reading lists.

Today it is not uncommon for university presses to publish fiction, but then it was seldom done. UQP, one of the major Australian publishers of novels, stories and poetry, was an exception. Frank Thompson, a transplanted American with a great interest in writing, was publishing some of the very best younger writers. Many are now at the peak of their careers, with American agents and publishers also. But it was not always so.

As I looked through UQP's 1970s list, I saw I could do justice to the reprint of C. E. W. Bean's *The Official History of Australia in the War of 1914–1918*, to *The Leader: A Political Biography of Gough Whitlam*, to *Migrant Crime in Australia* and to *The Genera of Australian Lichens*. I knew how to reach the library and specialist markets. But what about *The Frangipani Gardens* by Barbara Hanrahan or *First Things Last* by David Malouf or this Steele Rudd fellow? My brief stint in the trade marketing department of a major US publisher had not prepared me for handling all these exotic books on my own.

I fortunately knew another freelance optimist, Franklin Dennis, who did know his way around the media, and I persuaded Frank Thompson to let me use his services for the trade books. Because of Franklin Dennis's skills and contacts, we were able to get books reviewed in the trade and general media. We also had an arrangement with Columbia University Press, whose sales representatives — all three of them — carried our trade books when they called on booksellers and wholesalers.

Looking back, I see that UQP books were reviewed quite widely in the scholarly and specialist media. *Choice*, a review journal for college librarians, and *World Literature Today* frequently reviewed our books. *Library Journal*, the *Journal of Economic Literature*, *19th Century Theatre Research*, *Pacific Affairs*, *The Booklist*, the *American Association for the Advancement of Science*, *Parnassus: Poetry in Review*, *Theology Digest*, the *American Journal of Psychiatry*, *Law Books in Review*, the *Harvard International Law Journal*, *Publishers Weekly* and

Modern Fiction Studies all gave review space to appropriate books, as did a number of Canadian review journals.

American reviews and promotions also stimulated sales abroad. Orders often came in from Europe and even Asia. These were forwarded to the London office or the home office, as appropriate, and I never did keep track of them, but it was, as they say, icing on the sales cake.

So Franklin Dennis and I were pioneers in introducing Australian books to this market. Now just about any Australian writer of merit can get a respectful hearing from US agents and publishers, but as recently as fifteen years ago this was not the case.

At one point Frank Thompson asked me to take on some agenting duties, trying to sell US rights for some of the top writers. I agreed to try, but within a few months was pleading to be let off. Nothing I have ever done professionally has been as frustrating as sending a manuscript to an editor and having it back a few days later — rejected. Did they even bother to read it, I wondered? Soon we had an arrangement with a professional agent who was used to the ups and downs and not as personally involved as I was. Roger McDonald's novel *Slipstream* was sold to the major US publisher Little, Brown & Co.

Looking back, it is fascinating to see which books sold well in this market. *Challenging the Men: Women in Sport,*

Australia's Great Barrier Reef, *The Changing Role of Fathers*, the fiction of Thea Astley and reprints of Miles Franklin novels all did well, in some cases outselling the Australian market. There was interest in the Asian and Pacific Writing series, including works by writers such as Achdiat K. Mihardia, Manik Bandopadhyaya, Antonio Enriquez, Nick Joaquin, Raja Proctor, and Pramoedya Ananta Toer. A series of pamphlets called the Leaders of Asia featured brief lives of major figures such as Nehru, Chiang Kai-shek and Ho Chi Min, and was quite popular for school adoptions. A booklet in this series, *Aung San*, by the Burmese leader's daughter Aung San Suu Kyi, first introduced me to this now famous Asian woman. The fiction of Rodney Hall, Michael Wilding and Murray Bail proved popular in American literary circles.

Most of my activities consisted of producing catalogues, flyers and brochures and mailing them to the best prospects. I also placed space ads in appropriate journals and sent out review copies. I wrote lots of letters, kept track of stock, dealt with the distributor in Massachusetts (here a sense of humour was very helpful), and when possible went to book-trade and library meetings. The result was we actually managed to sell significant quantities of books.

I believe at one stage UQP exported more books to the US than any other comparable Australian publisher. But it was still very difficult to get the general book media to pay attention to Australian books. It became apparent that most American intellectuals had ties to Europe and were not terribly interested in small Antipodean nations. The Paul Hogan television commercials and Australian films probably did more to call attention to Australia among Americans at this time.

One thing I soon learned was that Australians were not attuned to the American conventions of book publishing as practised by all the major trade publishers. Seasonality was (and still is) everything. Books are almost never added at the last moment. The Fall season is the big one, with Christmas books accounting for a very large portion of total books sold each year. Books for Fall are announced and presented to the sales reps at a sales conference the preceding May, with Spring books presented in December. Some larger publishers add a Summer season. Selling books to bookstores and wholesalers that service them outside of this seasonal cycle is exceedingly difficult, a fact I had much trouble transmitting Down Under.

My own introduction to university press publishing in the United States was during the 1960s at New York University Press, then a very small publisher with a backlist of perhaps 300 titles. NYU and all other university presses were greatly affected by the launch of the Soviet sputnik in

1957 and the realisation that in this area the US was a distant second-best.

The American Congress reacted to this embarrassment by allocating large sums of money to libraries and schools for the purchase of books and other educational materials. Much of this largesse became available in the 1960s, and the effort to play catch-up yielded great bonanzas to American publishers in general, and in particular to those with scholarly or educationally oriented lists.

Working in its usually mysterious ways, the Congress would allocate certain sums but not make them available until the beginning or middle of June of a year, with the proviso that they must be spent by June 30, the end of the fiscal year.

I recall NYU Press receiving library requisitions for every book — all 300 of them — towards the end of June, with all the paperwork and processing to be done in a few days. All types of libraries — public, university, school and special — got these funds, known as 'Titles'. There were Title I, Title II, Title III, Title IV and perhaps others. Title II, I believe, was for libraries. I particularly remember a requisition from a school library to 'send everything that would be appropriate for a high school library and an invoice IMMEDIATELY'.

University presses rejoiced at these windfall years, but actually they set up an expectation of sales volume that was impossible to continue once the country caught up and the Congress cut off the funding. This contributed to some of the serious problems of university presses in the 1980s and beyond. Suddenly a press used to selling up to 2000 copies of its new books found it hard to move as few as 500.

Children's books presented another challenge. Breaking into this field is very difficult, with a few successful publishers controlling most of the bookstore and library sales. A group of influentials — librarians, editors, teachers — set the standards for books from the picture book through to books for elementary-school age-groups. They do the reviewing for the three major reviewing media in the field, and they will seldom bother with a book deemed unsuitable because of vocabulary level. Many Australian books do not thereby qualify and for this reason finding co-publishers proved very difficult. The boundaries for young adult books were less firm and greater success was achieved here. Truly, nothing in American publishing proved easy, as I learned, often to my dismay.

My usefulness to UQP diminished with the expiration of the export subsidy in the early 1980s, and although I have been able to work for some Australian publishers since, including the Australian Government Publishing Service, nothing has equalled those heady days of pioneering work for UQP.

My association with UQP opened many doorways for me. Two trips to the wonderful Land of Oz, personal friendships that still prevail, knowledge of a culture and literature that increasingly gain world recognition for their individuality as well as their universality — these are the intangibles. Because of this association, I was invited to be one of the founders of the American Association of Australian Literary Studies in 1986. From a base of twenty members, we have grown to over two hundred, and our splendid journal *Antipodes* has gained international recognition. Last year the Modern Language Association recognised the AAALS as an Allied Organisation.

Despite the distance, I was always fortunate to enjoy good relations with the UQP staff — with successive managers, editors, publicists, production and finance people, and all the many others who helped make the American operation possible and successful.

One of the most attractive aspects of the Australian literary world is its size relative to the US. Many writers seem to know each other and are acquainted with each other's work.

In the early days, I recall, I could get very annoyed with 'those Aussies'. Too self-effacing, too colonial British in mentality — they could use a dose of American chauvinism, I used to think. Now all this has changed. I have watched an emerging national consciousness. No longer are Australian children educated as though they were still in Britain, as Robert Hughes said of his own schooling. Now a truly multicultural society, Australia has achieved this enviable status in a manner others could usefully emulate. UQP's richly varied list reflects that new-found cultural maturity.

Fiction Fast Forward

D'ARCY RANDALL

I BEGAN WORKING FOR the University of Queensland Press in early 1980. I was hired by Frank Thompson as in-house editor, a title that made me the reader and editor for the fiction list, the copy editor for several scholarly titles and textbooks, and the chief paper-pusher for the Russian Writing Series and the Asian and Pacific Writing Series. As time passed, I took on more administrative duties, including working with the Literature Board of the Australia Council and UQP's agents for foreign rights, but my job became more and more focused on literature. When Laurie Muller took over as Manager, I continued running the fiction list, but also became the in-house liaison for Barbara Ker Wilson's new Young Adult Series and helped coordinate the paperback reprint series. Such was my job when I left UQP in 1989.

For me, my career at UQP was a fortunate fluke. When I started working there, my family and I had only recently migrated to Australia from the United States, and I knew next to nothing about contemporary Australian literature. On the other hand, I had grown up in a bookish publishing family and had worked with the Louisiana State University Press, so the literary culture of passionate affinities and bitter squabbling was nothing new. Moreover, the 'Australian renaissance' of the 1970s and 1980s — the obsessive artistic drive to explore Australia's past and to re-present its many faces to the world — resonated powerfully with me. Unlike most migrants, I had strong familial ties to Australia, through an Irish Australian grandfather. Although this grandfather died well before I was born, he was a mythic presence in my childhood. My mother had told me many stories about his youth in Western Victoria of the 1880s and 1890s, hunting with Aborigines, winning footraces and breaking horses. A great uncle had survived Gallipoli, and family gossip whispered that some of our in-laws had harboured Ned Kelly, so during my Australian years I would see variations of my own family history and mythos realised in book after book.

However, I soon discovered that UQP's position in the Australian literary renaissance was complex. In fact, I spent much of my first year or so puzzling over what was specifically 'Australian' about the famous fiction list that I had inherited. Of course, Roger McDonald's *1915* reimagined the Anzac tragedy at Gallipoli, and some of Peter Carey's stories and David Malouf's *Johnno* brooded on certain features of Australia's psychic landscape, but my first, overwhelming impression of the list was its eclectic worldliness.

During the 1970s, UQP's fiction list had developed largely around short stories, and the most influential story writers like Michael Wilding, Murray Bail, Peter Carey and Barry Oakley — not to mention the guiding absence of Frank Moorhouse — had created a list of sharp, urbane tales that clearly targeted a readership not just in Sydney and Melbourne but also in London and New York (especially New Yorkers). UQP even hosted a *New Yorker* writer on its list: John Updike. Frank Thompson had purchased an Australasian edition of *The Coup*, a title that meant a lot to UQP at the time. Lined up on the publishing list above 'John Updike', the names of the other UQP writers looked just fine. This 'American Dream' of publishing took on a surreal dimension during the Updike promotion, when for a month or so the central hallway between our offices sported a life-sized cardboard image of Updike in tennis gear, posed as if to lob any number of UQP writers over the net and into the court of the *New Yorker* itself.

This dream was, in one sense, not so far-fetched. Frank had spent much of the 1970s trying to educate American and other foreign publishers about Australian writers, and by 1980 he was justly proud of UQP's part in the writers' successes: Carey, Bail, Malouf and McDonald had found US and/or London publishers; their worldly careers were starting to take off.

One complication in this picture of ambitious internationalism was the Asian and Pacific Writing Series. This series, initiated by Frank in the early 1970s and edited by Michael Wilding and Harry Aveling, insistently positioned Australia as a South Pacific country with crucial, emerging ties to its Asian neighbours. Aside from its visionary purpose, many of the titles, like Nick Joaquin's *Tropical Gothic* or Ninotchka Rosca's *The Monsoon Collection*, were simply brilliant books to read, and everyone who worked on the series bemoaned its slow sales. One particular pride of the series was its edited anthologies: Ulli Beier's *Black Writing from New Guinea*, Bonnie S. McDougall's *Paths in Dreams: Selected Prose and Poetry of Ho Ch'i-fang*, Harry Aveling's *Contemporary Indonesian Poetry* and James Kirkup and A. R. Davis's *Contemporary Japanese Poetry*. In 1997 I was pleased to see the Asian and Pacific Series win points for integrity when the Kirkup and Davis was praised by Marjorie Perloff in her *Boston Review* account of the Araki Yasusada 'hoax', a scandal that recently stirred American poetry circles. Less immediately relevant to Australian culture, but still intriguing, was the Russian Writing Series, of which the house favourite was Vladimir ('the other') Rasputin's pair of novellas, *Money for Maria* and *Borrowed Time*, later republished in the UK by Quartet.

Yet despite their worthy aims, these various series and initiatives were quite time consuming, and distracted from my more pressing concern: the direction of the fiction list. UQP had developed its dynamic reputation largely because of its willingness to support new, unproven writers at a time when a new generation of Australian readers was seeking them and few other publishers responded. However, by 1980 UQP's competition among other fiction and poetry publishers, both Australian and foreign, was starting to grow.

A small but significant part of the competition came from British publishers. The fact that several high-profile writers first published by UQP sent their next manuscripts to London concerned all of us, not just because we had 'lost' authors, but because the pattern led other writers to speculate that maybe UQP was a good place to publish a first book, but after that it was 'time to move on'. Assuming the modest role of literary launching pad was a fate taken for granted by many small presses, but it was a fate UQP management resisted. Both Frank Thompson and, later, Laurie Muller were determined that UQP would not remain small, but would grow up with its writers.

Fortunately for UQP, this resistance was supported to an extent by some unglamorous but significant changes in

Athol Perkins, UQP's part-time manager from 1948 to 1961 (unsourced photographs are from UQP's archives)

The first bookshop at St Lucia (late 1950s)

Frank Thompson, UQP's youthful new manager, on his arrival in Brisbane, March 1961 (*Courier-Mail*)

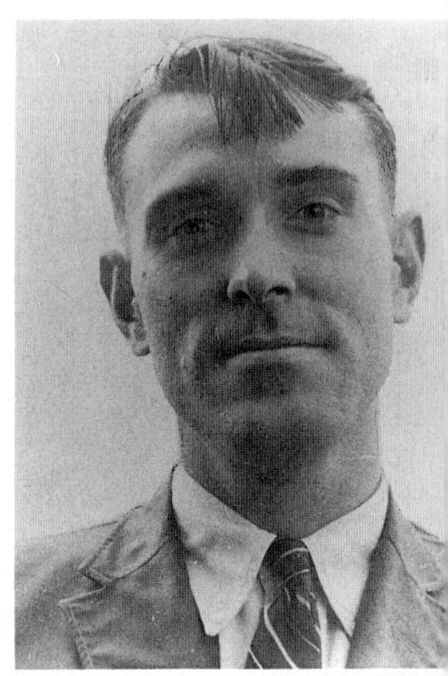

Frank outside the bookshop extension, September 1963

Frank Thompson with drama lecturer Eunice Hanger (left), Judith Wright and Kath Walker (Oodgeroo) at the 1964 Lennon's Hotel launch of Kath's first book *We Are Going* published by Jacaranda Press (Fryer Library)

Norfolk

UQP staff in 1969 celebrating publication of a book on Norfolk Island, with (from left): editor Sue Pechey, Frank Thompson, Cecily (journals), Joy Thompson (invoices), typesetter Wendy Kerr, senior editor Ann Lahey, editor Roger McDonald, manager's secretary Megan Gayler, sales secretary Barbara Absalon, editor Shirley Hockings, assistant Linda De Simone, editor Penelope Rogers, production manager Cyrelle Birt and storeman Malcolm Moffatt

David Malouf in late 1974, a few months before the publication of *Johnno* (*Courier-Mail*)

Michael Wilding, from the 1974 *Living Together* jacket (Richard Harris photograph)

Senior editor Ann Lahey at work in the mid 1970s on a scholarly manuscript — with sharp pencils and even sharper eye

Like a character from one of his own compelling stories, Peter Carey after the publication of *The Fat Man in History* (1974)

Roger McDonald at the time he was writing his first novel *1915*

Presentation in UQP's boardroom in May 1978 of a royalty cheque to Hugh Lunn for his Joh biography, with (back row, from left) Rosemary Chay (sales), Peter Lazzarini (accounts), Malcolm Beazley (sales), Maureen Easton (accounts), Craig Munro (editorial), Frank Thompson, Don Bradmore (deputy manager), Greg Spencer (bookshop); (front row) Dianne Muller (sales), Cyrelle Birt (production), Hugh Lunn, Joy Jackson (sales), Marilyn Bitomski (editorial), Merril Yule (editorial) and Jenny Bird (production)

Bookshop manager Frank Sandison (left) with his successor Greg Spencer (centre) and former staff member Peter Gates (late 1970s)

Production manager Cyrelle Birt (second from left) discussing the 1978 schedule with Marilyn Bitomski. Gail Curtis is on the left while editorial secretary Ailsa Mackintosh checks final blueprints

UQP poetry editor Tom Shapcott at his Ipswich house (Graeme Kinross Smith photograph)

Rodney Hall, from the jacket of his 1975 *Selected Poems* (*Bulletin*)

Barbara Hanrahan on her return from England in the late 1970s

Frank Thompson on his return from a trip to Russia, September 1979 (*Courier-Mail*)

Gerard Lee at the time of his first novel *True Love and how to get it* (1981)

Frank Thompson with Merril Yule and Faber & Faber's Robert McCrum at the Frankfurt Book Fair, October 1981

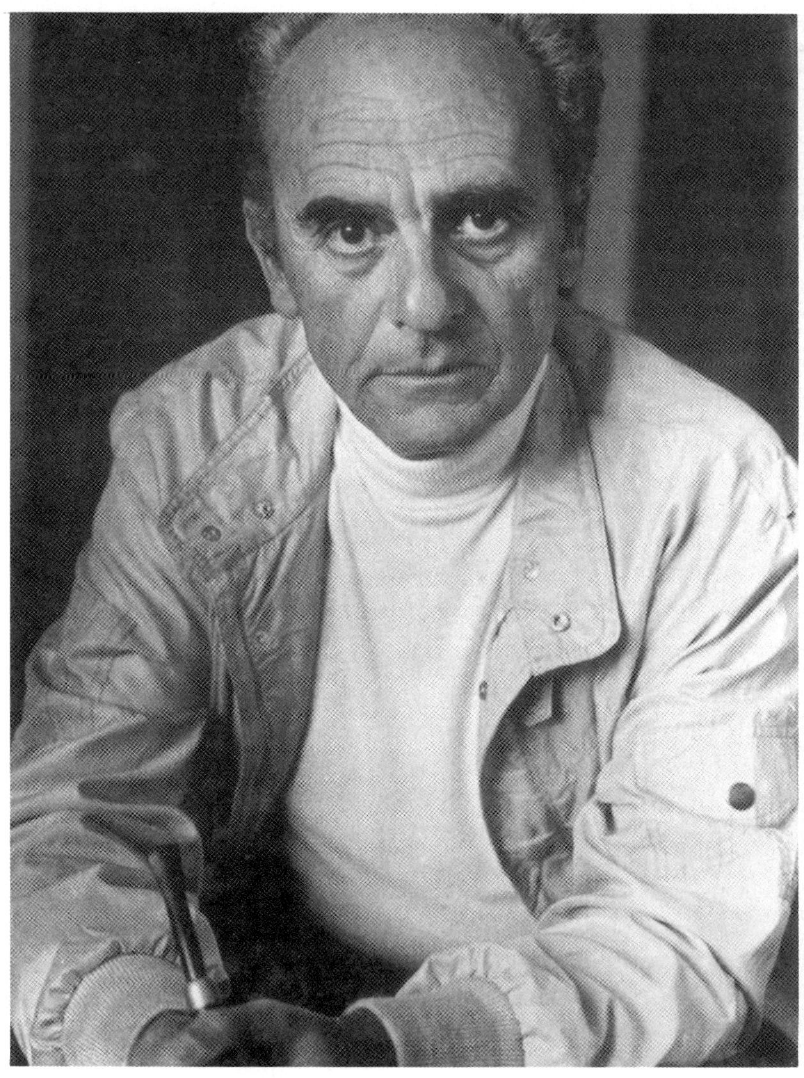

Dimitris Tsaloumas, from the jacket of his award winning 1983 dual-text poetry collection *The Observatory* (Jacqueline Mitelman photograph)

Olga Masters, from the jacket of her last novel *Amy's Children* — published posthumously in 1987 (Brendan Hennessy photograph)

Hugh Lunn at his 1984 *Queenslanders* launch in Brisbane's city Botanic Gardens, with the Phantom (aka John Henderson) and UQP publicist Anne Barkl

Queenslanders was launched by Flo Bjelke-Petersen who had earlier given Hugh secret access to the family photo album for his controversial Joh biography after the subject's refusal to cooperate

John Blight on his Brisbane verandah with his acclaimed 1985 collection *Holiday Sea Sonnets* (*Courier-Mail*)

Kate Grenville after the publication of her first book *Bearded Ladies* (1984)

anette Turner Hospital at the time of her first UQP edition of *Dislocations* (1987)

UQP's North American representative Pearl Bowman (right) on a 1987 visit to S
Lucia, with editors D'Arcy Randall (left) and Rosanne Fitzgibbon

The *Over the Top with Jim* '50s launch party at the Boomerang Theatre, Annerley Junction, 1989, with (from left): Shirley Brown, Jeanette Mastenbroek, Hugh Lunn and Rosemary Chay

ATION

UQP's 1989 Wivenhoe Dam picnic for staff and authors, including: (standing) Ross Patrick, Craig Munro, Terry Farley, Tonya Steffens, Judy McLean, Jeanette Mastenbroek, Rosanne Fitzgibbon, Kirsty-Ann Allen, Bill Gates, Yvie Fregon, Terry Gwynn-Jones; (sitting) Jan Bryant, Gerald Tooth, Clare Forster, Peter Evans, Nicola Evans, Gerard Tarte, Florence Reye, Gregory Rogers, Paul Rendle, Rosemary Chay, Keith McDonald, Paul Hodges, Kay Saunders and Erin, Ray Evans, Robert Brown, Hugh Lunn, Helen Dash, Laurie Muller, Dinah Johnson, Eileen Sneath, Sue Gough, Estelle and Peter Pinney, Heather Patrick, Sue Abbey and Ross Clark

Laurie Muller, UQP's general manager since 1983

Robert Brown (sales), Sue Abbey and Nicola Evans (editorial), Terry Farley (production) and Eileen Sneath (editorial), 1989

Marion Halligan receives the 1989 Steele Rudd Award for her story collection *The Living Hothouse* from Premier and Arts Minister Mike Ahern

Gillian Mears at the time of her first book *Fineflour* (1990)

Beverley Farmer, whose first book with UQP, *A Body of Water*, appeared in 1990

Mabel Edmund (left), author of *No Regrets* (1992), with her editor Helen Dash

Hugh Lunn with the book that became a popular favourite over the air waves when serialised on ABC radio in 1991 (*Courier-Mail*)

Carol Davidson, Barry Gibbins and Anna Stachewicz representing UQP at the Sydney Book Fair

Fiction editor Rosanne Fitzgibbon (left) with novelist Rosie Scott and Laurie Muller

Sue Gough at the time of her first young adult novel *A Long Way to Tipperary* (1992)

James Moloney, whose YA fiction career began with *Crossfire* (1992)

Liam Davidson, whose novels include *The White Woman* (1994) and the Banjo award winning *Soundings* (1993)

Laurie Muller accepts his 1993 National Book Council Gold Medal for services to publishing from state governor Leneen Forde (*Courier-Mail*)

The now New York-based Peter Carey, internationally acclaimed for his novels as well as for his 1995 children's book *The Big Bazoohley* (Craig Voevodin photograph)

Indigenous editor Sandra Phillips with Cunnamulla author and story-teller Herb Wharton — a regular performer at European festivals

Lisa Bellear after the publication of her first poetry collection *Dreaming in Urban Areas* (1996)

Novelist Melissa Lucashenko (left) with Kibble winner Bobbi Sykes after Melissa had won the 1998 Dobbie Award for her first novel *Steam Pigs*

Children's editor Leonie Tyle (left) with Melissa Lucashenko and Brian Caswell at the 1998 Children's Book Council Conference in Adelaide

Barbara Ker Wilson, UQP's inaugural children's editor

Cassandra Pybus, whose autobiographical essay collection *Till Apples Grow on an Orange Tree* was launched at the 1998 Adelaide Festival

US–British publishing law. Since 1947 the British Traditional Market Agreement had neatly divided the world's English-language marketing territories between American and British publishers, who controlled the sales in the postwar Commonwealth countries, including, of course, Australia. The Market Agreement had virtually forced ambitious Australian writers to sever whatever early ties they had with Australian publishers and send their manuscripts overseas. This artistic brain-drain had consequently impoverished (in both senses of the word) Australia's cultural life. On a more mundane level, Australians had to wait months, even years, to buy important 'new' books locally. However, in 1976 a suit filed by the US Justice Department eventually terminated the Traditional Market Agreement in favour of a Consent Decree, which stipulated that traditional 'Commonwealth' rights could no longer be licensed automatically. This summary certainly oversimplifies the whole story, but the point is that in the late 1970s a separate 'Australasian' or 'Australian and New Zealand' publishing territory became at last a theoretical option for ambitious writers and their publishers. Because few writers anywhere bother to keep up with the details of international publishing law, Frank's purchase of the John Updike edition can be seen, in retrospect, as a creative performance demonstrating serious new publishing possibilities. John Updike (or rather his publisher, or agent) could — and did — bypass the British and sell Australasian rights directly to a publisher like UQP.

Of course, for UQP and other Australian literary publishers, the real opportunity offered by the Consent Decree was less the option of purchasing prestigious (and expensive) American titles than it was the possibility of keeping their 'own' successful writers. Ideally, Australian writers could enjoy international careers through British and US houses while at the same time maintaining their ties at home; the Australian publishers need not be left behind. The example of Peter Carey, whose novels were published very successfully by UQP in Australia, Faber in the UK and Knopf in the US, illustrated this ideal. Penguin took over UQP's distribution in 1984 making it possible for UQP to publish even the trade paperback editions of Carey's immensely successful novels.

In the late 1970s and early 1980s UQP faced another more constructive challenge in the greater willingness of other Australian publishers to risk taking on new writers. The resignation of Beatrice Davis from Angus & Robertson in 1973 had closed one great era in that publisher's history, but A&R subsequently published Frank Moorhouse, giving it a significant stake in UQP's 'territory'. Fremantle Arts Centre Press had come out with Elizabeth Jolley's first story collection in 1976 and her second in 1979. In 1980 Penguin's splashy paperback publication of Blanche D'Alpuget's first novel *Monkeys in the Dark* impressed many writers. But the list I really coveted was that of McPhee Gribble, which included first works by Helen Garner and Beverley Farmer, whose novel *Alone* had me teary-eyed for days. This list drew attention to an evident bias at UQP: its overwhelming emphasis at that time on male writers.

UQP did list works by two prominent women novelists, Thea Astley and Barbara Hanrahan, but Thea was already well established when she first submitted a manuscript to us. My concern and frustration over the masculine aura of the 'new writers' list grew as I sifted through the pile of unsolicited manuscripts (it, too, contained work mostly from men) and spoke with women writers who had sent their first work elsewhere. Meanwhile, of course, excellent new male writers — such as Angelo Loukakis, James McQueen and Victor Kelleher — continued to send in work that I was proud to include on the list.

Finally, a female presence was established at UQP, not, as it turned out, by trendsetting women in their twenties, but by two older (trendsetting) women who had been writing for years: Olga Masters and Elizabeth Jolley. The manuscript of Olga Masters' *The Home Girls* arrived via Craig Munro. I have written at length about my and UQP's relationship with Olga Masters, so will not repeat myself here, but the influence of her personality and exceptional talent on me — and UQP's list — was profound. When her first collection of stories, *The Home Girls*, along with Dimitris Tsaloumas' *The Observatory* won a National Book Award the following year, the twin victory was like a blessing on UQP's new decade of publishing. The manuscript of Elizabeth Jolley's *Miss Peabody's Inheritance* arrived, I think, about that time. I had been very interested in Jolley's work and in 1981 had visited her in Western Australia. When her novel arrived, I read it quickly, and delighted in its multiple voices and exquisite pacing. I hoped that the presence of Masters and Jolley would encourage other women to submit manuscripts.

Then, in early 1983, Frank Thompson and head editor Merril Yule suddenly resigned. They left before the university could seek and hire people to replace them, so for a while other staff members and I struggled to resolve any problems that arose.

During this period I tried hard to read promising new manuscripts, but could not spare the time for any that needed work or that I didn't understand. All of a sudden, professional presentation counted: Marian Eldridge's immaculate manuscript of *Walking the Dog* invited me to slow down long enough to explore, and admire, her beautifully cultivated sketches of Australian domestic life. Still, the pile of unsolicited fiction manuscripts began to lean dangerously, like Peter Carey's horses about to fall into the pool.

One morning I received a note from one of the writers, Kate Grenville. She had submitted a manuscript and wondered what had happened to it. She was very polite, causing me to feel extremely guilty, although her manuscript was one that I had set aside to take home.

For me that week, taking manuscripts home was running a serious risk. Despite our collective crisis management, the offices of UQP offered me a daily haven of grown-up order. Going home was the real challenge. My husband was temporarily working in another city, leaving me in charge of our preschooler, who at 6 pm would unfurl the larrikin nature she had repressed all day at the sitter's. Then, a friend from out-of-town descended on my 1 1/2 bedroom house with her husband and two toddlers, one of whom kept me awake with his croupy cough and tore into my daughter's toys after we'd left in the morning. Fortunately, I do not remember the details of that particular evening, except that at around 11.30 pm everyone at last went to bed and I finally got to 'Bearded Ladies'.

I kept reading well beyond midnight. Like a good film-maker, Grenville set up a scene, delivered the goods and moved on efficiently. In a few stories, however, her powerful imagination broke through the discipline. I finally collapsed into a weird dream state after finishing the brilliantly nightmarish 'Country Pleasures'. I could think of no writer who evoked so well the horror of a bad relationship — and from a young woman's point of view. I was even more impressed a few years later, when in *Lilian's Story* and *Joan Makes History* she expanded her range, telling stories as intense and light as her earlier work is intense and dark.

During the 1980s and 1990s no one complained any more about the lack of women writers at UQP. In addition to three novels by Thea Astley and eight by Barbara Hanrahan, we published five books by Olga Masters, three by Elizabeth Jolley, three by Kate Grenville and two by Marian Eldridge. Later, these writers were joined by Janette Turner Hospital, Marion Halligan, Margaret Coombs, Beverley Farmer, Lily Brett, Suzanne Edgar, Lolo Houbein and Gillian Mears. Ironically, the new UQP 'Collected' series of short stories is almost entirely composed of women, Peter Carey being the 'token' male writer.

From 1981, the fiction list also developed another discernible direction which would become known as 'multicultural' or 'migrant' fiction. Writing in the 1990s, I find the term 'multiculturalism' sometimes confusing to contemporary readers; even during its heyday some writers resisted it as a label. However, at the time the term was meaningful. The growth of UQP's fiction list, along with the growth of the academic specialty 'Australian Literature', had been driven not only by males, but by Anglo-Irish males. Meanwhile, the ethnic background of Australia had changed dramatically after World War II, when migrants from Southern and Eastern Europe moved into the major Australian cities and quickly began to influence cultural life. Australia not only gained mature artists like Dimitris Tsaloumas and Maria Lewitt, but the children of this generation were beginning to write and publish. The second generation had grown up in two worlds, hearing (if not speaking) two languages, struggling with two sets of values: it was not surprising that many sought artistic expression of these tensions.

Meanwhile academics began to question just who/what was an 'Australian' writer, and educators in secondary and primary schools became concerned that their texts reflect more accurately the multicultural origins of their students. This trend was also supported politically when the Literature Board of the Australia Council added funding specifically directed toward multicultural writing, and the prestigious New South Wales Premier's Literary Award added a prize for multicultural fiction.

Angelo Loukakis' *For the Patriarch* was published just at the right time to take advantage of these academic, educational and political developments. I had a particular interest in this collection because it was one of the first I worked on at UQP, and Angelo later became a 'second-reader' and a good friend. The characters in his stories, mostly Greek migrants and their families living in Australian cities, also seemed like friends, and all of us at UQP were personally as well as professionally delighted when *For the Patriarch* and, later, *Vernacular Dreams* became successful in so many ways.

About the time UQP published *For the Patriarch* another, dramatically different migrant story arrived circuitously from Rosa Cappiello, who had moved to Sydney from Naples in the 1960s. Her first novel, *Paese Fortunato*, a scarifying but bracingly energetic account of some women migrants' experiences in Sydney, had been first published in Italy by the famous literary publisher Feltrinelli. UQP's Australian-English translation took a tremendous amount of time to organise and publish. Not everyone liked the Italian novel, and Cappiello herself was rightly concerned about who would translate her work. She eventually worked productively with Gaetano Rando, and the resulting novel, *Oh Lucky Country*, has become a favourite on Women's Studies syllabi.

Despite my sympathy with the initial motivations of 'multiculturalism', as time passed I began to wonder what the word actually meant. For one thing, the prohibition on Anglo-Irish excluded writers like Victor Kelleher, whose world view and thoughtful, moving responses to an enormous range of reading and experience in England, Africa, New Zealand and Australia seemed to me truly 'multicultural'. His writing and sensibility obviously owed much to his having moved, particularly as a young person, from one culture to a series of others. Yet aside from my own doubts, and some of the writers' grumbling over 'labels', the multicultural 'hook' was ultimately a positive and useful device to promote talented writers. *For the Patriarch*, *Oh Lucky Country*, Spiro Zavos' *Faith of Our Fathers*, Peter Skrzynecki's *The Wild Dogs* and Angelika Fremd's *Heartland* won literary prizes and/or found their way to school and university reading lists. We also published three anthologies of multicultural writing, R. F. Holt's *The Strength of Tradition* and *Neighbours*, plus Sneja Gunew and Jan Mahyuddin's *Beyond the Echo*, and some of the new writers in these anthologies later went on to publish their own books.

By the mid-1980s UQP was indeed growing up with its writers, and in 1989 it had become a commercial as well as a critical success. The fiction list gathered its own momentum. UQP became at once more regional and more worldly, and we were finally able to add staff, both permanent and freelance, to help with the burgeoning fiction and trade non-fiction lists. For the fiction, Rosanne Fitzgibbon and Jena Woodhouse handled most of the copyediting and much related correspondence, while Clare Forster helped me with the initial reading and selection. Sue Johnson and Mary Roberts' *Latitudes*, an anthology of Queensland writers, inspired me to write to Janette Turner Hospital, and before long we had another popular and internationally acclaimed writer. *Latitudes* also brought to my attention Matthew Condon and reaffirmed my and Craig Munro's determination to keep nagging Gerard Lee for a new manuscript: hence, *Troppo Man*.

This momentum, however, created new kinds of demands on me and other UQP staff. Australian fiction was flourishing around the world, but the emotional investment we all had in the writers was beginning to exact a price. In 1984 Barbara Hanrahan had moved to a London publisher, a loss that hurt terribly. In 1985 Peter Carey was short-listed for the Booker Prize, sending morale to the outer stratosphere. The following year, 1986, Olga Masters' sudden death slammed us back to earth. The expanding careers of writers like Kate Grenville and Angelo Loukakis caused pride; the loss of some writers to other lists caused grief, some deserved, some not. In 1988 it was as if the surges and troughs of the previous years repeated themselves, but with greater intensity and in shorter order: Janette Turner Hospital's novel *Charades* was launched with great fanfare at the Brisbane Expo; Olga Masters' last collection of stories was published, and the literary community mourned her loss and celebrated her memory; Peter Carey won the Booker Prize, suspending (momentarily) time and space …

That year, my family and I decided to return to the United States, and as I prepared to leave UQP, some strange and wonderful things happened. Barbara Hanrahan returned. Two strikingly good new manuscripts from Liam Davison and John Clanchy appeared at about the same time. Then, out of the blue, Beverley Farmer, the writer I had least expected to see on our list, sent us *A Body of Water*. Its form, content and grace once again asked me what was 'Australian', and now, ten years later, I still cannot answer the question. As I prepare to send a copy of Farmer to a friend writing his own eclectic, literary montage, I will simply write: 'Here is a brilliant book for you.'

As It Was, Nearer by Far

MARTIN DUWELL

TAKING OVER AS the University of Queensland Press's poetry editor in 1984 I stepped into large but comfortable shoes. Roger McDonald and Tom Shapcott were much admired predecessors as well as friends. Their contributions had developed an outstanding list. And I had been in a very good position to observe it, since through the 1970s and into the early eighties I had run my own Makar Press which was also in the poetry publishing business. Although Makar might have been expected to view UQP as a large rival, I had never felt the slightest tension between us. It was always good to talk to Roger who often contributed poems to *Makar*, and he may have been the first to suggest to Peter Annand that it would be a good idea to publish a series of books, smaller than the conventional sixty-four pager, as part of our journal's annual subscription. So Roger may also deserve acknowledgment as one of the founding fathers of what became *Makar*'s Gargoyle Poets series. At any rate it was always informative and instructive to keep an eye on what was happening in the Press's offices a hundred metres or so away from my room in the university's English Department and I think my attitude was simultaneously well-disposed and objective.

Though I had never discussed it with either Roger or Tom or, for that matter, David Malouf or Rodney Hall, I always felt that the essential motivation behind the first Paperback Poets series was to offer a publication venue to a whole host of fine poets who had been denied publication by the clogging up of the limited publishing channels in the sixties. These were from among the ranks of the 'New Impulses' poets, so called because an anthology which showcased them (edited by Hall and Shapcott and published by UQP in 1968) had been called *New Impulses in Australian Poetry*. They included poets such as Malouf and Judith Rodriguez who were yet to publish their first books. The series would also offer a local publisher to Tom Shapcott and Rodney Hall, poets much more prolific in terms of publishing history. At the same time, the youngest poet of the New Impulses group, Andrew Taylor, also had a first manuscript that would need publication.

I felt that this program, centering around people in their thirties, didn't emerge quite as planned. Almost immediately it was, if not hijacked, then at least altered, by younger poets — although the fact that I belonged to a generation that considered anybody over thirty to be aged and irrelevant might have coloured my view at the time. But the youthful Michael Dransfield's first book, *Streets of the Long Voyage*, arrived nestled between Malouf's *Bicycle* and Hall's *Heaven in a Way*. Although all three books are brilliant, *Streets of the Long Voyage* had a special potency and has remained popular with readers for a quarter of a century. Similarly, Richard Tipping's *Soft Riots* was a revelation, as was *The Deer under the Skin* by the then little-known J. S. Harry. The late sixties and early seventies was a time when an extraordinary number of new poets erupted on the scene. There seemed to be new names turning up continually in contributions to the little magazines of the time, especially *New Poetry* and *Makar*, and this first Paperback Poets series needed quickly to balance up the writers in their thirties with the new writers in their twenties. McDonald managed this with great skill and eventually the series published not only Dransfield, Harry, Tipping, Vicki Viidikas and Rhyll McMaster but also Alan Wearne, Jennifer Maiden and Martin Johnston.

The emergence of the New Impulses generation was quickly overtaken, in the early seventies, by the arrival of the group sometimes called the New Writing group or, to use John Tranter's phrase, 'the Generation of '68'. Generationally, Dransfield and Tipping were members of this group. Some preferred to publish in underground journals for aesthetic/political reasons, some published with *New Poetry*'s Prism Poets and some with Makar Press. John Tranter's anthology, *The New Australian Poetry* (Makar 1979), is a pretty definitive encapsulation of the boundaries and activities of this group. Later, a group of younger poets in Canberra, supported by Les Murray, became a kind of reaction to the New Writing poets, objecting to their dislike of existing Australian poetry and their tendency to look to American models. The position of this group is well summed up in Robert Gray's and Geoffrey Lehmann's anthology *The Younger Australian Poets* (Hale and Iremonger 1983). While Murray and Lehmann have been published by Angus & Robertson and, later, in the Heinemann poetry series edited by Jamie Grant, Robert Gray's first book, *Creekwater Journal*, was published by UQP early in the second series (in 1974), and the 'Canberra Poets', Mark O'Connor, Kevin Hart and Alan Gould, all published their first books with UQP. The tension between these two groups dominated the publishing of poetry until the second half of the eighties.

A tension like that poses a lot of problems for a poetry list and one of the great achievements of McDonald and Shapcott was to negotiate it so successfully. Everyone recognises that there are, essentially, two opposed types of editors: those with a narrow agenda who, at their best, effect really radical transformations of literary culture and those who want the best of a range of modes. Each type can caricature the other cruelly but they both seem viable to me — a statement which, of course, irrevocably places me in the latter category. A publisher who wants the best of a variety of modes, as I always have, and as Shapcott and McDonald have, runs a lot of risks. Your list can be stretched so wide that it can look gossamer thin and of course you risk the accusation that your list has no direction and that you are an editor without principles. But to me, editing has always been about a complicated process of self-education and this means the desire to stretch my responses as much as possible. I have always been more interested in poems that I expect to dislike (and do) than in those which I find immediately exciting and gratifying. This may appear deliberately perverse but it has been part of my wiring since I began editing contemporary poetry as an undergraduate in 1968. The fact that I am usually associated with the New Writing poets — whose work I know, love best, and have written most about — does not contradict this, since there is, within that group, a far larger range of opposing conceptions of poetry than is usually thought. Since I am not a poet myself, this pluralist approach causes me fewer problems than it must do for Shapcott — an indefatigable poet, editor and anthologist. Part of understanding such an interesting poet and the mechanisms of his career would have to accommodate the fact that he has edited poetry so utterly different from his own work, as though for him editing were a way of learning what can be done and thus, as Auden says, discovering 'from what we are not what we might be next'.

The word that Shapcott chose to summarise the period of the second Paperback Poets series and the later period of his own editorship, at least as far as 1978, is 'Consolidation', the title given to the second anthology made from the Press's list. In a publishing culture intoxicated with the idea of the 'new' and the concomitant totemic term of all editors, 'discovery', this is a very modest word. But it is an accurate one. Clearly neither Shapcott nor myself wanted a list given over, in the name of principle, to one or other of these groups and settled on the idea of trying to publish the best from a range of modes. Although Shapcott might well be remembered for having extracted from David Malouf his wonderful second book, *Neighbours in a Thicket*, it is worth recording that he also persuaded Bruce Beaver to write a book about his youth. And the result, *As It Was*, moved that poet into a quite different kind of literary activity and produced a new kind of autobiography. It is also worth pointing out that the second of the anthologies made from the Paperback Poets lists has always been more interesting than the first. It is organised according to the poets' ages and shows, for example, older poets like David Rowbotham as well as Beaver renewing themselves. This period also saw the publication of two posthumous books of previously unpublished Dransfield poems, *Voyage into Solitude* (1978) and *The Second Month of Spring* (1980). Edited by Rodney Hall, they added a priceless two hundred pages to the body of Dransfield's poetry available in print.

My own sense of what happened in the early to mid-eighties is that this division of the poetic imperium into, on the one hand, 'Les Murray, Geoffrey Lehmann and their friends' and, on the other, 'John Tranter, Robert Adamson and their friends' was rapidly overtaken by three developments which have characterised the period since and are only just being, in their turn, replaced. The first of these is the interest in women poets as an entity in themselves. The arrival of feminism first made its mark in readers' rather than in writers' practices. Although the list in the period from 1978 to 1989 contains Judith Rodriguez, it remains a very male list, more so in fact than the first Paperback Poets series. It is fairly likely that this is the result of the growth of specialist women's publishing houses. The second development has been the interest in black writing in English. Here UQP has been a pioneer but has developed this as a separate series.

The final difference is a strong interest in what was initially called multicultural writing. Here UQP led the way by publishing Dimitris Tsaloumas' selection of Greek poems with English translations, *The Observatory*. To me, perceiving the power and importance of Tsaloumas is one of Shapcott's great editorial triumphs. It is a book which for many months I found intoxicatingly incomprehensible. It was not until I read a prose translation of 'Introductory Note', made by Con Castan, that I had any inkling of what a great poet Tsaloumas is. During my editorship the Press published *The Book of Epigrams* and also Tsaloumas' first book of poems written in English, *Falcon Drinking*. His second, *The Barge*, was published after my tenure. In a sense this part of the program could be said to have begun even earlier with the publication of Maria Valli's *Poesie Australiane* in 1972. It could also be said to be the inspiration behind the two books of Aboriginal traditional poetry edited by myself and Professor R. M. W. Dixon of the Australian National University, *The Honey-ant Men's Love Song* and *Little Eva at Moonlight Creek*. My idea was, initially, to provide a book of Australian poetry which didn't happen to be written or composed in English. The strength of UQP's more conventional list provided a context in which to face up to the fact that not all Australian poetry is written in English and *The Observatory* provided the model for what I think is the best system for publishing translations: to include the original language version and the translation on facing pages.

Just as Shapcott's period as editor negotiates the difficult poetic politics of the period and simultaneously looks forward intelligently to the changes to come on the literary scene, so it also inaugurates an important series of Collected and Selected poems, beginning in 1975 with David Rowbotham's *Collected Poems* and Rodney Hall's *Selected Poems.* A second series was begun later, under the general control of in-house editor Sue Abbey, and in a solely paperback format, with a collection of all the published poems of Michael Dransfield in 1987. It is a valuable series which enables readers to do a number of things: to take a serious look at the poetry of people like Shapcott himself, Judith Rodriguez and Fay Zwicky; to look carefully at poets from the 'generation of '68' grouping such as Adamson, John Scott and Laurie Duggan whose work is not all easily available; to sample updated 'Selecteds' for really important older poets like Bruce Beaver and John Blight; and to assess properly edited final volumes for deceased poets Charles Buckmaster and Jennifer Rankin as well, of course, as Dransfield.

My policy as editor was to continue the width of the list and to try to live up to the quality of the existing program in being solid, open, adventurous and wide-ranging without being thin or eccentric. This included publishing two books by Gary Catalano, whose first book had appeared in the

Paperback Poets series, as well as works by Shapcott and Andrew Taylor. At the same time, I wanted to include as many as possible of the good poets from *The New Australian Poetry* and I am proud in this respect of John Tranter's brilliant *Under Berlin* — an accessible book by a great poet — and the two individual books of John Scott: *St Clair* and *Singles*. In the case of *St Clair* I can record what is, I think, the only example of a change imposed by UQP's publishing committee on the books I edited. It was initially titled *Two Poems* and I have always preferred this dry, aggressive title, though, since a third long poem, 'Preface', was added while the book was being considered, it would have had to be changed to *Three Poems* and that would have trespassed on Ashbery territory. The book was renamed after one of the original narrative poems and I still think this was a mistake. In this period, as well as later, UQP published selections of Adamson, Scott, Buckmaster, Beaver and Duggan.

Many of the books of this period remain among my favourite books of poetry and would be so had I been a reader rather than an editor. Apart from the three books by Tranter and Scott already mentioned, there was Tsaloumas' *Falcon Drinking*, Bruce Beaver's *Charmed Lives* which, I am ashamed to admit, turned up unsolicited, and the late John Blight's *Holiday Sea Sonnets* — a really distinctive poet's return at a late stage in his career to an earlier mode. There are also the pleasures of publishing the work of poets whom I had admired early in the seventies and whose work seemed to have ground to a halt. A huge manuscript arrived from Richard Tipping containing virtually everything he had written since the publication of *Domestic Hardcore* in the second Paperback Poets series in 1975. A heavily edited version of this was published as *Nearer by Far* in 1985.

There was also the case of Lewis Packer's *Serpentine Futures*. As Richard Packer, this poet had published a marvellous book with UQP in 1972 (though it was not part of the first Paperback Poets series) called *Being Out of Order*. It had made a big impression on me in my undergraduate days, especially in one poem, 'The American Age', which is a set of nightmare images of the 1970s but which has become, if anything, more suggestive as the millennium approaches. I had published Packer's poems in *Makar* and remembered reading a fascinating and mysterious poem called 'The History of Flight' which remains resonant but mysterious because it is one of those poems which disorients you by leaving you unclear as to what is metaphoric and what is literal — a tendency shared by many of the Tsaloumas epigrams. When a manuscript arrived, also unsolicited, with this as the first poem, I was interested and very receptive and *Serpentine Futures* duly appeared in 1986. Unfortunately its author was notorious for an aggressive litigiousness.

Although most authors content themselves with trying to sue those who have rejected them, I think Packer had sued, after publication, most of the publishers who had published him. I have always felt slightly uneasy that I loaded UQP with the burden of this developing saga, concluded only by Packer's premature death.

Since exchanging poetry editing for the role of reviewer and critic, I have been pleased to see the continuation of the model that my predecessors and I established. There have been new books by Catalano, Beaver, Tranter, Taylor, Shapcott and Tsaloumas as well as good books by other writers new to UQP. It has also been further developed so that, for example, in the case of the two books by Komninos there has been a refreshing ability to open the list to the best of 'performance' poetry.

To look back from this present to the mid-seventies and even further, it is hard not to be impressed by the University of Queensland Press's overall poetry list. It runs to over 100 volumes and stands squarely astride the Australian poetry of that period. Poets are often not easy authors to deal with, but they have usually responded to UQP, whether steered by Frank Thompson or Laurie Muller, as a sympathetic, supportive publisher with genuine vision and a commitment to quality. Though not all books have been greeted with equal rhapsody or comprehension, they have most often been well received. Sometimes, of course, good books ask a lot from readers. *The Observatory* is one example and so is John Scott's *St Clair.* If I had to nominate a single poem which gave me, as editor, most excitement, it would be 'Preface', that sixty-page-long, extraordinary, gothic fiction of the man who goes in search of A—, his ultimate female, enacting the major arcana of the Tarot pack as he does so. One reviewer in a West Australian newspaper called it a 'catalogue of obscenities'. While this did nothing to raise the spirits of its author, it gave its editor immense pleasure to be reminded that it is still possible for a great poem to outrage people.

Reaching Younger Readers

BARBARA KER WILSON

ONE DAY IN 1984 I had a fortuitous meeting at a literary gathering with Laurie Muller, the General Manager of the University of Queensland Press. I had just left The Reader's Digest, where I'd spent seven years as Editor of Condensed Books for Australia and New Zealand, and I now intended to resume my erratic career as a writer and to do some freelance editorial work. 'Life is what happens when you're making other plans' ... Out of the blue, Laurie told me that he was interested in starting an Australian teenage fiction list at UQP. I thought it was a most perceptive notion and that this was exactly the right time to launch such a list. No other specifically Australian teenage list existed (though plenty of other publishers were to latch onto the idea following UQP's lead), and teenage lists were extremely successful in the UK and the United States.

Given the established reputation of the adult fiction published by UQP, I knew that the proposed youth list would embody integrity of purpose and aim to establish new writers of quality. Laurie then asked me if I would like to develop this new series, taking on the role of Editor. He knew that I had previously developed the young books list at Angus & Robertson (from 1966 to 1972) and had subsequently started Hodder & Stoughton's children's list. In fact, my very enjoyable work with adult books at The Reader's Digest had been a new direction for me; before coming to Australia in 1964 I had begun my publishing career in the children's books department at Oxford University Press in the UK, and continued as Managing Editor for children's books at The Bodley Head and then at William Collins in London. As a writer, I had produced some 35 children's books, both fiction and non-fiction.

I was intrigued by the idea of a return to publishing books for younger readers, and accepted Laurie Muller's invitation. At this time I lived at Leura, in the Blue Mountains, out of Sydney, and to begin with I worked from home, visiting Brisbane from time to time to confer with my colleagues at the Press. From the beginning, Publishing Manager Craig Munro and fiction editor D'Arcy Randall, as well as the rest of UQP's editorial and marketing departments, were enthusiastic about this new development. Later, after the list was established, Clare Forster brought her own special insights to the young books.

I began UQP's Young Adult Fiction list, as we decided to name it, by renewing my contacts within the children's book world (especially the library and teaching areas, for the marketing of young books relies heavily on institutional budgets) and placing notices in the journals of the various Australian writers associations and literary magazines, announcing the new YAF list and inviting manuscripts for consideration.

Books are chosen for publication in a number of different ways: non-fiction, for instance, may be commissioned from certain authors on specific subjects; chance meetings with people who have fascinating experiences and unusual ideas can lead an editor to encourage them to start writing; perhaps a short story or novel by an adult writer seems to suggest that the author could write for a teenage audience; a work long out of print may be reissued in a new edition; literary agents solicit publishers' interest in their clients; Australian copyright may be obtained for a book originally published elsewhere ... and then, and then, there are those unsolicited manuscripts which arrive at publishers' offices every day, sent by aspiring authors who hopefully, eagerly, confidently, doubtfully wait to learn the fate of their 'dearly beloved child', as Jane Austen called her first published novel, *Pride and Prejudice.*

I have always, but always been a true believer in the

potential precious ore to be mined from those piles of typescripts and computer print-outs, my belief firmly founded on my experience throughout decades of publishing adventures. In former days, out of those hillocks of paper I had read first manuscripts by writers such as Gillian Avery, Michael Bond (creator of Paddington Bear), Alan Garner, Mollie Hunter, William Mayne, Philippa Pearce, Rosemary Sutcliff, John Ryan (the 'onlie begetter' of Captain Pugwash), to name a few outstanding children's writers (and, in John Ryan's case, an illustrator). There's an intense excitement in 'discovering' a new author. Sometimes the manuscript needs more work, occasionally it is the author's second manuscript which is eventually published; the important thing is to recognise a new and individual voice arising from the narrative, and to be able to encourage authors to fulfil and expand their talent.

From the flood of unsolicited manuscripts sent to UQP since the Young Adult Fiction list was started have emerged writers of the calibre of Maureen Pople, Donna Sharp, James Grieve, Brian Caswell, Gregory Bastian, Judith Clarke, James Moloney, Jill Dobson, Ian Ottley and Stephen Measday. Two notable Queensland authors, Sue Gough and Michael Noonan, expressed interest in writing for the new list, and their teenage books have been exceptionally well received, while Dorothy Porter, whose poetry had appeared under the UQP imprint, also produced two excellent YAF titles. Alan Collins and Rosemary Dobson are two other adult writers who successfully turned to young books. While our YAF list is essentially Australian, we have included a few books originally published elsewhere: from the United States Deborah Savage's novel *The Flight of the Albatross*, from New Zealand Diana Noonan's *Leaving the Snow Country*, and from Canada Budge Wilson's *My Cousin Clarette.*

The first three UQP Young Adult Fiction titles were published in 1986: Maureen Pople's brilliant, wryly humorous novel *The Other Side of the Family*, James Preston's *The Sky Between the Trees*, and Donna Sharp's *Blue Days*. These were followed by Nora Dugon's *Lonely Summers*, Michael Noonan's acclaimed novel *McKenzie's Boots*, James Grieve's *A Season of Grannies*, Alan Collins's *The Boys from Bondi*, and *Summer Press* by Rosemary Dobson. These eight titles appeared in the first YAF catalogue, which I took with me in 1988 to the London and Bologna Book Fairs. We sold several titles to overseas publishers, and in their US editions Michael Noonan's *McKenzie's Boots* was selected by the American Library Association as one of the Best Books for Young Adults, while Maureen Pople's *The Other Side of the Family* was chosen as Best Book of the Year (1988) by the American School Library Journal, and James Grieve's *A Season of Grannies* was shortlisted for the UK *Guardian* Award. *Blue*

Days by Donna Sharp was shortlisted for the Children's Book Council of Australia's 'Book of the Year' Award. These were the first of many awards for UQP's Young Adult Fiction list, culminating in James Moloney receiving the CBC 'Book of the Year' Award in 1997 for *A Bridge to Wiseman's Cove.*

In 1991 I proposed that we should extend our young books list to cover a lower age-group, as there appeared to be a market gap for quality fiction for young children. What should we call the new series? We wanted something that related to Queensland, and for a while we favoured 'Cane Toads'! However, this idea was squashed, and the series eventually became 'Storybridge', a name that occurred to me as I was driving over that well-known Brisbane river-mark one afternoon. The Storybridge Series was launched in July 1993 with two short novels — Brian Caswell's *Mike* and Mavis Scott's *The Magic Palace* — and John Fairbairn's collection of stories, *Green Slime.* By 1997 we had published a total of 30 titles, including Peter Carey's delicious story *The Big Bazoohley*, shortlisted for the 1996 CBC 'Book of the Year' Award in the younger category, and James Moloney's *Swashbuckler*, which won that year's Award.

I had now been working with UQP for almost a decade, and once again I decided it was time to make a bid for my elusive 'retirement'. The UQP young list now needed a full-time editor. At the Warana Festival of 1990 (now evolved into the Brisbane Writers' Festival), I had been asked to launch a new Queensland publishing company, Jam Roll Press, the brainchild of Leonie Tyle, Robyn Sheahan and Robyn Collins, which was to specialise in picture books. Jam Roll produced some outstanding titles and featured illustrators such as Gregory Rogers, David Mackintosh, Narelle Oliver and Annmarie Scott and authors who included Gary Crew, Mark Svendsen, Janeen Brian and Jena Woodhouse. But this was the start of difficult times for Australian book publishing, and the market for higher-priced picture books was diminishing. Jam Roll Press, and Leonie Tyle, became part of UQP, with Leonie as the full-time Managing Editor of children's books.

UQP's children's list is now one of the most highly regarded in Australia. Picture books as well as novels have achieved success in North America, the UK and Europe. In little more than a decade this prestigious list has emerged, encompassing the production of high-quality books for children of all ages.

Publishing Indigenous Writers

SANDRA PHILLIPS

[Interviewed by Louise Poland, May 1997]

SANDRA PHILLIPS was interviewed by researcher Louise Poland in Melbourne at the Australian Reconciliation Convention in May of 1997. It was a moment of reflection for Sandra after two years with UQP and, as it turned out, just one month before she moved into arts administration with the Australia Council in Sydney. Sandra is now living with her young family in Singapore.

Some of the titles Sandra worked on at UQP were: *Follow the Rabbit-Proof Fence* by Doris Pilkington, *Warrigal's Way* by Warrigal Anderson, *Our Land Is Our Life* edited by Galwaruy Yunupingu, *Dreaming in Urban Areas* by Lisa Bellear, *Talking About Celia — Community and Family Memories of Celia Smith* by Jeanie Bell, *Plains of Promise* by Alexis Wright, and *Steam Pigs* by Melissa Lucashenko.

Sandra, what makes Aboriginal publishing distinctive?

In publishing you make a lot of value judgments about

content, material, style, process, outcome, targets. With Aboriginal publishing, you're making all those value judgments on appropriate criteria, which include culturally appropriate criteria, as well as industry expectations. Aboriginal people need to be centrally involved in that publishing process, and non-Indigenous people involved in the publishing of Indigenous work also need to be sensitised to the relevant issues.

Sandra, you worked at Magabala prior to UQP. What are the major differences in what appear, from the outside, to be quite different publishing houses?

With a house like UQP which is not small and not big, a medium-size press, there are departments which can sometimes fall into a bit of bureaucratic rigidity. From my experience of working at those two quite different presses, probably the biggest thing that comes up is deadlines — the rigidity of the overall publishing program and schedule. At UQP the Indigenous titles are scheduled alongside every other title with the same time frames attached to them. My Aboriginal authors are usually working on their first titles. It's very necessary to establish that relationship of trust and dialogue in the development of the creative work for publication. A small Indigenous press could shape its processes to suit those needs better. I think at UQP, in the editorial department, there is a very good understanding about those processes because the Press would have to be the most prolific publisher of Aboriginal and Torres Strait Islander writers. Magabala Books, IAD Press and Aboriginal Studies Press produce many collaborative works with non-Indigenous writers holding the pen. These oral stories are recorded, transcribed, edited and then published. Usually linguists or anthropologists shape the texts. For Aboriginal and Torres Strait Islander people to do the writing, the initiation of the concept, the execution, the refinement, the development, and then to take their books through the whole maze of the publishing process, that's quite different. UQP makes this challenge a priority.

Who shapes the list for the Black Writers' Series at UQP?

The David Unaipon Award is UQP's annual award for unpublished Aboriginal and Torres Strait Islander writers. Between 20 and 30 manuscripts are entered each year. This award has been going since 1989, so we've had more than 160 manuscripts entered since then. That's 160 manuscripts by Aboriginal and Torres Strait Islander people that may never have seen the inside of a publishing house otherwise. That channel provides the primary source of manuscripts for appraisal. Of course the award itself is judged externally by three Aboriginal judges and their decision stands whatever their choice of winner or commended entries. UQP guarantees publication to the winner with possible publication to the highly commendeds. The Press has a chance to look at all the entered manuscripts and offer publication to some additional works.

That's something you decide then?

In-house editors are pivotal to that whole process of manuscript appraisal, and especially for manuscripts written by Aboriginal or Torres Strait Islander authors.

If we can look at Aboriginal publishing over the last fifteen years, what do you think are some of the most important steps and maybe some of the most contentious ones?

Obviously the thing that comes to mind is the success of Sally Morgan's *My Place*. The schools listing of *My Place* was a significant factor in the sales success of that book and I think it proved for the wider non-Indigenous community a means of accessing a story from Indigenous Australia. I think it was a palatable story from an Indigenous Australian person. The palatability led to schools listing it, eventually, and led to people saying 'Ah, have you read *My Place*?' or 'Oh, I'll buy this for my grandmother' ... The grandmothers can read it, the grandfathers can read it. That's fairly significant. It shows a lot about style, reception, the factors that lead to commercial success for some titles.

Also I couldn't go past mentioning some of the fine writers UQP has published, including Doris Pilkington's fiction, Alexis Wright's recent novel *Plains of Promise,* Melissa Lucashenko's fiction, Jeanie Bell's unique genre-blending history styles and voices of community and family, Lisa Bellear's debut poetry collection, Mabel Edmund's memoir ... the list goes on in terms of who has been achieving publication in the last fifteen years.

Would it be fair to say that women's autobiography has been an important part of distinctive Aboriginal writing?

I don't know that you have to make the distinction between women's and men's autobiography. It was more about getting people to understand the Aboriginal experience of living in Australia. People have used their own lives and the telling of their lives as a vehicle for their own expression and healing and validation. Publication makes it available to a wider understanding. In the *Australian Women's Book Review* I wrote that autobiography is a national obsession, biography is a national obsession, and I would suggest that it's connected with our continuing definition of who we are as peoples. I think you can get very good biography, very good autobiography. And you can read text that doesn't do much for you. It's really important to have the full range of biographical telling from the Indigenous community, as there are different kinds of people representing our communities. Autobiography, those sorts of tellings have dominated, but there's a whole range of ways for our people to explore the print media.

What do you think are the other key areas of publishing?

The other key area of writing is poetry. From the David Unaipon Award it is quite clear that poetry entries far outweigh anything else. Either it is the form most easily integrated into daily life, or it's connected with the song cycle of telling of things. There is poetry that achieves a lot for the individual writer and there is poetry that can transcend individual impact and make a difference to the readers or the listeners of that poetry. People get very emotional about what is good poetry, what is bad poetry — what is good writing, what is bad writing. That will always happen. It's either something that touches you or it doesn't.

Reading is obviously an intellectual activity but it is also about an emotional or philosophical engagement with what you are reading. So if you are responding to that on a number of different levels, then the work must be good. If you are not responding, it doesn't necessarily mean the work isn't good. I would recommend to non-Indigenous readers that they actually look at the impact that writing is having on them. This is especially relevant for reading across cultures. For example, if you feel too challenged by the contents, you may say the writer forgot that his or her task was to tell a story and not to beat the reader about the head; if you feel sympathetic, you may be afraid to criticise the work; if you feel angry, you may condemn the writing as entirely incompetent. If readers can allow for their emotional responses within such a rational appraisal, they can then avoid the extremes of interpretation.

Would those comments then inform the way you would define success as an editor? How do you, as an editor with your own list, define success? In a way, this ties in with another topic I'm interested in, that of commissioning. Anyway, what is success for you?

The bigger houses are now establishing the editorial in-house function as a commissioning function. But with a press the size of UQP, we're more than just commissioning editors. You work in detail on manuscripts, you appraise manuscripts, you take recommendations to your monthly publishing committee — so that's the commissioning element perhaps. Commissioning to me implies that you have a lot of resources behind you with which to go out into the wider world. I think that we've got enough channels open, for example, between UQP and the Indigenous writing community, that there is a flow and there is communication, without necessarily having to go out to get somebody to write something that you consider is important.

So there are more important or useful methods where you are?

It's about having a channel of communication. I think that's what a lot of Australian publishers don't have with Indigenous writers. Some of the bigger houses only accept manuscripts that come from a literary agent. So their contact with the overall writing community is fairly minimal, and their accessibility to publishing projects from the Indigenous writing community is even more minuscule.

What about the issue of reviewing?

Reviewing of Aboriginal writing is very important. I think too often judgments are made about those books without the reviewer having enough background or context, and without a willingness to engage with a form of writing that could be different. There don't seem to be any consistent credentials for reviewers of Aboriginal and Torres Strait Islander books. In order to understand them and in order to review them — to act as a mediator between them and the potential reading public — reviewers should have some specific cultural understanding or professional credentials. Most recently, with *Plains of Promise* by Alexis Wright you had the whole gamut from 'this is not a great book' to 'this is an exciting, very exciting new writer who deserves Rolls Royce treatment'. So you've got the ends of the spectrum there. Ultimately it's all about acknowledging that the writing is coming from a different source. The technique is similar, the whole medium is obviously the same, but the integrity and what informs the expression could be, and should be, and probably is in most cases, very different.

What is it about publishing that you find most challenging?

Well, I hate deadlines, but I love them as well. It's great to work on a project and have an outcome. You develop intense creative relationships that lead to the fulfilment of the book and that's all wonderful. I think you need to be a good communicator to be able to do that effectively. I think you need to have good language understandings, very strong language understandings and a love of language and a love of expression, a love of the written word as well. I think that I've moved into an area that few other Aboriginal people are involved in. It's very satisfying and very challenging, constantly challenging. You can't apply formula to process. You're working as part of a team and able to act as a mediator. I am acting as a mediator between a community which I'm a part of — the Indigenous community — and the wider Australian community.

What are your hopes for the future of publishing and, specifically, the future of Aboriginal publishing?

The more publishing opportunities for Indigenous writers the better. I hope those publishers who enter the area recognise the potential difference required in the publishing of those writers. Indigenous writers who do get published need support and encouragement to engage and communicate regularly about the process so they don't feel disempowered. In a smaller press it is essential to nurture your backlist and keep your titles in print. I hope publishers recognise this different journey taken by most of the books written by Aboriginal and Torres Strait Islander people.

There can be little doubt that UQP is leading the way in publishing creative writing by Aboriginal and Torres Strait Islander authors. This publishing is amply facilitated by the Press's commitment to the David Unaipon Award, but there are examples that existed before it, and there are examples that extend beyond just the opportunities afforded by it. UQP has actively fostered the writing careers of Aboriginal and Torres Strait Islander authors, with some seeing the publication of their second and third books.

I can only hope that other publishing houses catch on, so that they too can be part of this uniquely Australian field of writing and publishing.

Would you say that it is 'the coming of age', if you'll excuse the phrase, of Aboriginal publishing?

It's not so much the publishing — you can't publish something that hasn't been written! It's having the communication and then being prepared to put in the hard developmental work on those Indigenous writers. And that's where a lot of the reviewers have no understanding of the relationship between the publisher and the writer from the word go. It is a developing canon. It is a new canon. And I'm not too sure if it's 'the coming of age' or if it's the ongoing journey of creative expression. Awards like the David Unaipon provide incentives. Respected writers such as Jack Davis and Oodgeroo have acted as mentors and role models.

And the more creative writers we have the more there are going to be.

David Unaipon award winners:

- **1989** Graeme Dixon, *Holocaust Island* (poetry, published 1990)
- **1990** Doris Pilkington, *Caprice: A Stockman's Daughter* (fiction, published 1991)
- **1991** Bill Dodd, *Broken Dreams* (memoir, published 1992)
- **1992** Philip McLaren, *Sweet Water, Stolen Land* (novel, published 1993)
- **1993** John Muk Muk Burke, *Bridge of Triangles* (fiction, published 1994)
- **1994** Rosalie Medcraft & Valda Gee, *The Sausage Tree* (memoir, published 1995)
- **1995** Warrigal (Edward) Anderson, *Warrigal's Way* (memoir, published 1996)
- **1996** Steven McCarthy, *Black Angels, Red Blood* (novel, published 1998)
- **1997** John Bodey, *When Darkness Falls* (young adult, published 1998)

Highly commended entrants achieving publication:

- Joe McGinness, *Son of Alyandabu: My Fight for Aboriginal Rights* (memoir, 1991)
- Mabel Edmund, *No Regrets* (memoir, 1992)
- Herb Wharton, *Unbranded* (fiction, 1992)
- Eve Fesl, *Conned!* (nonfiction, 1993)
- Lisa Bellear, *Dreaming in Urban Areas* (poetry, 1996)
- Jeanie Bell, *Talking About Celia* (biography, 1997)
- Alexis Wright, *Plains of Promise* (novel, 1997)
- Melissa Lucashenko, *Steam Pigs* (novel, 1997)

On an Australian Selection

LAURIE HERGENHAN

THE AUSTRALIAN AUTHORS SERIES has developed over more than twenty years, beginning in 1976, with thirty-six volumes to date. To convey to readers some idea of its origins and background I need to go back in time before 1976 to sketch the circumstances of my initial involvement with Australian literature, and even a bit beyond that, for the series initially grew out of a very different cultural climate from this turn-of-the-century one.

In 1975 Frank Thompson, as manager of the University of Queensland Press, invited me to be the general editor of a new Portable Australian Authors series, as it was first called. As I remember, Roger McDonald was present at the first meeting and was an adviser in the early stages. The series was Frank's general concept, but he left it completely to me to develop. At the time I could not see where it would lead, but I'll always be grateful to have been given this opportunity.

It reminds me of another opportunity generously offered by James McAuley in 1963 when I was a new lecturer in

English at the University of Tasmania. I had arrived there in 1960, shortly before Jim took up the position, then unique in Australia, of Reader in Poetry. Not long after, with the sudden death of Professor Murray Todd, Jim was appointed to the Chair in English, his first academic appointment in the field. From a new and secure base he was keen to advance the interests of his small department of five staff as well as to pursue his own career in literature, as poet and critic, and in politics. In consultation with his old friend Alec Hope, fellow poet, critic and head of the Department of English at the Australian National University, and a leading proponent of the introduction of the academic study of Australian literature, Jim decided that there was a need for a scholarly journal exclusively devoted to this field. Both believed that it would encourage and draw upon a burgeoning in teaching and criticism that was becoming apparent. This was assisted by the vigorous growth of universities and of publications in the literary field, including moves to tap into the educational market, such as the beginning of the Australian Writers and Their Work series (Lansdowne, later Oxford) and an Australian Poets series (Angus & Robertson). Moreover, 1962 had marked the inauguration of the first ever Chair of Australian Literature, at Sydney University. The 1960s was also a decade which saw the consolidation of literary reputations, such as those of White, Wright and Slessor, and the emergence of others, such as Anderson, Harrower, Hazzard, Keneally and Stow, with fresh talent to gain attention in the early 1970s. Debate about such matters as traditions and styles enlivened the literary scene along with the political debate over the Vietnam War. *Australian Literary Studies* (*ALS*) was the journal that grew out of McAuley's vision and although beginning modestly it was to prove long-lived.

As with Frank Thompson's proposal over a decade later, McAuley's idea proved a prescient one and was similarly offered to me, no strings attached, to develop completely in my own way. Each indeed offered the proverbial lucky break. Jim and Frank, in their respective institutional and management roles, took care of the economic side of the ventures, leaving me to develop the literary possibilities, the building up and maintaining of quality productions. This was a luxury, as I was to discover later when I had to cope with the economic management of *ALS* as well as to edit it.

With both projects the question arises, 'Why me?', for I realise I was not offered these opportunities by chance, though serendipity contributed to my background and training and to my being in the right place at the opportune time.

The University of Sydney, where I was an undergraduate and postgraduate in the early 1950s, did not offer courses in Australian literature. A year's survey course in Australian history first awakened my interest in the study of the culture of my own country. The lecturer, Duncan McCallum, was learned, eccentric and dedicated, all attractive qualities to me. He brought to lectures a sea of detail, piles of loose-leaf notes, of which he was not always in command, and he was notorious for not launching the first fleet until third term. But it was the fascination of the rich detail, the scholarship behind it, and the opportunity to write essays using original historical documents that captured my imagination. This taught me that you did not have to go abroad — though I was to do so — to experience the excitement and rewards of such research.

At Sydney University an Honours course in literature called something like 'Scholarship and Bibliography' opened up a fascination of the ways in which English texts, including Shakespeare's — there were no Australian examples — were first printed, what the processes of transmission were, how versions could vary, how they might be edited. This was the origin of my lasting interest in editing.

Another Honours course introduced me to American literature, a new literature in English flowering in a new country. After writing an MA on Nathaniel Hawthorne, which confirmed my interest in the nineteenth century, the period when Australian literature began to develop, I went abroad in 1957 to study for a PhD. This was a move not encouraged by Australian academia at the time. Besides, unconventionally, I went not to Oxbridge but to London University, more by accident than choice, but to my good fortune. I revelled in using the great resources of the British Museum Library and its outlying newspaper depository at Colindale, at the virtual end of the Northern line. Here, in the days before later armies of researchers, I was allowed to roam the stacks.

I studied the contemporary reception of novelist George Meredith, never a popular writer, not realising that this kind of work would later feed indirectly into my studies in the Australian field. My research involved embarking upon the sea, or parts of it, of Victorian magazines and newspapers and the journalistic world of the times, pretty much uncharted then. Out of this grew a realisation of the interest and value of what my mentors in London, especially my admired PhD supervisor, Professor Geoffrey Tillotson, believed in: the importance of considering texts in what we then called 'the context of the times', in trying to recapture the circumstances of the production, circulation and consumption of literature. Of course, post-structuralist studies since the 1980s have transformed conceptions and methods of such approaches to what was for me an historical as well as a critical study, but there is continuity, if not often acknowledged, between what I learned then and what goes on now. What I came to love in London left a lasting impression.

Out of my Meredith research I published scholarly articles in English periodicals after I began teaching at the University of Tasmania in 1960, articles strong on historical context, with lots of detail and footnotes, and sifting the detail to build arguments. I think it was this background that prompted Jim McAuley to offer me the editorship of *ALS*. Even though I knew little about Australian literature at the time, Jim believed I could apply my training to its study. A generous Head, with a fine critical mind, who had himself not followed a conventional academic path, he valued historical scholarship and Australian literature, to which he made an important contribution as poet and critic.

When I became editor of *ALS* I had to learn fast about Australian literature and what had been written about it, and to learn through editing, gathering the knowledge and contacts it both built and demanded. *ALS* helped to pioneer at home and abroad the academic study of the field — it is still the only journal exclusively devoted to it — by extending it beyond the canon and beyond literary texts to embrace the contexts of biography, bibliography and social history.

In 1971 I moved from the University of Tasmania to the University of Queensland, attracted by the opportunity to teach Australian literature and the resources of a larger university, as well as warmer climes. I had already made contact with UQP through negotiating the publication of my first book in the Australian field, *A Colonial City: Selected Journalism of Marcus Clarke* (1972).

After my move to the University of Queensland I co-edited *ALS* with Ted Stokes, a former colleague from the University of Tasmania, but in 1976 it 'followed' me to Queensland and to UQP. Difficulty in continuing a subsidy at the Tasmanian end was offset by a special subsidy granted by the then Queensland Vice-Chancellor, Zelman Cowan. Frank Thompson had my work with *ALS* in mind when he asked me at this time to become general editor of the Portable series.

The American 'Portable' and 'Essential' series were a general model Frank suggested, perhaps partly out of his experience of teaching in that field. I was not familiar with them. What attracted me was the general concept of a collection of an author's work: a core selection (say, a novel) or core pieces (say, a selection of poems, stories) presented in the context of a selection from their representative writings across a variety of genres, which both adds to an appreciation of the central selection and at the same time suggests a writer's range. This flexible pattern allows for wide-ranging adaptation to individual careers.

With each volume care is taken to choose the most

accurate texts available for inexpensive reproduction, with provenance and major variations noted. This textual care, along with the central 'Portable' idea of building up a special kind of collection, a cross-section of an author's output instead of offering a single work, distinguishes the series in Australia from the usual commercial reprints. At the same time, the series does not aim at the definitiveness of the recently launched series of Academy Texts, also published by UQP. These are directed towards specialised use and will serve more as reference works than as widely used reading texts.

It was not long before the Portable series title was changed because of a legal challenge from its US counterpart. It was a sign of success, we thought, to be challenged by an American giant, so without fuss we changed the name to the Australian Authors series — the AAs as we call them now.

The first two published volumes in 1976, *Marcus Clarke* edited by Michael Wilding and *Henry Lawson* edited by Brian Kiernan, illustrate some of the possibilities of the flexible series format when adapted to Australian authors. One author was canonical and a national icon, while the other was not widely read or studied, though regarded as 'classic'. Frank later told me that when I chose these two authors to begin the series he had some misgivings: the Lawson has many competitors while the Clarke promised only limited readership. It was typical of Frank's generosity and willingness to take risks as a publisher that he kept any such misgivings to himself. Laurie Muller, Frank's successor, has kept these generous and encouraging attitudes alive. It is also appropriate to express here my appreciation of the valuable contribution over many years of Craig Munro and Rosanne Fitzgibbon as in-house editors and advisers, since the project has always been for me a team effort.

The *Henry Lawson* has proved one of the most widely read volumes of the series and remains in print while many other selections of that author have come and gone. Kiernan made his selection an individual one by using the series format to represent generously not only a substantial body of stories — some well known, others less so — but also selections of autobiography, poetry, letters and journalism. The collection, divided into chronological sections, indicates the course of Lawson's career and allows readers to see him more in the round, to grasp something of his range and the varying circumstances in which he wrote and which he wrote about, in a way that straight selections of his stories, the usual mode of representing him, cannot do.

Wilding's *Marcus Clarke* illustrates the difficulty of reproducing a long core novel, in this case *His Natural Life*, originally a Victorian 'three decker', which could hardly be bypassed as his most famous book, and along with it as generous a selection as possible of other writing: stories, journalism, essays. The bulky novel, photographically reproduced for economy's sake, left only a hundred pages for accompanying selections of these neglected writings, but these were enough to draw attention to Clarke's range and they are often cited from this selection. In addition, there were resulting problems of circulation, for the Clarke collection could not hope to compete commercially with reprints of the novel only. *Barbara Baynton*, edited by Alan Lawson and Sally Krimmer, faced a similar problem by including the important out-of-print novel, *Human Toll*, and some shorter pieces as well as the handful of famous stories, the only Baynton work available. Still, if economic viability, for at least some volumes, has always remained a consideration in planning the series, thanks to UQP this has not been at the expense of literary quality, the prime consideration. Individual editors and I have always kept in mind an audience of teachers, students and some general readership. Hence, while the *Lawson* volume is both popular and widely cited in literary studies, the *Clarke* serves mainly the latter purpose in appealing to scholars who are interested in him as much more than a one-book writer. Similarly, a volume like *The Jindyworobaks*, edited by Brian Elliott, while not circulating widely, remains a key text in understanding an important literary movement, more mocked than understood. *Nettie Palmer*, edited by Vivian Smith, is the only modern volume to reprint selections of her dispersed and influential critical journalism. Other volumes, such as *Colonial Voices* edited by Elizabeth Webby and *Eight Voices of the Eighties* edited by Gillian Whitlock, deal with literary movements and groupings and their contexts, not simply with individual writers.

Anyone, whether individual or institution, general reader or otherwise, who possesses the mini-library of the entire AA series has access to a substantial and wide-ranging body of Australian literature, and a continually expanding one. I see this as the achievement of the series, for which there are few, if any, Australian parallels. It is an achievement made possible by the riches of the literary material available and by the growing number of scholars who have provided the series with its individual editors. Indeed, these editors represent a roll-call of many of the most notable Australian scholars.

These developments cannot be graphed in a smooth upward curve. Changing technology affecting publishing and readership, changing literary tastes and approaches, the growth of overlapping studies such as feminism, cultural studies and Australian studies, continue to challenge the series, calling for constant inventiveness and imagination in choosing and designing individual volumes. Responding to this challenge, by building change into the series, is the only way to keep it vigorous.

The Pursuit of Literary Studies

ANTHONY J. HASSALL

IT IS NOW A DECADE since the Studies in Australian Literature (SAL) series was initiated by the University of Queensland Press and I was offered the role of founding General Editor. I doubt whether anyone ever sets out to become a series editor, and I was no exception. My encounters with Australian writing in the course of a fairly typical Australian education in the 1940s, 1950s and 1960s were limited to Paterson and Lawson in primary school, Judith Wright's poetry and, unforgettably, *Richard Mahony* in secondary school, and nothing at all in an English Honours course at university. These very limited contacts were, however, sufficiently engaging to encourage me to diversify my teaching and research interests in the 1970s. I had begun as an eighteenth-century scholar, with a PhD and a book on Henry Fielding. By the time that was published in 1979, I had begun reading, teaching and writing about Australian literature. I had also decided that my next book would be on the Western Australian poet and novelist Randolph Stow, whose work I greatly admired and whose achievement I thought was undervalued, something he had in common with many Australian writers at that time. My involvement with and commitment to Australian literature was intensified when I moved to the Chair of English at James Cook University in 1983, a position traditionally occupied by an Australian literature specialist, which carried with it the Executive Directorship of the Townsville Foundation for Australian Literary Studies. Since then I have written and edited mainly in the field of Australian literature.

On the basis of a generous assessment of *Strange Country*, my book on Randolph Stow (UQP 1986), Laurie Muller invited me to become General Editor of a proposed new series of critical studies of Australian writers, a series designed to strengthen and support UQP's already extensive Australian list. It was a meeting of like minds. There was a real passion for Australian literature at UQP, a passion I shared, and I was delighted to accept the proposal. It is a decision I have never regretted, though it has certainly involved a great deal of careful, patient and time-consuming work. Since 1990 I have had the assistance of two Advisory Editors, Jenny Strauss of Monash University and Bruce Bennett of the Australian Defence Force Academy, both of whom are strongly committed to the critical study of Australian literature and distinguished practitioners of it.

Back in 1987 there was very little critical writing on Australian literature. The only long-running series was the pamphlet-sized Australian Writers and Their Work, which Oxford University Press had taken over from Lansdowne Press in 1966. The abridged treatment this series afforded was evident in *Recent Fiction* (1973), which crammed Randolph Stow, Thomas Keneally, Shirley Hazzard and Elizabeth Harrower into 46 pages. There was also Edward Arnold's short-lived Studies in Australian Literature series, which produced two titles, again not much more than pamphlet length, though Dennis Douglas's *Maurice Guest* was a valuable contribution. In 1992 Oxford replaced Australian Writers and Their Work, discontinued in the early 1980s, with a new Australian Writers series. This published some dozen titles, still relatively slim, though larger than the earlier pamphlets, but ceased in 1996 because of what was judged to be a disappointing response. Those of us working on the SAL series at UQP have been aware of the disappointing track records of these other series, but we have continued to believe that substantial critical studies of Australian writers are needed, and we remain determined to succeed where others have failed or lost heart.

In addition to these rival series there were, when the SAL series began, very few book-length studies of Australian writers, and only a handful of histories of Australian literature. The best single-author study was Dorothy Green's *Ulysses Bound: Henry Handel Richardson and Her Fiction* (1973). The histories of Australian literature had enjoyed mixed success. H.M. Green's standard two-volume *A History of Australian Literature* (1961) was by then dated in content and approach. Leonie Kramer's *Oxford History of Australian Literature*, published in 1981, was widely dismissed as old-fashioned and authoritarian at a time of innovation, diversity and new theoretical insights.

There was clearly a need for a new and up-to-date history, and in 1986 I convinced the Executive of the Association for the Study of Australian Literature to undertake *The Penguin New Literary History of Australia* as a Bicentennial project, and I persuaded the distinguished and long-serving editor of *Australian Literary Studies*, Laurie Hergenhan, to accept the role of General Editor. It was an innovative and deliberately multivocal project, designed to reflect the many different theoretical and political approaches then being taken to the study of Australian literature. It was a timely volume, the reviews were generally favourable, and the Bicentennial fervour should have helped sales, but it was not a publishing success. This relative failure was the more striking, as the earlier Penguin, *The Literature of Australia*, edited by Geoffrey Dutton in two editions (1964 and 1976), which had been conventional in format and which reflected the critical orthodoxies of its time, had sold extremely well.

The contrasting sales of these Penguin histories clearly did not encourage the proposed new series to pursue the more esoteric trends in literary criticism too enthusiastically. On the other hand, the fate of the Leonie Kramer edited *Oxford History* did not recommend conservatism. If there was a lesson to be learnt, it was that the SAL series should aim to capture as much as possible of a limited market by being theoretically literate and up-to-date, while retaining a style that was lucid and accessible to non-professional readers. That represented quite a challenge.

With this in mind, we developed a set of guidelines for books in the series:

1. The SAL series would aim to produce a collection of critical studies of Australian Literature which would merit a place in every worthwhile library with a serious interest in Australian literature in Australia and overseas.
2. The books would be substantial, full-length critical studies, not patronisingly slight 'slim volumes' or pamphlets.
3. At least to begin with, the SAL series would address a concept of Australian literature that was constructed in a relatively straightforward and unproblematic manner. We would not indulge in the luxury of questioning at too great a length whether, or how, Australia should be

seeking its literary identity at a time when such concepts were under challenge, not least from the globalising of communications technology.

4. One of the urgent tasks confronting Australian literary criticism was to provide a context of sophisticated and informed critical discussion for the endeavours of writers such as David Malouf, Peter Carey and David Williamson, who were consciously seeking to create and consolidate distinctively Australian narratives.
5. The SAL series would not engage in agonised debates about what might or might not be classified as 'Australian' or 'literature'. It would not radically reappraise broadly agreed definitions of 'literature'. It would include within its brief all writing that was generally regarded as Australian, in all its current and future diversity. Elizabeth Jolley, for example, was an interesting test case, because she grew up in England and moved to Australia at the age of thirty-six. Almost all of her publishing history and a significant amount of her subject matter is Australian, and she is widely regarded as an Australian author. So a book on Jolley by Paul Salzman eventually became part of the series.
6. The question of how the series would reflect the increasing complexity and diversity of literary critical discourses had to be addressed. The view adopted was that SAL

volumes should be informed by current critical theory and practice, and that they should aim to interest academic readers and postgraduate students at the forefront of new critical and theoretical developments; but they should also be accessible to undergraduate readers and to senior high school students and their teachers. The market we were targeting was limited: we could afford neither to bore the sophisticated nor to exclude the relative newcomer with jargon or theoretical impenetrability. So prospective authors would be asked to write lucidly.

In designing the SAL series for a limited market, we were obliged from the beginning to address severe financial constraints. There is an opinion in the trade that in money terms literary criticism is not worth publishing. At the launch of the tenth SAL title a senior editor at Penguin Australia described book-length Australian literary criticism as 'vanity publishing'. Fortunately this view was not shared by Laurie Muller, Craig Munro, Rosanne Fitzgibbon and Clare Forster at UQP. But realism had to prevail. So the binding was paperback, the covers two-colour — green and gold of course — the paper quality basic, and the books limited to about 200 pages. Even so, the initial price was $29.95.

Reviewers generally welcomed each volume, but there were complaints about the paper quality, the binding and the price. In 1994 UQP responded by redesigning the books in a smaller format, adding full-colour covers, improving the quality of the paper and reducing the price. All previously published volumes are eventually to be reissued in the new format, in revised editions where appropriate.

Early in the life of the SAL series, UQP decided to ask all authors with institutional support to provide camera-ready copy. The technology was available in universities, and employing it transferred a significant component of the cost from the Press to the host university.

In recent years Australian universities have received some $3000 for each substantial book-length research publication as part of the Government's Research Quantum funding. This could be used by university departments to offset the costs of preparing camera-ready copy.

This strategy saved the Press a significant part of its previous costs, and was essential to the survival of the SAL series; but it was not without its effects on the finished product. One was that authors had to learn how to drive the software needed to produce a finished, formatted book in electronic form. This returned to the author an unprecedented degree of control over appearance and formatting, but it meant that the author and the General Editor had to do most of the editing formerly done by professional copy editors. UQP casts a technical and editorial eye over the camera-ready copy, and provides advice and support, but it does not undertake full copy-editing and proofreading in the traditional manner. Electronic correction and spell-checks still leave a considerable amount to be done by the General Editor and the author. Unfortunately, too many errors and typos survive this scrutiny, as reviewers properly remind us. They are corrected in second editions, of which there have been seven to date.

In a further cost-cutting development, the Press has recently acquired the technology to produce small runs of books on demand, in place of a single large print run. This obviates the need for expensive warehousing of stock, with concomitant remaindering and wastage. UQP are presently considering publishing the series in electronic form, but no decision has yet been made.

In the decade since the Studies in Australian Literature series began more than twenty titles have been published. As the following details indicate, the series is diverse and deliberately unformulaic. Five early books — J. J. Healy on *Literature and the Aborigine in Australia*, Anthony J. Hassall on Randolph Stow, Shirley Walker on Judith Wright, Laurie Hergenhan on convict fiction and Carole Ferrier's *Gender, Politics and Fiction* — were new and revised editions of existing books. Twelve are studies of single authors, all but one by single authors. Eight volumes address themes, periods or literary movements, such as *The 1890s* or *Michael Dransfield and the New Australian Poetry*, and of these, three are collections of essays by various hands. One volume, released in two editions to date, is a cumulation of the invaluable annual bibliographies in *Australian Literary Studies*.

Two of the first three titles concerned Aboriginal writing and writing about Aborigines, and the third, David Brooks and Brenda Walker's *Poetry and Gender*, was a collection of essays and statements on women's poetry and poetics. This demonstrated from the beginning that the series would reflect matters of current concern in Australian culture and welcome work on and from minority groups and writers. Three of the books have won the annual Walter McCrae Russell Award of the Association for the Study of Australian Literature for the best book of literary criticism: Adam Shoemaker's *Black Words White Page: Aboriginal Literature 1929–1988*, which is our bestseller to date, Clifford Hanna's *The Folly of Spring: A Study of John Shaw Neilson's Poetry*, and Julian Croft's *The Life and Opinions of Tom Collins: A Study of the Works of Joseph Furphy*. Many other series titles have been welcomed by reviewers as ground-breaking studies of major Australian writers and literary topics.

Although UQP has made a substantial contribution to its study, there is still not nearly enough Australian literature taught in our universities, and there are still only two Chairs of Australian Literature in Australia, one at Sydney University and one at James Cook University. When I began my university career in the 1960s, English literature precluded or marginalised Australian literature. Nowadays English departments give generous space to Literary Theory, Cultural Studies, Women's Studies and Postcolonial Studies, and while these are worthy in their own right, they continue to displace or marginalise Australian literature.

Nonetheless, I am heartened by the quality and volume of literary criticism that has appeared in the journals and from a number of publishers in the last decade. Although the support base seems likely to remain small, another decade of comparable productivity would establish a solid body of secondary literature, and ensure that Australian literature continues to be taken seriously by literary communities in Australia and throughout the world.

History on the Edge

RAYMOND EVANS

ACADEMIC HISTORIANS look to their home-based university press as a life-raft to help keep them professionally afloat. In a relatively small Western society like Australia, with low levels of tertiary achievement and an even lower regard, it would seem, for books with extensive footnotes and fat bibliographies, academic vulnerability is correspondingly enhanced. If the name of the intellectual game is 'Publish or Perish', then the university press virtually becomes a sanctuary from extinction. Yet serving the academic community can often fly in the face of any publishing press's impulse to profit and expand. After all, a biography entitled *Sir Matthew Nathan: British Colonial Governor and Civil Servant* is hardly likely to compete as exciting product on the shelves with one called *The Emperor Wally Lewis*. The high takings from one tend merely to contribute to the meagre sustenance of the other.

Yet historical publishing should hardly be regarded as a kind of cultural charity. Historians contribute to their society in the coin of general enlightenment, and that coin can sometimes be both a diverting and a priceless one. If anything has been learned from the convulsive debates presently shaking Australian society over race relations, it is that the past always has quite a stranglehold on the present, and that we can only know and be comfortable with ourselves by knowing and owning all of our history. Today, Australian historical publishing has burgeoned so dramatically that we now have various historical world-views in contention and a rich and stoutly contested historiographical tradition of debate has emerged. This is all a very recent development, however, occurring over only the last two decades.

In the 1960s and early 1970s the appearance of a new volume of Australian history was in itself still a notable event, irrespective of its theme or quality. At the University of Queensland, members of the History Department were probably no more remiss in their lack of attention to their own society's past than Australian academic historians elsewhere. Perhaps, indeed, they were more perspicacious, with Gordon Greenwood, and A. C. V. Melbourne before him, publishing significant volumes. During the 1970s UQP would produce editions by both of these men. These books, *The Future of Australian Federation* by Greenwood and *Early Constitutional Development in Australia* by Melbourne, were excellent exemplars of an early tendency in Australian historiography to produce tightly structured political and constitutional histories, exploring institutional forms and slow structural evolution. UQP presented them as reproduced classics, but the really exciting breakthroughs towards a more wide-ranging social and cultural analysis of the past would arrive only gradually, and largely from other quarters.

Continuing the project of political history, but blending it with the newer historical wave of the 1960s — labour history — Denis Murphy began in the 1970s to produce a range of authored and edited volumes exploring Queensland's and Australia's Labor history, as well as political biography, capped by his epic, *T.J. Ryan*. Murphy was, for a decade or so before his untimely death, UQP's major publishing Australian historian and, indeed, no one since has been capable of assuming that mantle. He was a committed labour historian, with a strong sense of Labor as the party of initiative and reform. There was not a great deal to be gained from arguing with Denis about that, and Queensland's second Labor Premier, T. J. Ryan, was to him solid proof of that legacy. I would work near Denis, researching my own historical agendas in the early 1970s, at the old Oxley Library in William Street; and he would position himself near a window where he could look down for inspiration at Ryan's bewigged statue in Queen's Park below. But whereas my field was social history Murphy stuck mainly with the political. Talk of class struggle, historically, disturbed him, and the new field of race relations history which emerged in the later 1970s seemed equally worrying, for how might white workers emerge morally unscathed from that sort of negative analysis?

Yet late in his short academic career, Murphy too began to venture into the realm of social history and conflict study with his synoptic, edited volume, *The Big Strikes*, which examined turbulent industrial struggles in Queensland history from the great urban and pastoral conflicts of the late nineteenth century to recent epic confrontations at Mt Isa. This book, in effect, was an academic reflection of Joe Harris's *The Bitter Fight: A Pictorial History of the Australian Labor Movement* which had appeared in a splendid, large-format edition from UQP in 1970. I had a particular affection for this book, for it was the archives of a doughty industrial activist, and a scrapbook — in more ways than one — of the great struggles waged among workers, bosses and governments in Australia over almost a century. Perhaps precisely because it was *not* an academic presentation, it resonated with a sense of issues which had really mattered to committed but ordinary Australian men and women. It was crammed with their cartoons, their handbills, and photographs of their stoical or hopeful faces. Its saga even occasionally ran with their blood.

It was the kind of book which presaged in spirit much of the social history to be published by UQP during its 'golden era' of historical publishing — the 1980s. The academic precursors to this substantial wave of significant volumes were Glen Lewis's *A History of the Ports of Queensland*, which despite its uninspiring title was a solid and ambitious attempt to produce a dynamic economic history of Queensland for the first time, and Ronald Lawson's *Brisbane in the 1890s*, a study which conversely eschewed conflict analysis and, using a truncated Weberian model, presented Brisbane society in a most angry and tautened decade as a cohesive, integrated and untroubled society.

The historians who published with UQP in the 1980s, however, would tend to follow more along the trail of Lewis than that of Lawson. They were often inspired to explore the past by the struggles in their own society during this era, usually against the ferocious right-wing initiatives of the Bjelke-Petersen government — struggles about industrial relations, race relations, gender relations and civil rights. They looked to the sources which Harris had produced, and to other books of documents such as J.G. Steele's *Brisbane Town in Convict Days*, as well as to reproduced nineteenth-century accounts, such as C. C. Petrie's *Reminiscences of Tom Petrie* and Anthony Trollope's *Australia*, for inspiration and awareness about wider issues than constitutional or parliamentary politics.

Early in the 1980s a group of young historians began meeting, soirée fashion, on odd Friday nights at the Paddington home of race relations historian Lyndal Ryan — a stone's throw away from Queensland's Government House. Lyndal would preside over proceedings like a latter-day, Antipodean Madame De Stael, and the little group who gathered to joust conversationally about the nature of Queensland's past began to dub themselves jocularly 'the Koala Club'. The group would talk untiringly late into the evening, debating over the essential features of Queensland's evolution, of which then so little was known. Firm bonds of camaraderie, extending well beyond the intellectual, were forged which in most cases have survived to this day. Apart from Lyndal, there were Jan Walker, Kay Saunders, Helen Taylor, Bill Thorpe, Tom Cochrane, Denis Cryle and myself — and one by one, as our independent historical studies were completed, either as theses or discrete research projects, UQP would gather us all in. Lyndal's path-breaking book, *The Aboriginal Tasmanians*, was published in 1981; Jan Walker followed with her classic study of Queensland's class and race relations in a rural setting, *Jondaryan Station*, in 1988. Tom Cochrane weighed in with his *Blockade* and Denis Cryle with *The Press in Colonial Queensland* in 1989. I wrote *The*

Red Flag Riots: A Study of Intolerance for UQP which they published in 1988. Kay Saunders later produced *War on the Homefront* (1993) and along with Helen Taylor and others compiled *Australia's Frontline*, an oral history in 1992. Further, in both 1989 and 1993, the Press also published new editions of the encompassing study *Race Relations in Colonial Queensland* which Kay Saunders and myself had first written with Kathy Cronin in the early 1970s. Finally, Bill Thorpe's *Colonial Queensland 1840–1900* brought up the rear in 1995, and in effect provided a high-water mark to what had been a substantial historiographical tidal wave.

This wave was, by and large, a fiercely critical one. The history written in this period was confronting and disturbing, and indeed had earlier set out very deliberately in Lyndal's soirées to be so. Emboldened by our critical unity, we believed we were finding a voice for things long buried which needed again to be said, and UQP was the tongue we would use. This kind of investigative analysis is now being derisively labelled 'black armband' history, for it refused to kowtow to popular sentiment by continually celebrating only white, Anglo-masculine achievement in Australia's past. In short, we former Koala Club members would still proclaim, 'Better a black armband than a white blindfold!' UQP, I believe, was bold and adventurous in publishing these penetrative books. Our only gripe was the often uninspiring appearance of many of these volumes — particularly the notorious red-cover series (edited by Lyndal herself) which did not really encourage the browser to lift them eagerly from the bookshop shelf. I comfort myself from time to time, however, with the rather sanguine hope that one day this brazenly crimson series will be regarded rather like the regimented orange-coloured volumes of Victor Gollancz's Left Book Club of interwar Britain, and just as fondly recalled.

I do not wish to leave the impression that historical publishing by UQP in the 1980s and early 1990s was nothing more than the outcome of a cabal it had formed with the shadowy Koala Club. It was merely that we local historians individually produced manuscripts of quality of the kind which UQP at the time was largely seeking. It had equal success with other notable authors: particularly Ross Fitzgerald's acerbic two-volume general history of Queensland, the latter of which ran the gauntlet of a pulping before it finally officially appeared, as well as his thoughtful and industrious political biographies on E. G. Theodore and Fred Paterson which have followed. And the Press did not have too far to look to find Craig Munro's acclaimed biography, *Wild Man of Letters*, about another Queensland tearaway, P. R. 'Inky' Stephensen. Stuart Svensen's *The Shearers' War* was a doughty piece of working-class history, written unashamedly and provocatively from that position, and placing Walker's Jondaryan story in a far wider perspective. W. Ross Johnston's handy, encapsulating *Documentary History of Queensland* added to the red-covered series in 1989.

Michael Sturma's *Vice in a Vicious Society*, which examined the moral backlash following the demise of convict society in New South Wales from the 1840s, and John Moore's more journalistic account, *Oversexed, Overpaid and Over Here*, which described further moral outrage as the American troops descended on the Antipodes a century later, were also significant studies in private passion and social control. Women's history was similarly well served with Daniels and Murnane's documentary account, *Uphill All the Way*, and Gail Reekie's later collection, *On the Edge: Women's Experiences of Queensland*, the latter significantly accepting only female applicants as literary participants. Regional studies like those of Lorna McDonald on Central Queensland, P. F. Donovan on the Northern Territory and Merval Hoare on Norfolk Island have been produced, as well as a wide-reaching though patchy historiographical overview, *Historical Disciplines and Culture in Australia*, edited by John Moses. Finally, one of the most ambitious of projects was the handsome reproduction of the *Official History of Australia in the War of 1914–1918*, with six of the twelve volumes written by the redoubtable and iconic war historian C. E. W. Bean.

Subsequently, quite a deal of UQP's historical production has centred around the theme of war, with studies on Vietnam by Terry Burstall and Hugh Lunn, a trio of arresting World War II reminiscences on Pacific campaigns by Peter Pinney, and books on Australian and Japanese internment in this war by Margaret Bevege and Yuriko Nagata respectively. The press has also continued conscientiously to profile race, ethnic and gender issues with such volumes as the widely received, interfacing studies *Sojourners* and *Citizens* on Chinese migration to Australia by Eric Rolls, an arresting account of Italians in North Queensland, *From Italy to Ingham*, Bill Rosser's colourful personal journey of discovery about frontier race war, *Up Rode the Troopers*, Stephenson and Ratnapala's important collections on the Mabo decision, John Singe's history of the Torres Strait, Dever's heterogeneous edited study *Wallflowers and Witches: Women and Culture in Australia 1910–1945* and Dornan and Cryle's meticulously cross-stitched *The Petrie Family: Building Colonial Brisbane*.

Overall, UQP offered increasingly, from the 1970s and on into the 1990s, sterling support for the task of building Australia's and particularly Queensland's historical awareness. In assessing its range of historical titles, one can clearly discern, in both terms of quantity and quality, a bias towards publishing the Queensland product. Queensland history is immensely fascinating. However, it is also relatively little known, and the local, educated community owes a debt to UQP for venturing to publish so much key research. It is clearly to its own financial disadvantage that it has done so, for Queensland's readership encompasses only some 12 per cent of the national book market. Working on the model of the North American university press, however, it has promoted regional understanding at the expense of quick sales, by observing a firm commitment to the belief that local historical knowledge is both liberating and endlessly captivating.

Yet, from where I sit, UQP's publishing policy on historical titles today seems to have lost some of the drive and coherence it attained in the 1980s. Economic exigencies appear to have often made a casualty of intellectual rigour, with manuscripts of popular appeal increasingly favoured over the exhaustively documented historical account, researched from primary data. High academic quality is no longer the *sine qua non* of the overall presentation; though, looking at the position more brightly, this departure at least places an increasing onus upon professional historians to communicate much more widely and, above all, to do so with flair and zest. In a time when so many chilling perceptual gaps have been detected in Australian society upon such fundamental matters as its race relations history, perhaps this pressure to speak broadly to people beyond the well-trodden academic circuits is not such a bad thing. Perhaps it is even worth the messy sacrifice of hundreds of meticulous little footnotes to do so. But I would continue to maintain that it is possible to write Australian histories which are both galvanic and intellectually precise, and that originally sourced accounts carry more reconstructive cultural potential than most other analyses manage to do. Historical scholarship will only move forward if it is kindly shepherded by publishers, and if originally researched and prescriptively argued manuscripts are to remain merely as unpublished theses on dusty departmental shelves then the cultural quality of Australian life will continue to diminish.

But it is an increasingly difficult task to ask university publishers to put their money where my mouth is; and I am myself presently preparing a volume on race relations for UQP which bows flexibly to the demands of the popular by closely integrating the colourful and personal with the scholarly throughout. After all, I suppose this is what academic publishing has always been about: we historians need our university press's attention much more than they financially require ours — and react accordingly. On the other hand, our University Press requires of us that we produce historical works of appealing literary as well as pedagogic quality which can hopefully inspire social and cultural change as much by the power of seductive expression as by the naked light of critical academic insight. By the same token, scholars must continue to resist falling under the spell of the popular. For their task has always been and must always be an intellectually subversive one.

The University as Publisher

Denis Cryle

THE PUBLICATION OF scholarly work and the distribution of textbooks were dual incentives in the development of university presses in Australia. The history of the University of Queensland Press, during its protracted genesis, was that of an in-house unit, serving the institution rather than Queensland as a whole. Although UQP was officially established after World War II, the Press's low public profile continued until 1961, when the first full-time manager was appointed. For most of the period under consideration, the University of Queensland was the entity responsible for overseeing the publication of academic work by its staff.

As early as 1916 when the Faculty of Science raised the issue of publishing papers, the university was supporting original work by its staff. On its 1916 publications list were such titles as H. G. Richards' *Volcanic Rocks of South-Eastern Queensland* and J. H. Johnson's Presidential Address to the Royal Society of Queensland.[1] A year later the Senate resolved that original publications be included in the University Calendar and that one hundred copies of each publication be purchased by the university. Despite the healthy output of Science and other faculties, attempts to centralise publication met with resistance during the 1920s and 1930s, slowing the early establishment of a press.

By 1922 commercial incentives associated with textbook supply began to play a part. The potential advantages enjoyed by the newly founded Melbourne University Press in obtaining wholesale reductions of 10–15 per cent from London book suppliers complemented the ongoing need for regular university-based publications. The Senate and its various committees entered into detailed correspondence with the fledging MUP, which after receiving a university loan of £300 had returned an early profit of £200.[2] Local prospects appeared sufficiently encouraging in March 1927 for J. D. Cramb, the University of Queensland Accountant, to recommend the establishment of a local press because of the 'very considerable savings' to be had on textbook purchases. From the beginning, the Student Union lobbied on the issue. In his detailed draft constitution, Cramb recommended that the press be funded with a £200 university loan and that its profits be retained for future expansion.[3]

It was a serious proposal, responsive to student requests for improved textbook supplies, and had it been implemented it would have seen the university follow its Melbourne counterpart promptly into the field. However, during the Depression years the mood of the university like that of the nation itself remained cautious. The Board of Faculties considered that the time was not opportune, while the Registrar, in referring the matter to the Senate, noted a significant difference in scale between the two universities:

> The difference in number in this University (annual enrolment about 500 including a large percentage of External Students) as compared with Melbourne's Annual Enrolment 2600 and the smaller annual expenditure on material and equipment, are of fundamental importance, as the operations of the Press and the profits of the annual turnover would necessarily be on a proportionately smaller and less profitable scale, in comparison with Melbourne operations.[4]

Still the matter of a press was not entirely laid to rest during this period. At the 1932 Universities Conference, Professor Henry Alcock, in the spirit of the Senate's 1916 resolution, employed more elevated and nationalistic arguments. Alcock, the first McCaughey Professor of History and Economics, was a distinguished Oxford graduate with an interest in local history. He was at this time President of the Professorial Board (1932–1937) and Chair of the Queensland Educational Broadcasting Committee.[5] Alcock recommended the establishment of a press to publish secondary and tertiary books 'written with a due knowledge of Australian conditions' and 'to afford an outlet for Australian scholarship'.[6] He envisaged a Combined Universities Press in Australia working in conjunction with a leading British publisher like Oxford. There seems to have been little formal canvassing of his proposal within the university. Nor was MUP enthusiastic about a joint venture. After some conference discussion, the resolution was dropped. But the success of MUP remained a guiding light in renewed calls for local establishment.

More sustained examination of a possible textbook outlet took place within the university during 1935. The Senate established a Special Committee to investigate claims that the establishment of a press would provide reductions of 10–20 per cent on textbook prices.[7] The Committee, comprising most of the interested parties — Archbishop Wand, Professors Alcock and Richards, Athol Perkins and a Student Union representative — undertook a survey of tertiary textbook selling in other capital cities and institutions. Advice from Western Australia against operating a bookshop solely for the purposes of price reduction was upheld by a Melbourne source who pointed out the sensitivities of local booksellers and the need for the university to join the Australian Booksellers Association. Caution again prevailed;

for despite the potential profits to be had from a bookshop, the prospect of short-term outlays and losses did not sit well with the university's system of annual financial allocations.

The issue was kept alive by the Student Association. On the eve of the war, the dental students' president outlined to the Registrar the ongoing disadvantages to fellow students:

> At present dental students have to buy all books from the retail booksellers and under existing conditions we find we are paying top price for all books purchased ... As the minimum expenditure on books by each student during the four years of the course is somewhere in the vicinity of £5 per annum you will see that this is quite a big item in the expense of the course ... There are many others which students feel they would like to have but owing to the high prices they cannot afford.[8]

To which the Registrar replied in confidence a year later that the Senate considered a bookshop 'undesirable'. The preferred model among administrators was the University of Sydney, where a second-hand book exchange supplemented the practice of advance book orders through the Union.

At the same period as the Senate rejected the bookshop option, the university, at the prompting of Professor Alcock, moved to centralise its publishing activities. A new Publications Board comprising the Vice-Chancellor, the President of the Academic Board, the Librarian, Archbishop Wand and Professor Goddard was created to oversee the allocation of £100 for publications in 1936.[9] The University of Queensland Papers, published in series from 1937 were not a profit-making activity. In the early years of the war, when the Board's expenditure exceeded income by more than two to one, the main benefits lay in the receipt and exchange of research papers from other universities and scholars. The Board's policy of centralising distribution and exchange met with ongoing resistance from departments like Geology which maintained its own 'very large exchange solely by the reprint system'.[10] In 1941, Professor Richards, still an active and influential researcher, wrote to Archbishop Wand complaining about 'the system of publication and distribution of reprints being taken out of this department's hands'.[11] Dorothy Hill recalled being equally horrified at the Board's willingness to duplicate exchanges with institutions already in correspondence with the Royal Society of Queensland.[12]

Not only did the Board's preference for original work over reprints remain contentious with individual departments, it was experiencing difficulty in maintaining output in the wartime conditions. Most of the wartime research in need of publication was exchange papers with limited capacity for local sales. A decision to support the publication of longer original works compounded the situation. Consequently, the Publications Board took the step of requesting that Senate funding be held over to enable the backlog to be met. After consideration by the Senate's Finance Committee, the request was referred to the Queensland Auditor-General who advised that all revenue associated with publishing be vested in the Senate alone.[13] It was in the wake of this advice that the Publications Board took the view that the establishment of a Press was 'the only way to continue its work'.[14] The concept of a trust fund and a capital reserve was gaining ground and, with it, the need to inaugurate a university press.

While the principle of establishment dates from the war years, the Senate took longer to act. In 1945 the Vice-Chancellor, J. D. Story, and the Auditor-General continued to correspond on the issue. In seeking to publish its backlog of work, the Board was making heavier demands on Senate support. In the case of an approved request to publish Bryan and Jones' 'Geological History of Queensland' at a cost of £150, the Board noted that 'although this paper will be valuable for reference and exchange purposes, it is very doubtful whether the amount received for sales will exceed £20'.[15] In 1945 the Senate agreed to provide £529 in the 1947 estimates for 'miscellaneous publications'. With establishment in 1948, the Senate's willingness to make up publication losses was confined to special circumstances. In retrospect Frank Thompson, the first full-time manager, considered that the need to renegotiate postwar financial support had led to the formation of the Press.[16] Certainly wartime publication delays and the 'need to be able to carry forward profits in any one year to offset any possible debits in another'[17] appear decisive for establishment. This necessity was recognised in the appropriate establishment statute to the effect that:

> The accounts of the Press shall be kept separate from other University accounts, and all funds acquired through the operation of the Press shall remain at its disposal, and shall not become a part of general University funds.[18]

Gazetted on 13 March 1948 as a university department, the Press began humbly with the occupation of a demountable at the back of the George Street complex. A Senate loan of £1000 proved inadequate because of the expenses the Press incurred in opening its Bookshop. Although the university already had a publication program prior to the Press's establishment, the Bookshop was an altogether new development. Strong wartime demand from the Student Union and the Medical School had developed for a facility to provide on-site textbooks, stationery, instruments and apparatus. The Bookshop, funded by a Senate loan of £4000 to be refunded from its profits, opened its doors in January 1949 and offered discounts of 10 per cent to students. It reserved part of its first-year profits (£3080) for the construction of additional premises at the St Lucia site.[19] This branch was constructed ten years later at a cost of £8250. However, staffing levels and space continued to lag behind as enrolments and demand spiralled upwards in the 1960s.

Despite a recommendation at the time of establishment that 'the essential part of the organisation is a really efficient manager, obtained from one of the large city bookstores',[20] the Bookshop, along with the Press, operated under part-time management until 1961. Complaints of poor service and an investigation into its activities prompted an upgrade by the late 1950s. Even then, the Bookshop faced criticism from academic staff as well as from competing publishers and retailers. Despite early advice, the university did not join the Australian Book Publishers Association until 1962. Commercial sensitivities among local traders erupted in a well-publicised incident when the Queensland Retailers Association alleged that the Bookshop had entered the toy-reselling business to undercut Brisbane outlets.[21]

After closing down its George Street operations in the early 1960s, the Bookshop was forced to canvass substantial finance for extensions at St Lucia. In 1963 it earned a net profit of £17 500 but had to raise £30 924 to fund the St

Lucia premises.[22] The Press, operating on the profit principle rather than through annual subsidy, continued to face financial uncertainty under full-time management as the Senate charged the Press fully for rates, phone and electricity and relinquished accountancy support. As manager Frank Thompson later reflected:

> The financial position of the Press had never been a very attractive one. Indeed the University has consistently followed a policy of making the Press pay for everything that could be conceivably charged to it. The Press paid for the original St Lucia bookshop and the first extension to it out of accumulated funds. This so depleted its accumulated funds that the Press has never since then had sufficient accumulated funds to meet its necessary capital outlays.[23]

The active involvement in the Press of Athol Perkins, dating from the formation of the early Publications Committee in the 1930s until 1961, provides an essential continuity between university publishing and the early UQP story. A distinguished entomologist and enthusiastic teacher, Perkins divided his time between his students, field work and a variety of administrative tasks. Born and educated in Sydney, Perkins joined the University of Queensland staff in 1922 as a Research Fellow into the fruit-fly problem, spending considerable time in field work at Stanthorpe over the next five years. At the time of his initial involvement on the Publications Committee, he was publishing a series of papers after conducting extensive research into the Queensland fruit-fly. Over the following quarter of a century, he was a member of the Publications Board (from 1936), Secretary of the Publications Committee (from 1944), then part-time manager of the Bookshop and Press (from 1948). Designated a lecturer in Entomology in 1938, Perkins demonstrated skill and industry in dealing with both students and administration. According to Elizabeth Marks:

> Perkins readily took on many other tasks for the University. In early days he was a Proctor, later Sub-dean of the Faculty of Science and, during Professor Teakle's absence, Dean of Agriculture for a year. He edited the Science Handbook, and the comments of grateful students and their parents attested his success as a Student Guidance Officer.[24]

These interpersonal and administrative skills were put to good use on the Publications Committee. In 1939 Perkins, as Staff Association representative, was appointed to a special committee established to inquire into the feasibility of a university bookshop.[25]

As the demands on his time increased, Perkins spent more time with tasks such as time-tabling than with his research interests. Although as a scientist his involvement with publishing was consistent with the university's early output and research profile, he mixed with a cross-section of staff in the closer academic environment. According to L. J. H. Teakle:

> Athol Perkins was a consistent member of the common room 'Club' on the first floor of the old Government House building, then the headquarters of the University. There was a group of select celebrities — Des Herbert, Walter Harrison, Athol Perkins, Henry Alcock, Gilbert Jones to name a few — who would foregather for morning and afternoon tea and the after lunch 'siesta'. This was the time for the exchange of views and ideas on any subject thrown in the ring.[26]

It was also Teakle's recollection that Perkins volunteered to manage the Press and Bookshop at one of these gatherings. At the time of the 1943 Press proposal Perkins had been heavily involved in the war effort as Secretary of the Queensland Government's Mosquito Control Committee before returning to his university position. Whether he volunteered for his Press assignment or had 'just been landed with it',[27] as another source implied, his renewed involvement as Press manager was to prove 'the most demanding of his varied administrative tasks for the University'.[28]

After the war Perkins visited southern universities to gather information for a commissioned Senate report on university presses and related activities. He was assisted by

Louis Livingston, a long-serving member of staff who was appointed Acting Accountant in 1943 and Accountant in 1946.[29] They were each requested to pay detailed attention to the commercial aspects of textbook sales. After receiving the scrutiny of the Finance Committee, their report was adopted in July 1948 including the recommendation that the university jointly operate a bookshop, store and publishing department.[30] Under the terms of appointment, the press manager was to be the Secretary of the Publications Committee and act under its direction. In this respect, Perkins' duties changed little, but he gained the additional responsibilities of the bookshop with only a clerk/storeman to assist him at George Street and a part-timer at St Lucia. Initially, most of the demand occurred at George Street but activity increased steadily at St Lucia over the next decade. During the first year of Bookshop operations, Elizabeth Exley remembered that 'he (Perkins) was seldom in the Department'.[31] The years immediately after establishment in 1948 proved the most demanding, until a separate Bookshop manager was appointed in the mid-1950s. According to colleagues, Perkins was 'run ragged' by the Press and continued to see himself as 'an interim appointment only'.[32]

Activity within Perkins' faculty also increased postwar. In 1948 Entomology became a separate sub-Department in the Faculty of Agriculture. Four years later, it became the first autonomous Department of Entomology with Perkins as Reader-in-charge.[33] During this time, the Press was largely run from Perkins' own office. Staff remembered the heavy responsibilities of their senior colleague and the patience of commercial printers waiting to see him on business. At the time of establishment, the university had hoped in future 'to be in a position to do its own printing' and to 'expand the range of publications and cater for an Australia-wide distribution'.[34] However, under the circumstances, the publication activities of the Press continued largely unchanged. One disadvantage of internal part-time management was a lack of publicity or capacity to canvass manuscripts and outside work. A monograph on Aborigines and the courts was rejected on the grounds that 'it was just not a work for general readers'.[35] In the post-establishment period (1947–61), the Press published some hundred titles, averaging 5–8 per year. Until 1960 its list comprised mostly scientific works and tertiary textbooks — Naylor's *Psychology*, Hajek's *Principles of Bankruptcy*, Sprent's *Parasitism*. Most successful was Gilford, Wood and Reitsma's *Australian Banking* which ran to four editions.

During the 1950s the technical and textbook output of the Press included May's *Anatomy of the Sheep*, Lee's *Physiology of Tissues and Organs* and Hill and Maxwell's *Elements of the Stratigraphy of Queensland*. No doubt Perkins' science background and interests were an influential factor. There were some exceptions. Schonell, Meddleton and Shaw's *Study of the Oral Vocabulary of Adults*, co-published with the University of London Press, was 'the first large scale investigation of the oral vocabulary of any group of adults' in the Commonwealth.[36] When debating the prospects of publishing Leopold's careful analysis of Thomas Mann's 'Joseph the Provider' in 1958, Perkins was able to conclude that, 'although very special in its context and appeal, I don't suppose it is any less special than some of the geology and botany papers we print'.[37]

Prior to the 1960s there was little attempt to establish an editorial direction or philosophy for the Press. It was the involvement of Frank Thompson, armed with commercial experience and a passion for literature, which later brought this about. During the Queensland Centenary in 1959 the Press had nevertheless responded with several local works, including Hadgraft's *Queensland and Its Writers* and Dick's *Five Towns of the Brigalow District.* Until that time the great majority of publications dealing with Queensland were devoted to science and economy — its flora, fauna, soils and primary industries. The Press continued to reject publication requests from talented Australian writers on the grounds that 'it is not the University's policy to publish contributions received from persons outside the University'.[38] With

Thompson's appointment in 1961, the Press became more responsive and entrepreneurial in attracting work, much of it literary and sustained by the interests and expertise of incoming staff. Perkins was no doubt relieved to relinquish his protracted role as 'Father of the Press'. At the time of his retirement in 1964, in circumstances of personal misfortune (he had begun to lose his sight), the Professorial Board noted appropriately the 'long period of service Mr Perkins has given to this University, not only in the field of Entomology but also by carrying extra duties in connection with the Bookshop and the Press'.[39]

Notes

The author acknowledges the valuable input and assistance of Elizabeth Exley, Mark Cryle (Main Library), Craig Munro (UQP), Phillippa Nelson (UQA) and Dr Elizabeth Marks in the preparation of this chapter.

1. Senate Paper, 9 August 1916, in Publications—Original Papers 1915–1947 (UQA S130).
2. Re a University of Queensland Press. Summary of Action Taken to Date, 3 July 1935, in Bookshop and Press—Establishment 1925–1947 (UQA S130).
3. Draft Constitution, J. D. Cramb to J. F. McCaffrey, 28 March 1927, in Bookshop and Press—Establishment 1925–1947.
4. Registrar to the Senate, 31 May 1927, in Bookshop and Press—Establishment 1925–1947.

5. Obituary, *University of Queensland Gazette*, 10 October 1948, pp. 4–5.
6. Summary of Action taken to date, 3 July 1935, in Bookshop and Press—Establishment 1925–1947.
7. Library Committee, 26 June 1935, in Bookshop and Press—Establishment 1925–1947.
8. President Queensland Dental Students' Association to the Registrar, 17 November 1939, in Bookshop and Press—Establishment 1925–1947.
9. Senate Minutes, 7 August 1936, in Publications—Original Papers 1915–1947.
10. H. C. Richards to the Registrar, n.d., in Publications—Original Papers 1915–1947.
11. Richards to Wand, 15 July 1941, in Publications—Original Papers 1915–1947.
12. Quoted in Elizabeth Marks, 'Frederick Athol Perkins 1897–1976', *Entomological Society of Queensland News Bulletin*, v. 4, no. 9, 1977, p. 14.
13. Auditor-General to J. D. Story, 3 December 1945, in Publications—Original Papers, 1915–1947.
14. Frank W. Thompson, 'The University of Queensland Press: Past, Present and Future', Typescript, UQP, 1973, p. 5.
15. Re The Revenue of the Publications Department being Regarded as a Trust Fund, Auditor-General to J. D. Story, in Publications—Original Papers 1915–1947.
16. Thompson, 'The University of Queensland Press', p. 4.
17. Report of the Sub-Committee appointed to consider the question of the establishment of a university press, in Bookshop and Press—Establishment 1947–1948 (UQA S130).
18. Statute XXIII C.(138) University of Queensland Press, University of Queensland Calendar 1949 (UQA S171).

19. University of Queensland Bookshop, in Bookshop and Press—Establishment 1947–1948.
20. Publications Committee, 1 May 1947, in Bookshop and Press—Establishment 1947–1948.
21. Retailers' Association of Queensland to the Vice-Chancellor, 8 November 1962, in Bookshop and Press—Establishment 1947–1948.
22. Thompson, 'The University of Queensland Press', p. 5.
23. Thompson, 'The University of Queensland Press', p. 8.
24. Marks, 'Frederick Athol Perkins', p. 174.
25. Registrar to Senate, 1939, in Bookshop and Press—Establishment 1925–1947.
26. Quoted in Marks, 'Frederick Athol Perkins', p. 174.
27. Elizabeth Exley, communication with author, August 1997.
28. Elizabeth Marks, 'Frederick Athol Perkins: 1897– 1976', *Proceedings of the Royal Society of Queensland*, no. 89, June 1978, p. xix.
29. Extract Staff Files (UQA S135).
30. Senate Minutes, 1 July 1948, in J. D. Story Papers 1948–1949 (UQA AC1).
31. Quoted in Marks, 'Frederick Athol Perkins', p. 174.
32. Elizabeth Exley, communication with author, August 1997.
33. Marks, 'Frederick Athol Perkins', p. 168.
34. *University of Queensland Gazette*, May 1949, No. 13 (UQA S170).
35. Correspondence October 1957, in Publications—Original Papers 1948–1962 (UQA S130).
36. *Study of the Oral Vocabulary of Adults*, Preface, p. 6.
37. Publications Committee, 2 May 1958, in Publications—Original Papers 1948–1962.

38. Correspondence, 26 February 1960, in Publications—Original Papers 1948–1962.
39. Extract Staff Files (UQA S135).

Reading the Community

ANNE GALLIGAN

THE UNIVERSITY OF QUEENSLAND PRESS was established in its present form under Statute 38 of the University of Queensland Act passed by the University Senate in 1948. This provided for the Press to function as a separate department of the University of Queensland, under a Board of Management appointed by the Senate. Provision was made in this original charter for the Press to be run in conjunction with a university bookshop, which is a continuing alliance.

The publishing program of the University of Queensland Press during the 1950s focused on scholarly publications by its own academics and official university handbooks. A rather narrow selection of books was published dealing mainly with science and mathematics. The Press was not especially concerned with financial return (that is, the business of publishing), relevance to the wider community or involvement in the literary community of the time.

This purely academic focus remained the emphasis until

Frank Thompson's appointment as Manager in 1961. His background was with Michigan State University Press, where 'it was taken for granted that university presses contribute to the cultural life of the nation'.[1] Thompson determined to broaden the base of activities of the obscure university press and 'actively canvassed for manuscripts' both within the university and throughout Australia.[2] UQP publications began to receive favourable reviews and an increasing number of manuscripts were submitted allowing greater selection freedom. Slowly cultural and artistic titles began to appear beside the more scholarly works. These included a study of Walter Burley Griffin by Jim Birrell and *The Drunken Buddha*, a Chinese novel translated and illustrated by Ian Fairweather.

In 1961 the staff consisted of Thompson and secretary Ann Lahey. Lahey had been introduced to publishing through working on an academic journal for the university History Department, and had worked with Reader's Digest in London. She was soon engrossed in editorial duties and became a great asset to UQP, training new staff as the Press expanded, and passing on editorial skills. As the number of publications grew through the 1960s, new staff were appointed, including editors Shirley Hockings (1963), Sue Pechey (1965), Roger McDonald (1969) and Penny Rogers (1969). Cyrelle Birt was appointed Production Manager in

1965 and proved to have considerable expertise as a book designer. She was joined by designer Norm Birrell in 1970.

The Press's first involvement in creative writing was a drama series, Contemporary Australian Plays, beginning in the early 1960s, with plays by Ray Mathew (1961) and David Ireland (1964). There was also a push into the general Australian market in response to a growing interest in Australian natural history and heritage.[3] When Roger McDonald was appointed poetry editor in 1969, a 'stronger literary direction' was set.[4] The Paperback Poets series was introduced in 1970 with volumes by David Malouf, Rodney Hall and Michael Dransfield published simultaneously. Priced at $1, the books were inexpensive, accessible and popular. The series continued for ten years and many of the poets published in this series have become major figures in contemporary Australian literature.

A number of significant factors combined in the early 1970s to create a dynamic publishing environment in Australia which launched UQP and a number of its authors into the larger domain of national and international publishing. In 1973 Thompson submitted a wide-ranging proposal to the University Senate advocating an expanded role for UQP. In the same year the Whitlam government greatly increased funding to the arts and broadened the role of the Australia Council. While government grants subsidised individual authors to write, the Press was also subsidised for specific publishing projects. The first two years of government grants for UQP in 1973 and 1974 produced works by David Malouf, Michael Wilding, Vicki Viidikas, Peter Porter (sound recording) and Murray Bail, an interesting cross-section of Australian writers.

This was a time of social change, of experimentation and innovation, and it could be assumed that the successful poetry and fiction list of the 1970s was the result of a carefully conceived editorial strategy by Thompson and his young staff. Publishing Manager Craig Munro (who was UQP's first fiction editor) has stated, however, that a new list grows more randomly, 'generating its own character as it develops'. 'There was initially no special commitment to experimental writing or to the work of younger writers',[5] although it was evident to Thompson that there were good writers not finding a publisher. It could also be argued that the avenue for publication provided by UQP and other small presses, such as Wild & Woolley and Outback Press, added a momentum for young Australian writers, a stimulus to greater creative effort.

The Press enlarged its publishing base, selectively creating a list of impressive authors, venturing into new areas of Australian publications and adding to the established academic interest. Series such as the Paperback Poets and

Portable Australian Authors introduced influential new directions and set new scholarly standards in Australian writing and publishing. The Asian and Pacific Writing and Leaders of Asia series ventured beyond the traditional Australian publishing program. These series were important to Thompson who considered that Australians 'should become more familiar with the cultures of their geographical area'.[6] History publications included regional and military history and an innovative audio-visual and microfilm program was introduced. By the late 1970s the dramatic expansion of UQP was restricted because of rising costs and accumulating warehouse stock, but a vigorous publishing program continued into the 1980s.

Laurie Muller, appointed Manager of UQP in 1983, continued this enthusiastic commitment to Australian publishing. Muller presided over a period of reorganisation and consolidation of UQP operations, which had been constrained by limited distribution arrangements and the difficulties of marketing such a diverse publishing list. There was a decision to focus on Australian Studies, particularly literature and history. Scholarly titles were to be published only in paperback. More popular-culture titles were also published, including books on football, community history and biography. In 1984 an important agreement was negotiated with Penguin to act as national distributor for UQP. This arrangement was broadened in 1989 so that Penguin became both the distribution agent and selling agent for UQP titles.

From the mid-1970s UQP had made a concerted effort to break into the international market, particularly the United States. At one stage UQP had a Manager, Pearl Bowman, sales representatives and a warehouse in New York stocking a wide range of titles. This marketing program was reduced when Austrade support was withdrawn, and was finally disbanded in 1989. A smaller-scale experiment in the UK ceased in 1988 after just a few years, because of the unsympathetic book market for Australian publications. The main demand for Australian titles overseas now is in the area of sale of rights rather than the exporting of physical books. This has continued to be an important subsidiary outlet for UQP publications, along with the sale of rights for film and stage adaptations.

One of the most exciting forces of the 1980s in Australian literary culture was the growing presence of talented and innovative women writers working across different genres. Among the male-dominated UQP list of the 1970s were Judith Rodriguez, Jennifer Maiden and Barbara Hanrahan, but the 1980s saw Olga Masters, Elizabeth Jolley, Kate Grenville, Janette Turner Hospital, Beverley Farmer and many other significant talents introduced as UQP authors. Thea Astley's work published prior to the 1980s now received greater recognition, and UQP was able to reprint selected earlier novels alongside new work. The interest in Women's Studies also produced challenging critiques of Australian history and culture including *Australia's Women: A Documentary History* by Kay Daniels and Mary Murnane, *Gender, Politics and Fiction* edited by Carole Ferrier, and *Women in Rural Australia* edited by Kerry James.

The highlight of the 1980s was Peter Carey's Booker Prize win for *Oscar and Lucinda* in 1988, arguably the most prestigious award for fiction in the English-speaking world. Carey also won the Miles Franklin Award in both 1981 and 1989 and has, over time, won most Australian literary awards for fiction. UQP has certainly benefited from the system of awards and prizes that operates in Australia and many UQP writers have won major awards across a wide range of titles. The poetry list has consistently attracted awards and critical praise for works by John Tranter, Thomas Shapcott, Fay Zwicky, Judith Beveridge, Laurie Duggan and others. The Young Adult Fiction and Children's titles regularly appear on the shortlists and award-winning lists of the Children's Book Council. The awards serve to raise the profile and prestige of the Press and its writers, highlighting the quality of Australian writing to the general public and providing a guide to the more notable publications each year.

UQP's commitment to publishing academic research and

critical material in the Humanities and Social Science areas remains strong, in contrast to the contraction or even demise of other university presses. Series such as Australian Authors and Studies in Australian Literature are effectively working in tandem, producing authoritative texts and complementing the teaching and appreciation of Australian literature. Anthologies of Australian writing such as *The Australian Short Story* edited by Laurie Hergenhan and *Colonial Voices* edited by Elizabeth Webby have been important educational texts. Historical and political titles continue to contribute to the documentation and discussion of past and contemporary Australian events, social issues and cultural institutions. These works include *The Concise History of Australia* by Russel Ward, *The Shearers' War* by Stuart Svenson, *Wallflowers and Witches: Women and Culture in Australia 1910–1945* edited by Maryanne Dever, *Politics of the High Court* by Brian Galligan, *Mabo: A Judicial Revolution* edited by M. A. Stephenson and Suri Ratnapala and *Son of Alyandabu: My Fight for Aboriginal Rights* by Joe McGinness.

Another important sign of UQP's commitment to academic publishing is its joint publishing, with the Australian Academy of the Humanities, of the landmark Academy Editions of Australian Literature. The first three volumes of this ambitious project were released by early 1998. UQP also provides a publishing outlet for seven scholarly journals, including *Journal of Australian Studies*, *Australian Literary Studies*, *Australian Journal of Politics and History*, *The Law Journal*, *Queensland Studies Journal*, *Crossings* and *Imago*. Although UQP involvement is usually limited to a production role, with the editorial work performed by academics, the fact is that at a time when financial and administrative support for journals is declining, these journals covering a wide range of disciplines continue to be published.

UQP has released an impressive range of military history titles. The backbone of this list has been the re-issuing of eleven volumes of the *Official History of Australia in the War of 1914–1918* under the general editorship of Robert O'Neill, and published in association with the Australian War Memorial. This highly acclaimed history was originally commissioned by the Australian Government in 1919 and is often referred to as Bean's history, after Charles Bean, Australia's first official war historian. Australian military and social history is detailed in other UQP titles such as *Australian War Strategy 1939–1945: A Documentary History* by John Robertson and John McCarthy, *Bluepencil Warriors: Censorship and Propaganda in World War II* by John Hilvert, and Terry Burstall's *The Soldiers' Story: The Battle at Xa Long Tan* and *Vietnam: The Australian Dilemma*. The tragedy and heroism of Australians at war are recorded in such accounts as *Captives: Australian Army Nurses in Japanese Prison Camps* by

Catherine Kenny, *We Survived: A Mother's Story of Japanese Captivity* by Nell van de Graaff and *Signaller Johnston's Secret War* by Peter Pinney based on his New Guinea diaries. *The War Diaries of Kenneth Slessor: Official Australian Correspondent 1940–1944*, edited by Clement Semmler, and Hugh Lunn's *Vietnam: A Reporter's War* are also significant personal memoirs and war narratives.

Although UQP's publishing strategy shifted away from the scientific emphasis of the pre-1960 era, there has been a continuing interest in natural history and the environmental sciences. The important reference text *Plant Life of the Great Barrier Reef and Adjacent Shores* was the result of extensive research and fieldwork by University of Queensland botany lecturers Alan and Joan Cribb. Other titles in the Ecology and the Environment list include *Insect Ecology* by Eric Matthews and Roger Kitching, and *Ecology of Mangroves* by Patricia Hutchings and Peter Saenger. Texts such as *Environmental Philosophy: A Collection of Readings*, edited by Robert Elliot and Arran Gore, and *Environmental Law in Australia: An Introduction* by D. E. Fisher provide an important theoretical and legal background for this expanding discipline. The four-volume Illustrated History of Humankind series, produced in conjunction with Weldon Owen, provides the latest world research in archaeology and anthropology in an illustrated reference format.

The development of the Black Writers series is an example of the key role a press can have in setting a timely new direction. This series grew from a decision in 1987 to favour black authors writing on black culture and to actively encourage black writing. The David Unaipon Award was established by the Press in conjunction with Arts Queensland and winners include Doris Pilkington, Bill Dodd and Phillip McLaren. This award is not genre specific, accepting any book-length manuscript by an unpublished Aboriginal or Torres Strait Islander author. The Queensland Government provides $5,000 in prize money with publication the following year by UQP. Sandra Phillips, an editor of the Black Writers series, referred to the 'escalating interest' in the Award, with 161 manuscripts entered since 1989. It has served to 'establish a national channel of communication with a community of writers ... that has a reverberating effect'[7] and provides an incentive to pursue publication among the Aboriginal and Torres Strait Islander communities. The UQP program is proving that there is no shortage of Aboriginal and Islander works waiting to be published and that there is an audience for these works. This series has an important role to play in contemporary Australian society as an educative tool, as a tool for social change and in providing a literary and cultural record.

Another aspect of the UQP publishing presence is its role

in 'growing' readers of Australian books. The Young Adult Fiction list, initiated in 1984 and developed under the direction of Barbara Ker Wilson, has been very successful. The current editor of this series, Leonie Tyle, stressed the importance of giving young people their own literature, 'books that reflected the interests of teenagers as opposed to adults'.[8] The Storybridge series and Jam Roll picture books also provide children's books that reflect the Australian community for young readers. The audience for children's and young adult literature is certainly appreciating the Australian product and there is a growing international market in this area.

Apart from its strong national role, UQP has always functioned as a regional publisher, providing an outlet for Queensland writers. The launching of first fiction from the pens of David Malouf, Roger McDonald and Janette Turner Hospital and more recently Matthew Condon and Robbie Lappan, for example, is indicative of UQP's policy of promoting Queensland writers and the unique northern perspective. Important works on Queensland history include *Race Relations in Colonial Queensland* by Ray Evans, a two-volume *History of Queensland* by Ross Fitzgerald and *The Road to Fitzgerald and Beyond* by Phil Dickie. Biographies such as *James Duhig* by Tom Boland, *Joh* by Hugh Lunn and *Oodgeroo* by Kath Cochrane add a richness and depth to understanding both the person and the period of Queensland social history. The commercial success of Adrian McGregor's *King Wally*, the Press's first sporting biography, indicates that the 'urge to culture as well as the pull to commerce can co-exist in the same publishing house'.[9] Ian Templeman, Cultural Director at the National Library of Australia, expressed an appreciation of UQP's 'sense of being very Queensland ... serving their writers and their kind of literary community, their sense of ideas'.[10]

There has been a range of publications crossing many cultural divisions throughout this period. In 1983 Dimitris Tsaloumas published the award-winning *The Observatory* in both the original Greek and the English translation. Rosa Cappiello's novel *Oh Lucky Country*, an expose of Australian attitudes to migrants, was published in 1984. Works by Peter Skrzynecki, Ania Walwicz and Angelo Loukakis and various collections of multicultural writings enlarged the scope of Australian writing. There is a focus on examining aspects of Asian/Australian relations with titles such as *Japanese Internment* by Yuriko Nagata, *The Year the Dragon Came* by Sang Ye, recording a unique social history, and *Sojourners: Flowers and the Wide Sea* by Eric Rolls, a study of Chinese culture.

Developments in technology have made a huge impact on the publishing industry in almost every area, from the writing process to the production process and bookshop ordering systems. UQP is taking seriously the opportunities offered by electronic publishing, although it is acknowledged that there is not the development capital available to pursue electronic options. Perhaps the most relevant, current benefit is in the licensing of electronic rights for UQP titles. Several journals are licensed to electronic publishers and short-term, non-exclusive licences have been given for particular groups of titles. The other applications of immediate interest are various CD-ROM marketing tools, such as the Book Wizard and the potential for promotion on the Internet.

Publishing for the Australian market has always been an economically precarious proposition. In the 1990s the nation-wide depression has seriously affected book sales and government funding has been reduced. The Australian marketplace is increasingly governed by multinational forces which are adding to the traditional difficulties of too many imported books in a small market. Like many other independent Australian publishing houses, UQP is dealing in original publishing with full editorial work, full production and marketing in its particular niche areas. There is a pragmatic approach to the realities of the market. Craig Munro commented that 'we are a university press, but we'll do the most commercial books we can if they will assist the least commercial. We do have a kind of Robin Hood philosophy'.[11]

As a general publisher operating across the intellectual, literary and popular cultures, UQP has developed a range of financial and marketing strategies for different groups of titles. There is an unashamedly vigorous approach to the more popular commercial titles or established author. Poetry and scholarly works operate on a pure cost-recovery basis, this being 'the equivalent of a big profit' for a commercial house,[12] with minimal promotion available for these titles. Academic titles circulate within a particular arena where reviews and conferences, scholarly organisations and subject area networks are most important.

Promotion dollars are spread thinly and sometimes the networks, the timing and/or the market misfire. One author expressed concern at the tendency to promote a few writers who achieve high sales rather than aiming for a more equitable promotion strategy. Marketing and Sales Manager Robert Brown explained that UQP has experimented with various levels of promotional activity and found that even when large amounts of advertising and publicity are invested in the promotion of certain books, the rewards in terms of sales are often limited.

Current marketing practice has resulted in an intense focusing on the covers of books, which can provide that 'make-or-break impetus to a publication's buyer appeal'. A recognisable house style has evolved with UQP publications, from the small-format $1.00 Paperback Poets series to the maroon or dark green covers of the academic titles, or the colourful artwork and designs of Cynthia Breusch and Christopher McVinish or Greg Rogers' earlier young adult covers. A great deal of attention is focused on this design element: covers can be 'a very emotive thing'.[13] It is one area of production where the author is often involved.

Despite this emphasis on the look of a book, publishers are still restricted by the need to make commercial decisions based on perceived market potential, and various rationalisms in the publishing process can offend an author. The basic production decisions are largely cost driven and it is in cutting production costs that publishing houses usually seek cost efficiencies. As Production Manager Terry Farley explains: 'If you go for a $9.95 book then you can't put it on beautiful paper and do all the things you'd like to do'.[14] The great difficulty in publishing into the depressed and saturated Australian market has been the steady decrease in the size of print runs, with an average commercial first printing being from 3,000 to 5,000 copies. With UQP, a smaller print run usually means cheaper paper, since the paper content accounts for 'around 38 per cent' of the printing cost.[15] Several authors expressed their disappointment with this practice and commented on possible negative effects in the marketplace. The larger print runs of more commercial books, however, allow greater flexibility and choice in the final design and presentation.

UQP has endeavoured to maintain a strong commitment to being an editorially driven rather than a market- or sales-driven press. The decision to publish can be based on the perceived cultural value of a work rather than on a purely commercial evaluation. In referring to the 'self-imposed responsibilities' involved in publishing decisions at UQP, Robert Brown commented that 'we publish books that we think are important, to fill in the gaps. We have to [do that] if we are going to have a viable Australian culture in the future, rather than one that is purely adopted from overseas.'[16]

One advantage of publishing with UQP has been the continuity and quality of its editorial commitment. There is a strong focus on working with the author to achieve the best possible text and a recognition that authors are concerned about, and appreciate, 'good editorial engagement with their work'.[17] The many fine editors and consultant editors working with UQP have included D'Arcy Randall, Martin Duwell, Rosanne Fitzgibbon (who won the inaugural Beatrice Davis Editorial Fellowship in 1992), Sue Abbey,

Barbara Ker Wilson, Clare Forster, Leonie Tyle and Sandra Phillips.

Developing a good author/publisher relationship is regarded as essential, although there are always individual differences in the needs and expectations of authors, and authors writing in diverse fields often require different kinds of support. An academic author, for example, does not usually require the same support as a novelist. Former UQP editor Sandra Phillips is aware of the struggle inherent in journeying Indigenous writing through established publishing structures in order for a work to reach the public domain.[18] She stresses the need to have 'a sense of working together', a recognition of complementary roles. 'The author obviously owns the writing, but the publisher is the one who takes the risk in moving that writing into the public domain. So they own the responsibility for making it the best it can be.'[19] Editor Sue Abbey agrees it is 'an association of trust. You have to win the trust of a writer ... That is why you find so many writers that have allegiance to the one house, often the one editor'.[20]

It should be acknowledged that UQP's success in many ways has been built on an ability to maintain a certain degree of author loyalty as writers are established and reputations grow. Author loyalty is regarded as vital to UQP. 'The term "stable of writers" is very important — we regard it more as a family of writers … We have very long-term commitments to our writers as creative artists.'[21] There has been increasing pressure in this area as other publishers with 'seemingly unlimited budgets'[22] search for authors with reputations, a marketable commodity. However, the fact that Peter Carey has published all of his books with UQP, and continues to maintain this association even from New York, is a significant endorsement of his Australian publisher.

The publishing achievements of UQP should be measured against the background of social change and cultural response that created a breakthrough in Australian consciousness and an appreciation of its own national identity. One result was an increasingly assertive and confident literary community. Frank Thompson provided the leadership and momentum to establish UQP as an academic and general trade publishing house of national significance. His adventurous approach to Australian publishing broke through traditional attitudes and practices. This combination of risk taking and the sheer talent of the discovered authors allowed UQP to develop a substantial and pivotal role in supporting the dynamic cultural resurgence of this period. It is also interesting to trace how government policy can have a significant impact on the literary community and on a publisher's program. The important role of awards and prizes is obvious in helping to create the aura of success, concentrating prestige and publicity around successful authors and their publishers.

The task of remaining innovative and competitive in the difficult and unstable publishing environment of the 1990s remains central to UQP's continuing success. In receiving the National Book Council Gold Medal for services to publishing (ironically described as an Award for Bravery), Laurie Muller commented on the UQP perspective that 'publishing is about judgment and enthusiasm, about caring and being passionate, about risk taking and giving new writers a go'.[23]

There is a sense of adventure and a definite cultural responsibility that perhaps assume a greater significance for a university press than for a purely commercial enterprise. Today UQP remains an integral part of the University of Queensland, perhaps its most highly visible department. UQP has contributed to a flourishing of Australian publications in scholarly, literary and general trade areas. It has a proven ability to 'read' the community and to produce innovative and wide-ranging Australian material for purposes of scholarship and the cultural record — an appropriate mission for a university press.

Notes

1. Thompson, Frank, 'Legends in Their Own Lunchtimes: Australian Publishing Since 1960', *Publishing Studies*, 1, Spring 1995: 30.
2. Thompson, Frank, 'The University of Queensland Press: Past, Present and Future', UQP Files 1973: 6.
3. Bowman, Pearl, ed., 'Frank Thompson: An American's Career in Australian Publishing', *Antipodes*, Winter 1989: 115.
4. Thompson, 1995: 33.
5. Munro, Craig, 'Editor's Statements', *Australian Literary Studies*, 10.2, 1981: 262.
6. Bowman, 1989: 118.
7. Phillips, Sandra, Interview with Anne Galligan, UQP, Brisbane, April 1997.
8. Tyle', Leonie, Interview with Anne Galligan, UQP, Brisbane, April 1997.
9. Moran, Albert, 'Inside Publishing: Environments of the Publishing House', *Continuum: The Media of Publishing*, 4.1, 1990: 132.
10. Templeman, Ian, Interview with Anne Galligan, National Library, Canberra, September 1996.
11. Munro, Craig, Interview with Anne Galligan, UQP, Brisbane, August 1996.
12. Ibid.
13. Fitzgibbon, Rosanne, Interview with Anne Galligan, UQP, Brisbane, August 1996.
14. Farley, Terry, Interview with Anne Galligan, UQP, Brisbane, August 1996.
15. Ibid.
16. Brown, Robert, Interview with Anne Galligan, UQP, Brisbane, April 1997.

17. Munro interview.
18. Phillips, Sandra, 'Mogwi Djan. National Indigenous Writers and Playwrights Conference and Workshop', *Queensland Writers' Centre Newsletter*, July 1996: 6.
19. Phillips interview.
20. Abbey, Sue, Interview with Anne Galligan, UQP, Brisbane, August 1996.
21. Munro interview.
22. Fitzgibbon interview.
23. Muller, Laurie, National Book Council Dinner, Brisbane, February 1993, UQP Files.

Appendix I

Books Published 1948–98, A Checklist

[*Note*: This list does not include the hundreds of UQP non-book publications, such as long-running scholarly journals (*Australian Journal of Politics and History*, the *University of Queensland Law Journal*, and *Australian Literary Studies*, for example), microfilms (including theses, *Nation Review*, early Queensland newspapers and many Papua New Guinea newspapers), audio cassette series (Writers on Tape, Public Figures & Issues on Tape), and medical teaching materials (including slides, radiographs and films). Overseas editions are usually not listed. Grateful acknowledgment is made to the University of Queensland Library Information Technology Service for the catalogue information on which this list is based.]

Establishment of the University of Queensland Press

The University of Queensland Press was established in its present form in 1948. Statute 38 of the Senate of the University of Queensland reads:

The University of Queensland Press

1. There shall be a department within the University to be called the University of Queensland Press, hereafter referred to as "the Press".
2. The functions of the Press shall be —
   (a) to publish and to sell or otherwise appropriately deal with official University publications, works of learning, literary matter used in connection with University teaching, past examination papers, and such other matter as the Board of Management may determine;
   (b) to acquire and sell books and others things used for academic purposes.
3. Subject to the supreme authority of Senate and to the provisions of this Statute, the control of the Press shall be vested in the Board of Management, which may do all things incidental to the carrying out of the functions of the Press.
4. Senate shall appoint a person to be manager of the Press, on such terms as to salary and otherwise as it may determine, and such officer shall act under the direction of the Board of Management.

5. The accounts of the Press shall be kept separate from other University accounts, and all funds acquired through the operations of the Press shall remain at its disposal and shall not become a part of general University funds. The accounts shall be balanced annually as at 31st August, and trading and profit and loss accounts and a balance sheet shall, when audited, be submitted to Senate.
6. From time to time Senate may make such grants as it sees fit out of general revenue for the purposes of the Press.

1948

Address on citizenship / by W. Forgan Smith to the International Knowledge of Living Fellowship
Psychology: an evolutionary introduction / by G.F.K. Naylor
The applications of atomic energy / by H.C. Webster
Medical and biological physics / by H.C. Webster, D.F. Robertson
Physiology and hygiene / by Margaret I.R. Scott
Notes on some fungi from New Guinea / by R.F.N. Langdon
Introduction to Greek philosophy / by Elsie Harwood
Prose selections / by J.J. Stable, A.K. Thomson

1949

The University of Queensland: its development and future expansion
Tropical fatigue: being an account of a preliminary enquiry, conducted in the field, into the effects of service in the Netherlands EastIndies, New Guinea, and the Solomon islands on R.A.A.F. ground crew, R.N.Z.A.F. ground crew and A.I.F. soldiers / by R.K. Macpherson
Secondary school junior physics / by Isaac Waddle
Personality deviations occurring in children of pre-school age / by John Bostock and Edna Hill

1950

The atom and its nucleus / by Sir H.S.W. Massey
Studies in Australian ergots / by R.F.N. Langdon
The technique of rabbit blastoderm culture / by Wharton B. Mather
Surgery of the rabbit embryo "in utero" / by Wharton B. Mather
Artificial insemination in the rabbit / by Wharton B. Mather
Useful formulae in physics expressed in MKS units. Part 1, Elementary
The deep cervical fascia: a study in structural, functional and applied anatomy / by E.S. Meyers
A junior physics test: an attainment test in physics / compiled and standardized by R.A. Squire

Notes on the soils of coastal Queensland and portions of the hinterland: with special reference to the tropical latitudes / by L.J.H. Teakle

1951

Physiology and hygiene / by Margaret I. R. Scott (2nd ed)
Classics in modern education / by Charles Gordon Cooper
Introduction to calculus / by H.M. Finucan
Projection methods and co-ordinate geometry of two dimensions / by H.K. Powell

1952

The life and work of Sir William Bragg / Macrossan lecture by Sir Kerr Grant
A concise trigonometry / by Stanley G. Brown
Laboratory manual for bacteriology / Bacteriology Department
Elements of deductive logic / by W.M. Kyle
Faunistic records from Queensland: Part 1. — General instruction. Part II. — Adult Stomatopoda (Crustacea) / by W. Stephenson
Community support for the university / by J. D. Story

1953

Liberal education: an introduction to the faculties of Arts, Law and Commerce
A study of the factors responsible for the fluctuation of sheep numbers in the Charleville district of South-Western Queensland 1939–1949 / by A.R. Bird
A bibliography of the marine invertebrates of Queensland / by W. Dall and W. Stephenson
Echinodermata (excluding Crinoidea) / by R. Endean
Affine transformation theory of the cuspidal cubics / by E.F. Simonds

1954

Proofs of theorems in the analysis of variance / by I.A. Evans
Enclosing of vines by trunks of rain forest trees / by D.A. Herbert
Three species of fungi parasitic on marine algae in Tasmania / by A.B. Cribb and Joan W. Herbert
The origin and differentiation of Claviceps species / by R.F.N. Langdon
The origin and distribution of Cynodon dactylon (L.) Pers. / by R.F.N. Langdon
New species of Claviceps / by R.F.N. Langdon
The Mitchell grass association of the Longreach district / by D. Davidson
Records of marine algae from south-eastern Queensland / by A.B. Cribb (1954–60)

1955

Colonial society, 1860–90: Queensland / by A.A. Morrison
Australian banking / by J.K. Gifford, J. Vivian Wood and A.J. Reitsma (2nd ed — 1st published 1947)
An engineer looks in on the pastoral industry in the far west / by Alex J. Gibson
The anatomy of the sheep / by N. D. S. May
Community support for the university / by J.D. Story
Puccinia visci sp. n. on Viscum in Queensland / by Joan W. Cribb
Quantitative methods for estimating the distribution of soil fungi / J.E.C. Aberdeen
Marine fungi from Queensland / by A.B. Cribb and Joan W. Cribb (1955–60)
The gasteromycetes of Queensland / by Joan W. Cribb (1955–58)
Payment of debts by executors in Queensland / by E. I. Sykes
Studies on Queensland Hemiptera / by T.E. Woodward

1956

The story of the sugar industry in Queensland / by A. F. Bell
A study of the oral vocabulary of adults: (An investigation into the spoken vocabulary of the Australian worker) / [F.J. Schonell et al]
Mind and experience / by W.M. Kyle
Factors influencing the distribution of the fungi on plant roots. Part 1, Different host species and fungal interactions / by J.E.C. Aberdeen
On Australian and New Zealand Peloridiidae (Homoptera: Coleorrhyncha) / by T.E. Woodward
John Anderson Gilruth: the influence of his life and work on the development of the livestock industries of the Commonwealth / Macrossan lecture by Sir Ian Clunies Ross
Projection methods and co-ordinate geometry of two dimensions / by H. K. Powell (2nd ed)
The corals of Low Isles, Queensland / by W. Stephenson and J.W. Wells
Further records of Echinodermata (excluding Crinoidea) / by R. Endean

1957

The subgenus Ochlerotatus in the Australian region (Diptera: Culicidae) / by Elizabeth N. Marks (1957–64)
Outdoor studies on living animals in Queensland / by W. Stephenson
Chemistry. Part I, Laboratory notes for students of medicine, dentistry and veterinary science / E.C.M. Grigg, E.A. Connor
The University of Queensland, St. Lucia, Brisbane / by F. W. Robinson
An introduction to psychological medicine / by B.F.R. Stafford
Philosophy: a synopsis / by Gordon James

1958

Socrates and Plato / Macrossan lecture by W. K. C. Guthrie
The time levels in Thomas Mann's Joseph the Provider / K. Leopold
John Murtagh Macrossan: his life and career / Macrossan lecture by Harrison Bryan
Australian banking / by J.K. Gifford, J. Vivian Wood and A.J. Reitsma (3rd ed)
Australian Plecoptera. Part I, Genus Trinotoperla Tillyard / by F.A. Perkins
Further experiments on the influence of light intensity on the growth of the sunflower (Helianthus annuus): with a discussion on some pot culture difficulties and possible shortcomings of growth analysis comparisons / by G.L. Wilson
Records of Trentepohlieae from Papua / by A.B. Cribb
The genus Trentepohlia in South-eastern Queensland / by A.B. Cribb
A note on the structure of green alga Callipsygma wilsonis J. Ag. / by A.B. Cribb
Two species of Tuberales from Queensland / by Joan W. Cribb
Cropping for fodder conservation and pasture production in the wool-growing areas of western Queensland / by P.J. Skerman

1959

Queensland and its writers: 100 years — 100 authors / by Cecil Hadgraft
The Latin extracts of [Virgil's] Journey to Hesperia / translated into English by C.G. Cooper
The vocational contributions of women graduates of the University of Queensland / by Margaret W. Rorke
The effects of a subnormal child on the family unit: first and second surveys / by F.J. Schonell [et al]
The effect of "trace elements" on experimental dental caries in the albino rat / by B.J. Kruger
Marine and brackish water hydroids / by Pamela R. Pennycuik
Outdoor studies on living animals in Queensland / by W. Stephenson

1960

Meyer and Merimee / by K. Leopold
School attainments and home backgrounds of Aboriginal children in Queensland / by F.J. Schonell, I.G. Meddleton, B.H. Watts
Australian banking / by J.K. Gifford, J. Vivian Wood and A.J. Reitsma (4th ed)
Explosives for engineers: a primer of Australasian industrial practice / by Cedric E. Gregory
Alfred Deakin: two lectures / Macrossan lecture by J. A. La Nauze
Dentistry in Queensland / S.A. Rayner and B.J. Kruger

The fluid intake of under eight year old Queensland children / B.J. Kruger
A phonetic system for Middle High German / by Gunther M. Bonnin
Trade protection in Australia / by A.J. Reitsma
Problems and trends in American education / Macrossan lecture by D. H. Russell
Studies on the life-history and biology of Choerocoris paganus (Fabricius), (Heteroptera: Pentatomidae: Scutellerinae) / by F.J.D. McDonald
Two new species of subterranean Ascomycetes from Queensland / by Joan W. Cribb
Some marine fungi on algae in European herbaria / by A.B. Cribb and Joan W. Cribb
Five towns of the brigalow country of south-eastern Queensland: Goondiwindi, Miles, Tara, Taroom, Wandoan / by R.S. Dick
Biochemistry: Laboratory manual for Elementary biochemistry, Biochemistry II and Clinical Biochemistry III / by Margaret S. Gilliland
A guide to canine radiography / by S. E. Gould
The dermestid beetle method of skull preparation / by B.J. Kruger
An investigation of the coral deaths at Peel Island, Moreton Bay, in early 1956 / by R.J. Slack-Smith
Additions to the Drosophila fauna of Australia / by Wharton B. Mather

1961

A spring song: a comedy / by Ray Mathew ; with an introduction by Eunice Hanger (Contemporary Australian plays series, 1961) Published with the assistance of the Commonwealth Literary Fund
Some observations on the rural-urban interdependence problems in Queensland: with particular reference to the Shire of Bowen and a method of procedure towards a rural-urban synthesis / by M. Juppenlatz
How to study at the university / by Sir Fred Schonell
Medical and biological physics / by H.C. Webster, D.F. Robertson (2nd ed)
Useful formulae in physics expressed in MKSA units. Part 1 — Elementary / Physics Department
Projection methods and co-ordinate geometry of two dimensions / by H.K. Powell (3rd ed)
An environmental lipofuscin pigmentation of livers: studies on the pigmentation affecting the sheep and other animals in certain districts of Australia / by Hans Winter
Observations of the life histories of the stick insects Acrophylla tessellata Gray and Extatosoma tiaratum Macleay / by Katherine Korboot
A comparative study of the male genitalia of Queensland Scutellerinae Leach (Hemiptera: Pentatomidae) / by F.J.D. McDonald
Some marine algae from Thursday Island and surrounding areas / by A.B. Cribb

The biology of Callianassa (Trypaea) australiensis Dana 1852 (Crustacea, Thalassinidea) / by T.S. Hailstone and W. Stephenson
Additional records of Echinodermata (excluding Crinoidea) / by R. Endean
Outdoor studies on living animals in Queensland / by W. Stephenson (2nd ed)
D. Pararubida: a new species of Drosophila from New Guinea / by Wharton B. Mather

1962

Australian painting today / Macrossan lecture by Bernard Smith
Australia and the Antarctic / Macrossan lecture by Phillip Law
Promise and performance: a study of student progress at University level / by Fred J. Schonell [et al]
The slow learner: segregation or integration / edited by F.J. Schonell, J.M. McLeod, R.G. Cochrane
Principles of bankruptcy in Australia / by E.J. Hajek [later Hayek]
Stresses in ships / Evans memorial lecture by F.B. Bull
Further surveys of public opinion on some dental health problems / by B.J. Kruger
Some nereid polychaetes from Queensland / by Eleanor Russell
Anglo-Dutch rivalry in the Malay world 1780–1824 / by Nicholas Tarling
Veterinary science in Queensland / by S.A. Rayner, J.W. Watson
Elements of the stratigraphy of Queensland / by Dorothy Hill and W.G.H. Maxwell
A revision of the subgenus Chaetocruiomyia Theobald (Diptera: Culicidae) / by Elizabeth N. Marks
Cleistogamy in Microlaena stipoides (Labill.) R.Br. / by H.T. Clifford
Trace elements in dental morphology: an investigation into the effect of boron, Fluorine and molybdenum on the morphology of the crown of the first mandibular molar of the rat / by B.J. Kruger
Ricarda Huch's Der letzte Sommer: an example of epistolary fiction in the twentieth century / by Keith Leopold

1963

The elements of poetry / by Robert D. FitzGerald
The constitutions of the Australian states / by R.D. Lumb
The life and work of Robin John Tillyard, 1881–1937 / Macrossan lecture by J.W. Evans
The Latin extracts of Cicero on himself / translated into English by C. G. Cooper
The Babylonian Talmud / by A. Fabian
Air conditioning: a guide for architects, engineers and prospective purchasers / by N.R. Sheridan [et al]

Fishes of Heron Island, Capricorn Group, Great Barrier Reef / by D.J. Woodland and R.J. Slack-Smith

Adagnesia opaca gen. nov., sp. nov.: a remarkable ascidian of the family Agnesiidae from Moreton Bay, Queensland / by Patricia Kott (Mrs W.B. Mather)

A new species of mysid (Mysidacea: Crustacea) from the Brisbane River / by Dinah Hodge

Francis Ponge and the new problem of the epos / by Antoine Denat

Top public servants in two states / by B.B. Schaffer and K.W. Knight

Early constitutional development in Australia: New South Wales, 1788–1856, Queensland 1859–1922 (with notes to 1963 by the editor) / by A.C.V. Melbourne, edited and introduced by R.B. Joyce (2nd ed)

A new species of Tomocoris Woodward and a new related genus (Hemiptera: Lygaeidae: Rhyparochrominae) / by T.E. Woodward

A comparative study of the female genitalia of Queensland Scutellerinae Leach (Hemiptera: Pentatomidae) / by F.J.D. McDonald

Biological studies of some caddis flies (Trichoptera) from southeast Queensland / by Katherine Korboot

Nymphal systematics and life histories of some Queensland Scutellerinae Leach (Hemiptera: Pentatomidae) / by F.J.D. McDonald

Further records of Trentepohlia from south-eastern Queensland / by A.B. Cribb

Biochemistry: laboratory manual for Biochemistry II and Clinical Biochemistry III / by Margaret S. Gilliland (2nd ed)

Genetics: introductory notes / by W.B. Mather

Genetics: advanced notes / by W.B. Mather

Headmasters for better schools / G.W. Bassett, A.R. Crane, W.G. Walker

India and Afghanistan, 1876–1907: a study in diplomatic relations / by D.P. Singhal

Parasitism: an introduction to parasitology and immunology for students of biology, veterinary science and medicine / by J.F.A. Sprent

The story of King's College, within the University of Queensland: commemorating the first fifty years 1913 to 1963

1964

Image in the clay / by David Ireland, with preface by Norman McVicker (Contemporary Australian plays series)

Walter Burley Griffin / by J. Birrell, with a foreword by Robin Boyd

Architecture in Queensland / by S.A. Rayner, F.B. Lucas

A general theory of social organization and behaviour / by G. McBride

The reading attainments of primary school children in three Queensland schools / by R.J. Andrews

Elements of horseshoeing / by J.A. Springhall

The anatomy of the sheep / by N.D.S. May (2nd ed)
The development of veterinary science in Australia / by H.R. Seddon
A study of some accounting problems in the oil industry / by F.K. Alfredson
Administrative control of capital expenditure: a survey of Australian public companies / by G.G. Meredith
Ahermatypic corals from Queensland / by J.W. Wells
Stolidobranch and Phlebobranch ascidians of the Queensland coast / by Patricia Kott (Mrs. W.B. Mather)
D.tetrachaeta: a new species of Drosophila from New Guinea / by D. Angus
Comparative studies of the external and internal anatomy of three species of caddis flies (Trichoptera) / by Katherine Korboot
Eight new species of caddis flies (Trichoptera) from the Australian region / by Katherine Korboot
The hermit in Van Diemen's Land / by Henry Savery, edited with a biographical introduction by Cecil Hadgraft and notes by Margriet Roe (first published 1829)
The maritime boundaries of Queensland and New South Wales / by R.D. Lumb
The systematic position of the grass genus Micraira F. Muell / by H.T. Clifford
Notes on Trentepohlia from Queensland: including one growing on spider / by A.B. Cribb
Erysiphaceae of south-eastern Queensland / by B.G. Clare
Ampelomyces quisqualis (Cicinnobolus cesatii) on Queensland Erysiphaceae / by B.G. Clare
The mountain mallee heath of the McPherson Ranges / by Richard Jones
Genetics: advanced notes / by W.B. Mather (2nd ed)
Pasture investigations in the Yalleroi district of Central Queensland / by L.A. Eyde [et al]
Pharmacy in Queensland / by H.W. Thiele

1965

The drunken Buddha / translated and illustrated by Ian Fairweather
The constitutions of the Australian states / by R.D. Lumb (2nd ed)
Britain and American imperialism, 1898–1900 / by R.G. Neale
A newspaper's role in modern society / public lecture by T.C. Bray
The future of nuclear power / Macrossan lecture by Sir J.D. Cockcroft
The theory of profit determination on long term contracts and an appraisal of Australian practice / by G.W. Beck
Contribution a la faune des annelides polychetes de l'Australie / by F. Rullier
Ecological and life history studies upon a large foraminiferan (Discobotellina biperforata Collins 1958) from Moreton Bay, Queensland / by W. Stephenson and May Rees

Further records of Echinodermata (excluding Crinoidea) from Southern Queensland / by R. Endean
Surveying in Queensland / by S.A. Rayner, J.V. Buley
The bone marrow cells of sheep / by Hans Winter
Ideological groups in the Australian Labor Party and their attitudes / by Tom Truman
The structure and function of a university department of surgery / inaugural lecture by William Burnett
The influence of shoot removal on drought survival of sorghum / by G.L. Wilson and P.C. Whiteman
Effects of water stress on the reproductive development of Sorghum vulgare Pers. / by P.C. Whiteman and G.L. Wilson
The classification of the Poaceae: a statistical study / by H.T. Clifford
An ecological and taxonomic account of the algae of the semi-marine cavern, Paradise Cave, Queensland / by A.B. Cribb
Precept and practice in the university: education or vocational training / inaugural lecture by G.N. Davies
Developments in early adolescence and the structure of secondary education: an interstate survey / by D.J. Drinkwater
Capital rationing and the determination of the firm's performance standards for capital investment analysis / by G.G. Meredith
Genetics: introductory notes / by W.B. Mather (3rd ed)
The University of Queensland, St. Lucia, Brisbane
The principal at work: case studies in school administration / edited by W.G. Walker
Graduation and employment: a survey of the graduates of the University of Queensland 1961, and their employment / by C. Williams
Geological excursions in Southeast Queensland / by N.C. Stevens

1966

The fiction fields of Australia / by Frederick Sinnett, edited with a biographical introduction and notes by Cecil Hadgraft
Germany and the European novel / inaugural lecture by K. Leopold
How to study at the university / by F.J. Schonell
Dunwich: a study of Aboriginal and European integration by J.A. Keats [et al]
The law of the sea and Australian offshore areas / by R.D. Lumb
Jubilee celebrations, 25, 26, and 27 May, 1960
Explosives for engineers: a primer of Australasian industrial practice / by C.E. Gregory (2nd ed)
Interim financial reports: the cash basis / by D.R. Barnett
D.argentostriata: a new species of Drosophila from New Guinea / by I.R. Bock

Ascidians from Northern Australia / by Patricia Kott

Studies on the direct visualization of the bovine ovaries through a retained cannula in the paralumbar fossa / by A.A. Baker

Morphology of the external genitalia of some Pentatominae (Heteroptera) / by E.B. Tay

Muscles of the ox / by R.M. Butterfield, N.D.S. May

What is applied mathematics / inaugural lecture by A.F. Pillow

Practical chemistry. I, Notes for: agriculture, engineering, forestry, pharmacy, physiotherapy (degree), science, surveying / by E.C.M. Grigg and R.A. Plowman (2nd ed)

Practical chemistry for medical students: Notes for medicine, dentistry, veterinary science / by E.C.M. Grigg (2nd ed)

Useful formulae in physics: (elementary) and international standard units (2nd ed)

Capital investment decisions: a manual for managerial planning and control / by G.G. Meredith

Grassland improvement in tropical territories / inaugural lecture by R.J. McIlroy

Post mortem examination of ruminants / by H. Winter

Society, the offender and the psychiatrist / inaugural lecture by F.A. Whitlock

Linear programming and practicable farm plans: a case study in the Goondiwindi district, Queensland / by P.A. Rickards and W.O. McCarthy

1967

Focus on Charles Blackman / by Thomas Shapcott (Artists in Queensland series)

Focus on Judith Wright / by W.N. Scott (Artists in Queensland series)

Focus on Milton Moon / by D. Pryor (Artists in Queensland series)

Focus on Andrew Sibley / by Rodney Hall (Artists in Queensland series)

John Dryden and the poetry of statement / by K.G. Hamilton

Australia / by Anthony Trollope, edited by P.D. Edwards and R.B. Joyce

Education through music / inaugural lecture by Noel Nickson

Existence and imagination: the theatre of Henry de Montherlant / by J. Batchelor

Andreas Gryphius and the Sieur de Saint-Lazare: A study of the tragedy Catharina von Georgien in relation to its French source / Keith Leopold

Australian banking / by J.K. Gifford, J. Vivian Wood and A.J. Reitsma (5th ed)

Principles of bankruptcy in Australia / by E.J. Hayek (2nd ed)

Practising accountants in Australia: an analytical study / by R.S. Gynther

Sir Winston Churchill and the Commonwealth of Nations / Macrossan lecture by J.D.B. Miller

Armchair, board room, cabinet: the province of economics / inaugural lecture by R.C. Gates
The Catholic Church and freedom: the Vatican Council and some modern issues / by D. Kenny
Don Juan in Melanesia / by Peter Lawrence, with an introduction by James McAuley
Animals in the service of man / inaugural lecture by P.B. English
A scale to measure the reading difficulty of children's books / by J. Anderson
An inventory to measure students' attitudes / by D.S. Anderson and J.S. Western
Gene frequency in laboratory populations of Drosophila melanogaster / by D. Angus
D. silvistriata: a new species of Drosophila from New Guinea / by I.R. Bock and V. Baimai
Additions to the Drosophila fauna of New Guinea / by D. Angus
The identity theory of mind / edited by C.F. Presley
Elements of the stratigraphy of Queensland / Dorothy Hill, W.G.H. Maxwell (2nd ed)
Raw cane sugar manufacture and the chemical engineer / C.W. Davis
The quest for dentistry without discomfort / inaugural lecture by R.R. Stephens
Headmasters for better schools / G.W. Bassett, A.R. Crane, W.G. Walker (2nd ed)
Medical and biological physics / by H.C. Webster, D.F. Robertson (2nd ed, rev.)
Voice without a larynx / by J. Sawkins
Practices in range forage production / by H.F. Heady

1968

Citizens of mist / by Roger McDonald (UQP's first book of original poetry)
New impulses in Australian poetry / edited by Rodney Hall and Thomas W. Shapcott
Keats (Plain texts of the poets series)
Browning (Plain texts of the poets series)
Shelley (Plain texts of the poets series)
Wordsworth (Plain texts of the poets series)
Milton (Plain texts of the poets series)
Tennyson (Plain texts of the poets series)
Pope and the Neo-classicists (Plain texts of the poets series)
The little lives of certain chairs, a table or two and other inanimates of our acquaintance / by Barbara Blackman, illustrations by Charles Blackman
Khaki, bush and bigotry: three Australian plays / edited by Eunice Hanger (Contemporary Australian plays series)

The poor parson / by Steele Rudd (A.H. Davis), illustrations by Syd Smith and Harry Julius
In Australia / by Steele Rudd (A.H. Davis)
For life: and other stories / by Steele Rudd (A.H. Davis), illustrations by H.J. Weston
Dad in politics and other stories / by Steele Rudd (A.H. Davis), illustrations by H.J. Weston
The unknown Japanese / by Joyce I. Ackroyd
Sir John Forrest / Macrossan lecture by F.K. Crowley
The art of prolonging the musical tone / by Colin Brumby
Conscription in Australia / edited by Roy Forward and Bob Reece
Political stability and political behaviour / inaugural lecture by Colin A. Hughes
Readings in Australian government / edited by Colin A. Hughes
Pacific circle 1: proceedings of the second biennial conference of the Australian and New Zealand American Studies Association / edited by Norman Harper
Daughter of time / inaugural lecture by P. Lawrence
Old people at home: an exploratory study of the aged population in the City of Brisbane / by Hazel M. Smith, Alma E. Hartshorn and Verna E. Graham
The constitutions of the Australian states / by R. D. Lumb (2nd ed)
The war aims of imperial Germany: Professor Fritz Fischer and his critics / by John A. Moses
Analysis for replacement of fixed assets / by Merle M. Gynther
The principal at work: case studies in school administration / edited by W.G. Walker (2nd ed)
The genus Drosophila in New Guinea and Sabah / by Wharton B. Mather
Macquaridrilus: a new genus of Tubificidae (Oligochaeta) from Macquarie Island / by B.G.M. Jamieson
A third race of Drosophila rubida / by Wharton B. Mather
Psychology: an evolutionary introduction / by G.F.K. Naylor (2nd ed)
Master of none / inaugural lecture by Derek Fielding
Resistance to insecticides in some Australian populations of
Blattella germanica (L.) / by G.H.S. Hooper and J.L. Goward
Revisional studies of Australian and Indomalayan Luciolini (Coleoptera: Lampyridae: Luciolinae) / by Lesley A. Ballantyne
The technical and administrative problems of a state road authority / by C.N. Barton
The nature and resolution of role conflicts among Queensland primary school teachers: an application of field theory / by M.J. Dunkin
Fortran programmes for crystallographers. I., Calculation of cell dimensions from oscillation and Weissenberg photographs / by J.C. Mills and C.H.L. Kennard

1969

Inwards to the sun: poems / by Thomas W. Shapcott

Focus on David Rowbotham / by John Strugnell (Artists in Queensland series)

On an Australian farm / by Steele Rudd (A.H. Davis), illustrations by Ben Jordan

From selection to city / by Steele Rudd (A.H. Davis), illustrated by Lionel Lindsay

James Brunton Stephens / literary biography by Cecil Hadgraft

Norfolk Island: an outline of its history 1774–1968 / by Merval Hoare

A glossary of grammatical terms: an aid to the student of languages / by S.H. Gerson

The statistician: his mode of reasoning / inaugural lecture by S. Lipton

Science and the future of Australia / Macrossan lecture by S. Encel

The civil engineer in modern society / inaugural lecture by G.R. McKay

Riding the minerals boom / inaugural lecture by R.L. Whitmore

What is architecture / inaugural lecture by G.E. Roberts

Apologia pro vita decani / inaugural lecture by E.G. Saint

The police and the public in Australia and New Zealand / by D. Chappell, P.R. Wilson

Least squares method in data analysis / by R.S. Anderssen

New perspectives on British Far Eastern policy, 1913–19 / by Don Dignan

A description of the Yugumbir dialect of Bandjalang / by Margaret C. Cunningham [Sharpe]

People working together / by L.M. Halliwell

Schools of Mapleton in-baskets / W.G. Walker, Peter Rich, Robert Teasdale

Prospects for mathematics in the life sciences / inaugural lecture by L. Bass

Behaviour therapy: proceedings of a symposium held by the Queensland Branch of the Australian Psychological Society, 1967 / edited by G.L. Mangan and L.D. Bainbridge

A critical analysis of some behavioural assumptions underlying R.J. Chambers' Accounting, evaluation and economic behavior / by Richard W. Leftwich

Handbook for dyslexia schedule and school entrance check list / by J. McLeod

Profit-volume decisions: a manual for managerial planning and control / by G. G. Meredith

1970

Bicycle: and other poems / by David Malouf (Paperback poets series)

Streets of the long voyage / poems by Michael Dransfield (Paperback poets series)

Heaven, in a way / poems by Rodney Hall (Paperback poets series)

Rodney Hall reads Romulus & Remus (Poets on record series)
Rosemary Dobson reads from her own work (Poets on record series)
James McAuley reads from his own work (Poets on record series)
6 one-act plays / edited by Eunice Hanger
Vance Palmer / by Harry Heseltine
The Dashwoods: a sequel to "On an Australian farm" / by Steele Rudd, illustrations by Claude Marquet
Grandpa's selection: and other stories / by Steele Rudd, drawings by Lionel Lindsay
Stocking our selection / by Steele Rudd, illustrated by A.J. Fischer [et al]
The book of Dan / by Steele Rudd, illustrated by Lionel Lindsay
Harold Pinter / by Alrene Sykes (US edn by Humanities Press)
Mystical symbolism in the poetry of Thomas Traherne / by Alison J. Sherrington
C.E.W. Bean, Australian historian / Macrossan lecture by K.S. Inglis
Myths and legends of Torres Strait / collected and translated by Margaret Lawrie
The provisional government / by V. D. Nabokov, translated by A.G.E. Speirs and edited by Andrew Field
The bitter fight: a pictorial history of the Australian labor movement / by Joe Harris
Commonwealth or Europe / by G. St.J. Barclay
The law and computers / by D.J. Whalan
The pattern of law reform in Australia / inaugural lecture by K.C.T. Sutton
Cities in transformation: the urban squatter problem of the developing world / by M. Juppenlatz
The literature of state budgeting in Australia, Canada, and the United States of America: a survey and select bibliography / by Kenneth W. Knight
The anatomy of the sheep: a dissection manual / by N. D. S. May (3rd ed)
A second collection of opisthobranch molluscs from Queensland / by Ron Kenny
A study of verbal interaction in science classes and its association with pupils' understanding in science / by R.P. Tisher
A syntactical study of epic formulas and formulaic expressions containing the -ant forms in twelfth century French verse / by C.W. Aspland
The ecological backlash: nature versus man / inaugural lecture by J.M. Thomson
The accounting valuation of beef cattle and sheep for Queensland primary production businesses / by G.W. Beck
Problems of insect control / by D. S. Kettle
Survey of the incidence of speech defects in south-east Queensland / by Mary A. Macfadyen

From amber to zener: the electrical engineer's progress / inaugural lecture by M.W. Gunn
Relationship between text-book orientation and mathematics achievement and attitude / by K.F. Collis
Theory and practice in educational administration / by W.G. Walker
Data representation / edited by R. S. Anderssen and M. R. Osborne
Submission to the Committee on Post-Graduate Education for Management
Directory of Australian grassland and animal production research centres / compiled by H. R. Webb

1971

The cool change / Andrew Taylor (Paperback poets series)
Two poets: The question, by Geoff Page; Single eye, by Philip Roberts (Paperback poets series)
The deer under the skin / poems by J. S. Harry (Paperback poets series)
Being out of order: some poems and "The uncommercial traveller" / by Richard [Lewis] Packer
Op. 8: poems 1961–69 / by J. S. Manifold
Douglas Stewart reads from his own work (Poets on record series)
R.D. Fitzgerald reads from his own work (Poets on record series)
Bruce Dawe reads from his own work (Poets on record series)
Apparition: poems / by A. Alvarez, paintings by Charles Blackman (also in limited edition)
The old homestead / by Steele Rudd (A.H. Davis), illustrations by Lionel Lindsay
Memoirs of corporal Keeley / by Steele Rudd (A.H. Davis), drawings by Lionel Lindsay
Focus on Ray Crooke / by Rosemary Dobson (Artists in Queensland series)
Drama for high schools / by Eunice Hanger
Some mid-Victorian thrillers: the sensation novel, its friends and its foes / inaugural lecture by P.D. Edwards
Theatre comes to Australia / by Eric Irvin
Style and meaning / by David J. Lake
This their dreaming: legends of the panels of Aboriginal art in the Yirrkala Church / by Ann E. Wells, photography by E. James Wells
The mass media in Australia: use and evaluation / by J.S. Western and Colin A. Hughes
The sexual dilemma: abortion, homosexuality, prostitution, and the criminal threshold / by Paul Wilson
Air pollution / by Alan Gilpin
Forrest 1847–1918 / by F.K. Crowley
Comparative education: purpose and method / by Phillip E. Jones

Useful formulae in Physics (elementary) and international standard units (3rd ed)
The Australian planner's dilemma / inaugural lecture by L. B. Keeble
The Christian future: a strategy for Catholic renewal / by Denis Kenny
Data acquisition and real-time systems / edited by D.E. Lawrence, P.M. Fenwick
Philippine nationalism: external challenge and Filipino response, 1565–1946 / by Usha Mahajani
School-to-university transition as a change of environmental press / by J.M. Genn
Rail movement of fruit in Queensland: a study of patterns and trends in the transport of a perishable commodity / by Donald B. Freeman
In defence of technology / inaugural lecture by D.J. Nicklin
The objectives of accounting in an accounting theory based on deductive methodology / by Errol R. Iselin
The aquatic oligochaeta known from Australia, New Zealand, Tasmania, and the adjacent islands / by R.O. Brinkhurst
The autistic syndrome: proceedings of the Sandoz Working Party on Definition, Nomenclature, and Classification: held August 1969 / edited by John Rendle-Short and Helen Clancy
The identity theory of mind / edited by C.F. Presley (2nd ed)

1972

The inspector of tides / Michael Dransfield (Paperback poets series)
The brineshrimp / by Rhyll McMaster (Paperback poets series)
Begin with walking / by Thomas W. Shapcott (Paperback poets series)
Diver / by R. A. Simpson (Paperback poets series)
Slade's anatomy of the horse / by Leon Slade (Paperback poets series)
Soft riots / by Richard Tipping (Paperback poets series)
Bruce Beaver reads from his own work (Poets on record series)
A.D. Hope reads from his own work (Poets on record series)
Poesie australiane = Australian poems / by Maria Valli, with English versions by A.G.E. Speirs
Aspects of the dying process: short stories / by Michael Wilding (UQP's first original story collection)
The ship on the coin: a fable of the bourgeoisie / satirical novel by Rodney Hall (UQP's first original novel)
Tropical gothic / stories by Nick Joaquin (Asian and Pacific writing series)
Atheis / novel by Achdiat K. Mihardja, translated from the Indonesian by R.J. Maguire (Asian and Pacific writing series)
Golconda / novel by Vance Palmer
We Kaytons / by Steele Rudd (A.H. Davis)
On Emu Creek / by Steele Rudd, illustrations by Percy Lindsay

A colonial city: high and low life: selected journalism of Marcus Clarke / edited by L. T. Hergenhan
The mystery of unity: theme and technique in the novels of Patrick White / by Patricia A. Morley
The art of Brian James: and other essays on Australian literature / by Clement Semmler
The explorers of the Moreton Bay District, 1770–1830 / by J.G. Steele
The constitutions of the Australian states / by R.D. Lumb (3rd ed)
Questioning the past: a selection of papers in history and government / edited by D.P. Crook (essays in honour of Gordon Greenwood)
Kalparrin: a voluntary agency looks to itself / by Stephanie Gardan, Alec Pemberton and Verna Graham
Tales from Torres Strait / collected and translated by Margaret Lawrie (children's edition)
An examination of cut-off rates for capital expenditure analysis under capital rationing / by Richard D. Morris
The economics of leasing plant and equipment / by F.J. Finn
Optimization / edited by R.S. Anderssen, L.S. Jennings and D.M. Ryan
British reactions to the French Revolution, 1789–1815 / edited by G.D. Story (Themes in modern history: documentary series)
Liberty and the struggle for the franchise, 1768–1848 / by G.D. Story (Themes in modern history series)
Pacific circle 2: proceedings of the third biennial conference of the Australian and New Zealand American Studies Association / edited by Norman Harper
Keys to the families and genera of Queensland flowering plants (Magnoliophyta) / by H. T. Clifford, Gwen Ludlow
The use of soluble silicates in Hawaiian agriculture / by Donald L. Plucknett
School, college, and university: the administration of education in Australia / edited by W. G. Walker
The policeman's position today and tomorrow: an examination of the Victoria Police Force / by Paul R. Wilson and John S. Western
Feature analysis in the human visual system / inaugural lecture by Ray Over
A framework for the development of a theory of financial accounting / by Stephen H. Penman

1973

A framework for the development of a theory of financial accounting / by Stephen H. Penman
Australian fiscal policy / by Douglas A.L. Auld
The miserable clerk / by Steele Rudd, illustrated by Percy Lindsay
The Rudd family / by Steele Rudd, illustrated by Percy Lindsay
Judith Wright reads from her own work (Poets on record series)

Chris Wallace-Crabbe reads from his own work (Poets on record series)
Black writing from New Guinea / edited by Ulli Beier (Asian and Pacific writing series)
Not slaves not citizens: the Aboriginal problem in Western Australia, 1898–1954 by Peter Biskup
Padma River boatman / by Manik Bandopadhyaya. Translated from the Bengali by Barbara Painter and Yann Lovelock (Asian and Pacific writing series)
Legalized pollution: the PIRG report on pollution control laws in Queensland
Credit and security in the Philippines: the legal problems of development finance / by Sixto T.J. de Guzman [et al]
Church, state, and conscience: collected essays by Max Charlesworth
Seedtime / by Vance Palmer
The big fellow by Vance Palmer
Consensus and conflict in agricultural education: a comparative study of four Australian agricultural colleges [check authors]
Credit and security in Ceylon (Sri Lanka): the legal problems of development finance / by Wickrema Weerasooria [et al]
Credit and security in Indonesia: the legal problems of development finance / by Sudargo Gautama (Gouwgioksiong) [et al]
Credit and security in Japan: the legal problems of development finance / by Hisashi Tanikawa [et al]
Credit and security in Korea: the legal problems of development finance / by Yoon Chick Kwack [et al]
Credit and security in Singapore: the legal problems of development finance / by Koh Kheng Lian [et al]
Credit and security in the Republic of China: the legal problems of development finance / by Loh Jen-kong [et al]
A soapbox omnibus / by Rodney Hall (Paperback poets series)
Alcoholism as a social problem / by Margaret J. Sargent
Signs & voices / by Manfred Jurgensen (Paperback poets series)
Hornpipes & funerals: forty-two poems and six odes of Horace / by David Lake (Paperback poets series)
Brisbane in the 1890s: a study of an Australian urban society by Ronald Lawson
A history of the ports of Queensland: a study in economic
nationalism by Glen Lewis
Logic: theory and practice / by M.K. Rennie, R.A. Girle
Policy and planning in higher education / edited by Robert McCaig
The tins: and other stories / by Peter Cowan
Error, approximation, and accuracy / edited by F.R. de Hoog, C.L. Jarvis
Poems from prison / by Jack Murray [and others] edited by Rodney Hall

Peanuts in Penang / a novel by David Richards

Nu-plastik fanfare red: and other poems / by Judith Rodriguez (Paperback Poets series)

4 Australian plays / by Barbara Stellmach (Contemporary Australian plays series)

Ice fishing / by Andrew Taylor (Paperback poets series)

The grasses of southeast Queensland / by J.C. Tothill, J.B. Hacker; illustrated by J.B. Hacker

The Industrial Revolution and its social impact 1750–1850 / compiled and edited by G.D. Story, J.J. Hayes (Themes in modern history series)

Condition red / by Vicki Viidikas (Paperback poets series)

A glossary of educational terms: usage in five English-speaking countries / by W. G. Walker, J. E. Mumford and Carolyn Steel

Explorations in educational administration / edited by W. G. Walker, A. R. Crane and A. Ross Thomas.

Aufsatzubungen: a programmed workbook for free essay writing in German / by G.W. Wagner, J. Resuhr

Crime and the community / by P. R. Wilson, J. W. Brown

Drieu la Rochelle: decadence in love: a study of the effects of social decadence on man-woman relationships in the non-political writings of Pierre Drieu la Rochelle / by R. B. Leal

The administration of solvent deceased estates in Queensland / by W.A. (William Anthony) Lee

A guidebook to field geology in southeast Queensland / by N. C. Stevens

The revolution of 1848 in France / compiled and edited by G.D. Story and J.J. Hayes (Themes in modern history series)

1974

The great tradition: a history of adult education in Australia / by Derek Whitelock.

Mischief in the air: radio and stage plays / by Max Afford

Better health for Aborigines?: report of a National Seminar at Monash University / edited by Basil S. Hetzel [et al]

Credit and security: the legal problems of development financing / by David E. Allan, Mary E. Hiscock, Derek Roebuck

Neighbours in a thicket: poems / by David Malouf

Consideration reconsidered: studies on the doctrine of consideration of the law of contract / by K.C.T. Sutton

He knew he was right / by Anthony Trollope, edited by P.D. Edwards (Victorian texts series)

The Banjo of the bush: the life and times of A.B. "Banjo" Paterson / by Clement Semmler

The First paperback poets anthology / edited by Roger McDonald

Maoism in action: the cultural revolution / by C. L. Chiou
Amours de voyage / by Arthur Hugh Clough, edited by Patrick Scott (Victorian texts series)
The fat man in history: short stories / by Peter Carey
Water pollution: causes and effects in Australia / by D. W. Connell
Credit and security in Thailand: the legal problems of development finance / by Chitti Tingsabadh [et al]
Patrick White as playwright / by J. R. Dyce
Design in balance: designing the national area of Canberra, 1968–72 / by Roger Johnson
Wild honey / by Paul Kavanagh (Paperback poets series)
The Samoan tangle: a study in Anglo-German-American relations, 1878–1900 / by Paul M. Kennedy
The history of the Australian steel industry / Macrossan lecture by Sir Ian McLennan
A dictionary of Australian education / by John McLaren
Tactics / by Jennifer Maiden (Paperback poets series)
Mateship in local organization: a study of egalitarianism, stratification, leadership and amenities projects in a semi-industrial community of inland New South Wales / by H. G. Oxley
Using "The first Paperback poets anthology": talking points for students and teachers / by Geoff Page
Peter Porter reads from his own work (Poets on record series)
Young America and Australian gold: Americans and the gold rush of the 1850's / by E. Daniel Potts, and Annette Potts
Randolph Stow reads from his own work (Poets on record series)
Creek water journal / by Robert Gray (Paperback poets series)
Useful formulae in physics (4th ed)
Living together / novel by Michael Wilding
The French Revolution: introductory documents / edited by D.I. Wright.
The tidal forest / novel by Geoff Wyatt
Australian town planning law: uniformity and change / by A. S. Fogg
The politics of education: a bibliographical guide / by G. S. Harman
University teaching — antique or antic? / inaugural lecture by Ernest Roe

1975

Airship / poems by Roger McDonald
One of our conquerors / by George Meredith, edited by Margaret Harris (Victorian texts series)
The psychology of Hardy's novels: the nervous and the statuesque / by Geoffrey Thurley

The organization and administration of Catholic education in Australia / edited by P. D. Tannock
Teachers, education and politics: a history of organizations of public school teachers in New South Wales / by Bruce Mitchell
Tales of the convict system: selected stories of Price Warung / edited by B.G. Andrews
Johnno: a novel / by David Malouf
The romance of Runnibede / by Steele Rudd
Green grey homestead / by Steele Rudd
Elements of horseshoeing / by J.A. Springhall (2nd ed)
Contemporary portraits: and other stories / by Murray Bail
The anatomy of accounting / by A. D. Barton
Contemporary Indonesian poetry: poems in Bahasa Indonesia and English / edited and translated by Harry Aveling (Asian and Pacific writing series)
People, problems and pills / inaugural lecture by Janet Irwin
Who owns the unexpected? A perspective on the nation's information industry / inaugural lecture by D. Meh. Lamberton
The existentialists and Jean-Paul Sartre / by Max Charlesworth
Australia in figures: a handbook of economic, political and social statistics / by W.G. Coppell
T.J. Ryan: a political biography / by D.J. Murphy
Labor in politics: the state Labor parties in Australia, 1880–1920 / edited by D.J. Murphy
The puffing pioneers and Queensland's railway builders / by Viv Daddow
A handbook of American literature: a comprehensive study from colonial times to the present day / by Martin S. Day
Computational methods in mathematical physics / edited by R. S. Anderssen, R. O. Watts
Passages of time: an Australian woman, 1890–1974 / by Mary Edgeworth David
Educational administration in Australia and abroad: analyses and challenges / edited by A. Ross Thomas, R. H. Farquhar, W. Taylor
A Victorian engagement: letters and journals of Walter Hume and Anna Kate Fowler during the 1860s / edited by Bertram Hume
Will's dream / by Philip Roberts (Paperback poets series)
Believed dangerous: fifty eight poems / by Robin Thurston (Paperback poets series)
Volunteers at heart: the Queensland defence forces 1860–1901 / by D.H. Johnson
The other side of the fence / by Peter Kocan (Paperback poets series)
Psychological deprivation in childhood / by J. Langmeier and Z. Matejcek. [translated by Peter Anger] (3rd ed)

The design of bridges: an historical study / inaugural lecture by C. O'Connor
David Campbell reads from his own work (Poets on record series)
Kafka's Trial: the case against Josef K. / by Eric Marson
Trade unions in Australia / by Ross M. Martin
The politics of illusion: the Fischer controversy in German historiography / by John A. Moses
The war aims of imperial Germany: Professor Fritz Fischer and his critics / by John A. Moses
The organization of labour: a response to a challenge, 1800–1850 / compiled and edited by Gordon D. Story, J. J. Hayes (Themes in modern history series)
Smalltown memorials / by Geoff Page (Paperback poets series)
Shabbytown calendar / poems by Thomas W. Shapcott
Selected poems / by David Rowbotham
Numerical methods for nonlinear regression / By D. R. Sadler
Immigrant chronicle / by Peter Skrzynecki (Paperback poets series)
How to study at the University / by Sir Fred Schonell, Jonathan Anderson (rev ed)
Police of the pastoral frontier: native police, 1849–1859 / by L. E. Skinner
Turn left at any time with care: poems / by Graeme Kinross Smith and Jamie Grant (Paperback poets series)
Social work: radical essays / edited by Harold Throssell
Brisbane Town in convict days, 1824–1842 / by J. G. Steele
Selected poems / by Rodney Hall
A place among people / a novel by Rodney Hall
Domestic hardcore / by Richard Tipping (Paperback poets series)
A heap of ashes / by Pramoedya Ananta Toer, edited and translated from the Indonesian by Harry Aveling (Asian and Pacific writing series)
Francis Webb reads from his own work (Poets on record series)
Drugs, morality, and the law / by F. A. Whitlock
The West Midland Underground: stories / by Michael Wilding
The burden of the public debt / by A. W. Hooke
The dis-honourable / by John David Hennessey, with introduction by Nancy Bonnin

1976

Melba / by Paul Sherman (Contemporary Australian plays series)
"The vailala madness", and other essays / by Francis Edgar Williams, edited with an introduction by Erik Schwimmer
Bards, bohemians, and bookmen: essays in Australian literature / edited by Leon Cantrell (for Cecil Hadgraft)
Henry Lawson / selected and edited with an introduction and bibliography by Brian Kiernan (Portable Australian authors series)

Health, sickness, and society: theoretical concepts in social and preventive medicine / by Douglas Gordon
Insect ecology / by E.G. Matthews
Organizational genesis and development: a study of Australian agricultural colleges / by Alan W. Black
The South Pole: an account of the Norwegian Antarctic expedition in the "Fram", 1910–1912 / by Roald Amundsen, translated from the Norwegian by A.G. Chater
The Professions in Australia: a critical appraisal / edited by Paul Boreham, Alec Pemberton, Paul Wilson
What is this thing called science?: an assessment of the nature and status of science and its methods / by A.F. Chalmers
Behaviour modification in Australia / edited by Peter W. Sheehan, Kenneth D. White
Of places and poetry / by Robert D. Fitzgerald
Patrick White: a general introduction / by Ingmar Bjorksten, translated from the Swedish by Stanley Gerson
Flame and shadow: selected stories of David Campbell
Mister Maloga: Daniel Matthews and his mission, Murray River, 1864–1902 / by Nancy Cato
Marcus Clarke / selected and edited with an introduction and bibliography by Michael Wilding (Portable Australian authors series)
The Bothie / by Arthur Hugh Clough, edited by Patrick Scott (Victorian texts series)
Principles and practice of nursing / by M.D. Emerton
American studies down under: proceedings of the fourth and fifth biennial conferences of the Australian and New Zealand American Studies Association / edited by Norman Harper
The Complexity of computational problem solving / edited by R. S. Anderssen, R. P. Brent
Contemporary American & Australian poetry / edited by Thomas Shapcott
Absence in strange countries / by Andrew McDonald (Paperback poets series)
Pictorial anatomy of the cat / by Stephen G. Gilbert (rev ed)
Paths in dreams: selected prose and poetry of Ho Ch'i-fang / translated and edited by Bonnie S. McDougall (Asian and Pacific writing series)
Alpine skiing / by Nancy Greene, Al Raine
The future of Australian federalism: a commentary on the working of the constitution / by Gordon Greenwood (2nd ed)
New devil, new parish / by Alan Wearne (Paperback poets series)
Radical cousins: nineteenth century American & Australian writers / by Joseph Jones
The schizoid world of Jean-Paul Sartre and R. D. Laing / by Douglas Kirsner

The VD epidemic: how it started, where it's going, and what to do about it / by Louis Lasagna
Australia and imperial defence, 1918–39: a study in air and sea power / by John McCarthy
When schools are gone: a projection of the thought of Ivan Illich / by Michael Macklin
Reef poems / by Mark O'Connor
Social class and language utilization at the tertiary level / by Millicent E. Poole
Schooling for the mentally retarded: a historical perspective / by Brian Preen
Mr. Chairman: a guide to meeting procedure, ceremonial procedure, and forms of address, with specimen meetings, and standing orders / by Marjorie Puregger (3rd ed)
Water life / poems by Judith Rodriguez, with author's linocuts
Poems from Murrumbeena / by R. A. Simpson (Paperback poets series)
Fundamentals of social and preventive medicine / by B. A. Smithurst
Dictionary of environmental terms / by Alan Gilpin (Australian environment series)
Sound pollution / edited by R. G. Barden (Australian environment series)
The invention of fire / poems by Andrew Taylor
An archaeological analysis of the Broadbeach Aboriginal burial ground / by Laila Haglund
The most noble art of them all: the selected writings of Laurie Thomas / introduced by Charles Blackman, John Olsen
The Dickens myth: its genesis and structure / by Geoffrey Thurley
The government of Tasmania / by W. A. Townsley
Public housing for Australia / by Paul Wilson
Around Mt Isa: a guide to the flora and fauna / by Helen Horton, with the section on reptiles by David Stammer and line drawings by Elizabeth McKenzie
Sir Matthew Nathan: British colonial governor and civil servant / by Anthony P. Haydon
Reptile ecology / by Harold Heatwole (Australian ecology series)
The government of Victoria / by Jean Holmes

1977

Accountability in education / edited by P.R. Chippendale and Paula V. Wilkes
Reluctant mission: the Anglican Church in Papua New Guinea, 1891–1942 / by David Wetherell
Administrative federalism: selected documents in Australian intergovernmental relations / edited by Kenneth W. Wiltshire
Formulating government budgets: aspects of Australian and North American experience / by Kenneth W. Knight, Kenneth W. Wiltshire

Australian external policy under Labor: content, process and the national debate / by Henry S. Albinski (N. Amer. ed Univ. British Columbia Press)
From Derby round to Burketown: the A.U.S.N. story / by N.L. McKellar
Tourist to the Antipodes: William Archer's "Australian journey, 1876–77" / edited by Raymond Stanley
Australians in America, 1876–1976 / edited with an introduction by John Hammond Moore
Models of madness / by Erica M. Bates
Anthony Trollope: his art and scope / by P.D. Edwards (US ed St Martin's Press)
Tables for statisticians / compiled by John White, Alan Yeats, Gordon Skipworth (2nd ed)
The Queensland years of Robert Herbert, Premier: letters and papers / edited with an introduction by Bruce Knox
Industrialization, history and ideology / inaugural lecture by Malcolm I. Thomis
Snakes: a natural history / by H.W. Parker
Antarctica, or, Two years amongst the ice of the South Pole / by Otto Nordenskjold and Joh Gunnar Andersson, with a foreword by Sir Vivian Fuchs and a biographical note
The journal of John Sweatman: a nineteenth century surveying voyage in North Australia and Torres Strait / edited by Jim Allen, Peter Corris
Foreign affairs for new states: some questions of credentials / by P. J. Boyce (US ed St Martin's Press)
Volcanoes of the earth / by Fred M. Bullard
Five plays for stage, radio, and television / edited with an introduction by Alrene Sykes (Portable Australian authors series)
Confessions of William James Chidley / edited by S. McInerney
The 1890s: stories, verse and essays / edited with an introduction by Leon Cantrell (Portable Australian authors series)
Credit and security in Australia: the legal problems of development finance / by David Allan [et al]
Sentencing in Western Australia / by Mary W. Daunton-Fear
Values, ends, and society / by Ian Davison
Delinquency in Australia: a critical appraisal / edited by Paul R. Wilson
Design for diversity: library services for higher education and research in Australia / edited by Harrison Bryan and Gordon Greenwood
Crows of the world / by Derek Goodwin, illustrations by Robert Gillmor
Explosives for Australasian engineers / by C. E. Gregory (3rd ed)
The pocket calculator pocket book / by R.J. Goult, M.J. Pratt
Children and screen violence / by Patricia Edgar
Dance a white horse to sleep: stories / by Antonio Enriquez (Asian and Pacific writing series)

Fathers, mothers, and others: towards new alliances / by Rhona Rapoport [et al]
Indonesia: selected documents on colonialism and nationalism, 1830–1942 / edited and translated by Chris L. M. Penders
The government of South Australia / by Dean Jaensch
Australian schools and the law: principal, teacher and student / by A.E. Knott, K.E. Tronc, J.L. Middleton
The constitutions of the Australian states / R.D. Lumb (4th ed)
Mangroves of Australia / by Richard Lear, Tom Turner
Australian primitive painters / by Geoffrey Lehmann; foreword Charles Blackman
The Lessons of Vietnam / edited by W. Scott Thompson, Donaldson D. Frizzell
Mungo's Canberra / by Mungo Maccallum; with drawings by Michael Leunig
The anatomy of accounting / by A.D. Barton (2nd ed)
The see-through revolver / novel by Craig McGregor
Identifying grasses: data, methods and illustrations / by H. T. Clifford and L. Watson
Philosophy and school administration / by Margaret Mackie
Principles of pediatrics / by G. M. Maxwell
The environmental crisis: a systems approach / by William James Metcalf (Australian environment series) (US ed St Martin's Press)
Race and politics in Fiji / by Robert Norton
Walking through tigerland: stories / by Barry Oakley
Of public concern: contemporary Australian social issues / edited by Paul R. Wilson
Planning in turbulent environments / edited by John S. Western, Paul R. Wilson
A Principal's workbook: simulations of school administration / edited by Keith Tronc
Aboriginal men of high degree / by A.P. Elkin (2nd ed) (US ed St Martin's Press)
The sorrow of the lonely and the burning of the dancers / by Edward L. Schieffelin
Geological oceanography: evolution of coasts, continental margins & the deep-sea floor / by Francis P. Shepard
Simulation and modelling / edited by M. R. Osborne, R. O. Watts
Germany in the Pacific and Far East, 1870–1914 / edited by John A. Moses, Paul M. Kennedy
Soil factors in crop production in a semi-arid environment / edited by J. S. Russell, E. L. Greacen
Textbook of sport for the disabled / by Ludwig Guttmann

The right to choose / by Gisele Halimi, translated by Rosemary Morgan
Cultural change and identity: Mandailing immigrants in West Malaysia / by Donald Tugby
Asian insight / by John Temple
Memories of a country childhood / by Judith Wallace
Women of value, men of renown: new perspectives in Trobriand exchange / by Annette B. Weiner
Papua New Guinea: initiation and independence / by Don Woolford
The Worker in Australia: contributions from research / edited by Allan Bordow, Helen Hurwitz [et al]
Intentions, motives and human action: an argument for free will / by P.N. O'Sullivan
Financial management in school administration / edited by Keith Tronc
Adelaide, 1836–1976: a history of difference / by Derek Whitelock
Recollections of an Indonesian diplomat in the Sukarno era / by Ganis Harsono, edited by C. L. M. Penders, B. B. Hering
From pasta to pavlova: a comparative study of Italian settlers in Sydney and Griffith / by Rina Huber

1978

Joh: the life and political adventures of Johannes Bjelke-Petersen / by Hugh Lunn
Federal aid to Australian schools / by Don Smart
Professionals and management: a study of behaviour in organizations / by Russell D. Lansbury
Unemployed workers: a social history of the Great Depression in Adelaide / by Ray Broomhill
The book of snobs / by William Makepeace Thackeray, edited by John Sutherland (Victorian texts series)
The coup / novel by John Updike
Society and electoral behaviour in Australia: a study of three decades / by D.A. Kemp
The government of the Australian Capital Territory / by Ruth Atkins
Film censorship in Australia / by Ina Bertrand
The peasant mandarin: prose pieces / by Les Murray
Queensland political portraits, 1859–1952 / edited by D.J. Murphy, and R.B. Joyce
Postal unions and politics: a history of the Amalgamated Postal Workers' Union of Australia / by Frank Waters, edited by Denis Murphy
Bundaberg: history and people / by Janette Nolan
Australian poems in perspective: a collection of poems and critical commentaries / edited by P.K. Elkin
Public service inquiries in Australia / edited by R.F.I. Smith, Patrick Weller

The Mungana affair: state mining and political corruption in the 1920s / by K.H. Kennedy
Ian Fairweather: profile of a painter / by Nourma Abbott-Smith
Jessie Street: a rewarding but unrewarded life / by Peter Sekuless
Changes, issues and prospects in Australian education / edited by S. D'Urso, R. A. Smith
Remembering the rural life / by Gary Catalano (Paperback poets series)
Japanese prisoners of war in revolt: the outbreaks at Featherston and Cowra during World War II / by Charlotte Carr-Gregg (US ed St Martin's Press)
Can't you hear me talking to you?: eight short plays about lovers and others / edited by Alrene Sykes (Contemporary Australian plays series)
Working couples / edited by Rhona Rapoport and Robert N. Rapoport, with Janice M. Bumstead
Air pollution / by Alan Gilpin (2nd ed)
Birds of man's world / by Derek Goodwin, illustrations by Robin Prytherch
Icelandic solitaries / by Alan Gould (Paperback poets series)
Hargrave and son: a biography of John Fletcher Hargrave and his son Lawrence Hargrave / by Elena Grainger
Programming for minicomputers / by J.C. Cluley (US ed Crane Russak)
The logical processing of digital signals / by S. L. Hurst
The sea-cucumber / by Martin Johnston (Paperback poets series)
East Timor: nationalism and colonialism / by Jill Jolliffe
The law of the sea and the Australian offshore areas / by R.D. Lumb (2nd ed)
Pieces for a glass piano / stories by Gerard Lee
Mungo on the zoo plane: elections 1972–77 / by Mungo MacCallum, drawings by Patrick Cook
Collected verse / by John Manifold
Two faces of deviance: crimes of the powerless and the powerful / edited by Paul R. Wilson, John Braithwaite
Modern Japanese poetry / translated by James Kirkup, edited and introduced by A. R. Davis (Asian and Pacific writing series)
The government of New South Wales / by R. S. Parker
Mateship in local organization: a study of egalitarianism, stratification, leadership, and amenities projects in a semi-industrial community of inland New South Wales / by H.G. Oxley
Ecology and ekistics / by C. A. Doxiadis, edited by Gerald Dix (Australian environment series)
Dransfield, Michael, 1948–1973
Voyage into solitude / poems by Michael Dransfield ; collected and edited by Rodney Hall
Selected poems / by Thomas W. Shapcott
Sigmund Freud: his life in pictures and words / edited by Ernst Freud, Lucie

Freud and Ilse Grubrich-Simitis, with a biographical sketch by K.R. Eissler, translated by Christine Trollope

People are legends: Aboriginal poems / by Kevin Gilbert

Conrad Martens in Queensland: the frontier travels of a colonial artist / text by John Steele

Studies in the recent Australian novel / edited by K. G. Hamilton

Black bagatelles / poems by Rodney Hall

J.S. Manifold: an introduction to the man and his work / by Rodney Hall

The departure / by Kevin Hart (Paperback poets series)

The other side of rape / by Paul R. Wilson

Evolution / by Colin Patterson

2D and other plays / by Eunice Hanger, edited by Alrene Sykes

Where the queens all strayed / novel by Barbara Hanrahan

Elota's story: the life and times of a Solomon Islands big man / edited by R.M. Keesing

Literature and the Aborigine in Australia, 1770–1975 / by J.J. Healy

God's gentlemen: a history of the Melanesian Mission, 1849–1942 / by David Hilliard

1979

Australia through American eyes 1935–1945: observations by American diplomats / selected, edited with introduction by P.G. Edwards

Rolf Boldrewood / edited with an introduction by Alan Brissenden (Portable Australian authors series)

They crossed the river: the founding of the Mater Misericordiae Hospital, Brisbane, by the Sisters of Mercy / by H.J. Summers

Historical disciplines and culture in Australasia: an assessment / edited by John A. Moses

As it was / poems by Bruce Beaver

Financial tables / compiled by Alan Yeats, John White, Gordon Skipworth

The plight of the Australian clergy: to convert, care or challenge? / by Norman W.H. Blaikie

A guide to Marxism / by Joseph Martin

The future with microelectronics: forcasting the effects of information technology / by Iann Barron, Ray Curnow [et al]

Political language and rhetoric / by Paul E. Corcoran

Memoirs of gold-digging in Australia / by Seweryn Korzelinski, translated and edited by Stanley Robe, foreword and notes by Lloyd Robson

A majority of one: Tom Aikens and independent politics in Townsville / by Ian Moles

Politics and policy in Australia / by Geoffrey Hawker, R.F.I. Smith, Patrick Weller

After the Odyssey: a study of Greek Australians / by Gillian Bottomley

Studies in comparative semantics / by Paul Canart, edited by Wendy Cobcroft, with a foreword by A. R. Chisholm

War crimes: short stories / by Peter Carey

Master mariner: Capt. James Cook and the peoples of the Pacific / by Daniel Conner, Lorraine Miller

The Development of Indonesian society: from the coming of Islam to the present day / edited by Harry Aveling (US ed St Martin's Press)

The mystery of wealth: political economy—its development and impact on world events / by John Hutton

The Indo-Fijian experience / edited and introduced by Subramani (Asian and Pacific writing series)

The Jindyworobaks / selected and edited with an introduction and bibliography by Brian Elliott (Portable Australian authors series)

Fuzzy switching and automata: theory and applications / by Abraham Kandel, Samuel C. Lee

Brain drain and foreign students: a study of the attitudes and intentions of foreign students in Australia, the U.S.A., Canada, and France / by G. Lakshmana Rao

My journey through dance / by Charles Lisner

1915: a novel / by Roger McDonald

The vegetation of North Stradbroke Island, Queensland / by H.T. Clifford, R.L. Specht, with notes on the fauna of mangrove and marine meadow ecosystems by Marion M. Specht

The management of the Australian economy / by Joseph Martin

Mental disorder or madness?: alternative theories / by Erica M. Bates, Paul R. Wilson

Valid for all countries: stories / by Desmond O'Grady

Politics between departments: the fragmentation of executive control in Australian government / by Martin Painter, Bernard Carey

Surfing subcultures of Australia and New Zealand / by Kent Pearson

Industrial relations in the public sector: the firemen / by N.F. Dufty

The struggle of the Naga tribe: a play / by W. S. Rendra, translated and introduced by Max Lane (Asian and Pacific writing series)

Milestones on my journey: the memoirs of Ali Sastroamidjojo, Indonesian patriot and political leader / edited by C.L.M. Penders

Seven Russian poets: imitations / by Rosemary Dobson, David Campbell

Something in the blood: short stories / by Trevor Shearston

The myth of Tantalus: a scaffolding for an ontological personality theory / by S. Giora Shoham

The Torres Strait: people and history / by John Singe

Sport in history: the making of modern sporting history / edited by Richard Cashman, Michael McKernan

Melanesian cargo cults: new salvation movements in the South Pacific / by Friedrich Steinbauer, translated by Max Wohlwill
The South American variant / by Sergei Zalygin, translated by Kevin Windle (Contemporary Russian writing series)
Rolf Boldrewood: Robbery under arms, essays and short stories / edited by Alan Brissenden (Portable Australian authors series)
The peach groves / novel by Barbara Hanrahan
The government of the Northern Territory / by Alistair Heatley
The adventures of Sumiyakist Q / by Yumiko Kurahashi, translated by Dennis Keene (Asian and Pacific writing series)

1980

Problems and other stories / by John Updike
First things last: poems / by David Malouf
Barbara Baynton / edited by Sally Krimmer, Alan Lawson (Portable Australian authors series)
The Acolyte / novel by Thea Astley
The nature of mind: and other essays / by D.M. Armstrong (US ed Cornell University Press)
Sun Yat-sen / by Richard Rigby (Leaders of Asia series)
Rethinking Australia's defence / by Ross Babbage
Prisons, education, and work: towards a national employment strategy for prisoners / by John Braithwaite
Fox Talbot and the invention of photography / by Gail Buckland
Labor in power: the Labor Party and governments in Queensland, 1915–57 / edited by D.J. Murphy, R.B. Joyce, Colin A. Hughes
Uphill all the way: a documentary history of women in Australia / compiled and introduced by Kay Daniels, Mary Murnane
Industrialization and dependence: Australia's road to economic development, 1870–1939 / by Peter Cochrane
Treasure in earthen vessels: Protestant Christianity in New South Wales Society 1900–1914 / by Richard Broome
Principles and practice of nursing / by M.D. Emerton (2nd ed)
Politics in Queensland: 1977 and beyond / edited by Margaret Bridson Cribb, P.J. Boyce
Share markets and portfolio theory: readings and Australian evidence / edited by Ray Ball [et al]
Mobility and community change in Australia / edited by I.H. Burnley, R.J. Pryor and D.T. Rowland
Jawaharlal Nehru of India, 1889–1964 / by Ian Copland (Leaders of Asia series)
Credit and security in West Malaysia: the legal problems of development finance / by Jaginder Singh [et al]

Environment policy in Australia / by Alan Gilpin (Australian environment series)
Summer ends now: stories / by John Emery
An Introduction to the Australian economy / by Ron Hefford [et al]
Gentleman George, king of melodrama: the theatrical life and times of George Darrell, 1841–1921 / by Eric Irvin
The haphazard amorist / novel by Graham Jackson
Singapore: its past, present, and future / by Alex Josey
The possession of amber / stories by Nicholas Jose
Will she be right?: the future of Australia / by Herman Kahn, Thomas Pepper
Australian schools and the law: principal, teacher and student / by A.E. Knott, K.E. Tronc, J.L. Middleton
Hal Porter / selected and edited with an introduction and bibliography by Mary Lord (Portable Australian authors series)
The paper chase / memoir by Hal Porter
Behind the banana curtain / by Hugh Lunn, with drawings by Alan Moir
Ferns, fern allies and conifers of Australia: a laboratory manual / by H.T. Clifford, J. Constantine
Jinnah / by K. McPherson (Leaders of Asia series)
Meetings and farewells: modern Korean stories / edited by Chung Chong-wha (Asian and Pacific writing series)
The wind commands: sailors and sailing ships in the Pacific / by Harry A. Morton, drawings by Don Hermansen and Paul Dwillies from original drawings and research by Peggy Morton
Seven sixes are forty-three / by Kiran Nagarkar, translated by Shubha Slee (Asian and Pacific writing series)
The great god Mogadon: and other plays / by Barry Oakley
Electrical properties of wood and line design / by M. Darveniza, foreword by S.A. Prentice
Sporting injuries: a trainer's guide / by Peter Dornan
The second month of spring / poems by Michael Dransfield, collected and edited by Rodney Hall
Mr. Chairman: a guide to meeting procedure, ceremonial procedure, and forms of address, with specimen meetings and standing orders / by Marjorie Puregger (4th ed)
Mudcrab at Gambaro's / poems by Judith Rodriguez
Maydays: poems / by David Rowbotham
Spotlight on possums / by Rupert Russell, illustrated by Kay Russell
Class, race, and colonialism in West Malaysia: the Indian case / by Michael Stenson
Wines & wineries of New South Wales / by James Halliday
Field Marshal Plaek Phibun Songkhram / by B. J. Terwiel (Leaders of Asia series)

Three political plays / edited by Alrene Sykes (Contemporary Australian plays series)
Chairman Hua: leader of the Chinese Communists / by Ting Wang
Voices of independence: new Black writing from Papua New Guinea / edited by Ulli Beier (Asian and Pacific writing series) (US ed St Martin's Press)
The leader: a political biography of Gough Whitlam / by James Walter
Do polar bears experience religious ecstasy? / by Ian Warden, drawings by Donald Greenfield
Victoria and Albert at home / by Tyler Whittle
The Canadians / by George Woodcock
Understanding cancer / by Ron Hicks
Famine / novel by Liam O'Flaherty
Environmental law in Australia: an introduction / by D.E. Fisher (Australian environment series)
The frangipani gardens / novel by Barbara Hanrahan
The voyage of Torres: the discovery of the southern coastline of New Guinea and Torres Strait by Captain Luis Baez de Torres in 1606 / by Brett Hilder

1981

Towards an older Australia: readings in social gerontology / edited by Anna L. Howe
Coal in Queensland: the first fifty years: a history of early coal mining in Queensland / by R.L. Whitmore
True love and how to get it / novel by Gerard Lee
Over-sexed, over-paid, & over here: Americans in Australia 1941-1945 / by John Hammond Moore
Regional economics: an Australian introduction / by G.J. Butler, T.D. Mandeville
His battalion and, Live until dawn / by Vasil Bykov, translated by Jennifer and Robert Woodhouse (Contemporary Russian writing)
Winding engine calculations for the mining engineer / P.K. Chatterjee, P.J. Wetherall (2nd ed)
Water pollution: causes and effects in Australia and New Zealand / by D.W. Connell (Australian environment series)
Breast feeding / cartoons by Patrick Cook
Paradise lost: a humanist approach / by K.G. Hamilton
Defending "a Christian country": churchmen and society in New South Wales in the 1880s and after / by Walter Phillips
Rockhampton: a history of city and district / by Lorna McDonald
The first UQP story book / edited by Craig Munro (published in the US as New Australian Short Stories)

A land full of possibilities: a history of South Australia's Northern Territory / by P.F. Donovan
Surveyors of the Liguasan Marsh / by Antonio Reyes Enriquez (Asian and Pacific writing series)
The End of a golden age: higher education in a steady state / edited by Edward Gross, John S. Western
Teach to the difference: cross-cultural studies in Australian education / by Russell Francis
Migrant crime in Australia / by Ronald D. Francis
Joseph Furphy / edited with an introduction by John Barnes (Portable Australian authors series)
On Dearborn Street / novel by Miles Franklin, with an introduction by Roy Duncan
Bliss / novel by Peter Carey
The story of ANZAC from the outbreak of war to the end of the first phase of the Gallipoli campaign, May 4, 1915 / by C.E.W. Bean (Official history of Australia in the war of 1914–1918, vol 1)
The story of ANZAC from 4 May, 1915, to the evacuation of the Gallipoli Peninsula / by C.E.W. Bean (Official history of Australia in the war of 1914–1918, vol 2)
Great Britain, great empire: an evaluation of the British imperial experience / by W. Ross Johnston
The Aboriginal Tasmanians / by Lyndall Ryan
Square crib / novel by Graham Jackson
Letters from the Antipodes / by Michel Butor, translated from Boomerang with an introduction and afterword by Michael Spencer (US ed Ohio University Press)
For the patriarch / stories by Angelo Loukakis
Changes, issues and prospects in Australian education / edited by S. D'Urso, R.A. Smith (2nd ed)
The escape machine / stories by James McQueen
The gentle art of cat surfing: cartoons / by Matt Mawson
Australian marketing casebook / by David L. Rados, Peter Gilmour
Black sands: a history of the mineral sand mining industry in eastern Australia / by I.W. Morley
Sketches of old Rockhampton / sketches by Edith Neish, text by Lorna McDonald
Marsupials and, Politics: two comedies / by Barry Oakley (Contemporary Australian plays series)
Policy-making in a new state: Papua New Guinea, 1972–1977 / edited by J.A. Ballard
Waiting for Surabiel / by Raja Proctor (Asian and Pacific writing series)
The pink triangle / by Roger Raftery

Money for Maria and Borrowed time: two village tales / by Valentin Rasputin; translated by Kevin Windle and Margaret Wettlin (Contemporary Russian writing series)

The genera of Australian lichens (Lichenized fungi) / by Roderick W. Roger

Shadow people / by Leon Saunders

Fred: an Australian hero / by Peter Sekuless

Selected poems / by R.A. Simpson

Mr. Sponge's sporting tour / by R.S. Surtees, edited by Virginia Blain (Victorian texts series)

As the saying goes: an annotated anthology of Chinese and equivalent English sayings and expressions, and an introduction to Xiehoy u (Chinese wit) / by C.C. Sun

Wines & wineries of South Australia / by James Halliday

The True life story of — / stories edited by Jan Craney, Esther Caldwell

Both sides of the door: an insight into the therapeutic experience / by Clive Williams, Kristine Sodersten

Henry James's ultimate narrative: The golden bowl / by R.B.J. Wilson

Towards achievement and acceptance: class-room studies of mildly intellectually handicapped children / by Margaret Henry

Joseph Furphy: such is life, stories, verse, essays and letters / edited by John Barnes (Portable Australian authors series)

The most beautiful world: fictions and sermons / by Rodney Hall

Race and politics in the Bahamas / by Colin A. Hughes

1982

Promoting industry: recent Australian political experience / by P. Loveday

The Australian-American security relationship: a regional and international perspective / by Henry S. Albinski (US ed St Martin's Press)

Body, land, and spirit: health and healing in Aboriginal society / edited by Janice Reid

An item from the late news / novel by Thea Astley

Fever, squalor, and vice: sanitation and social policy in Victorian Sydney / by A.J.C. Mayne

Lessons from history: the Tokushi yoron / by Arai Hakuseki, translation and commentary by Joyce Ackroyd

A Comintern agent in China 1932–1939 / by Otto Braun, translated from the German by Jeanne Moore, with introduction by Dick Wilson

Australian science fiction / edited and introduced by Van Ikin (Portable Australian authors series)

Regional and urban location / by Colin Clark

Consolidation: the second paperback poets anthology / edited by Thomas Shapcott

Anthony Trollope's son in Australia: the life and letters of F.J.A. Trollope (1847–1910) / by P.D. Edwards
From the dreaming to 1915: a history of Queensland / by Ross Fitzgerald
Workers in bondage: the origins and bases of unfree labour in Queensland, 1824–1916 / by Kay Saunders
Deutsch-lernen macht Spass / by Rosalie M. Russell
Aboriginal power in Australian society / edited by Michael C. Howard
Henry Kingsley / edited with an introduction by J.S.D. Mellick (Portable Australian authors series)
Democracy in trade unions: studies in membership participation and control / by Mary Dickenson
The eye opener / novel by Geoffrey Dutton
An introduction to the New Zealand economy / by B.H. Easton, N.J. Thomson
Challenging the men: the social biology of female sporting achievement / by K.F. Dyer
Australia's Great Barrier Reef / by Robert Endean
Australian town planning law: uniformity and change / by A.S. Fogg
Coordinating Australian university development: a study of the Australian Universities Commission, 1959–1970 / by A.P. Gallagher
When Sunday comes / poems by Silvana Gardner
The Australian Imperial Force in France, 1916 / by C.E.W. Bean (Official history of Australia in the war of 1914–1918 vol 3)
The Australian Imperial Force in France, 1917 / by C.E.W. Bean ((Official history of Australia in the war of 1914–1918 vol 4)
Australian defence policy for the 1980s / edited by Robert O'Neill, D.M. Horner
Australian education in the Second World War / by Andrew Spaull
The five faces of Thailand: an economic geography / by Wolf Donner
What is this thing called science?: an assessment of the nature and status of science and its methods / by A.F. Chalmers (2nd ed)
Tropical baroque: four Malineno theatricals / by Nick Joaquin (Asian and Pacific writing series)
The teachers of Mad Dog Swamp / by Khammaan Khonkhai, translated by Gehan Wijeyewardene (Asian and Pacific writing series)
Separation, divorce, and after / by Lynne McNamara, Jennifer Morrison
Jobs or dogma?: the Industries Assistance Commission and Australian politics / by John Warhurst
Slipstream / novel by Roger McDonald
Impressions of the University of Queensland / drawings by Christopher McVinish, text by Susan Pechey
The home girls / stories by Olga Masters

The University of Papua New Guinea: a case study in the sociology of higher education / by V. Lynn Meek
The drama of discrimination in Henry James / by Susan Reibel Moore
New Guinea images in Australian literature / edited and introduced by Nigel Krauth (Portable Australian authors series)
Nakano Seigo (1886–1943) / by L.R. Oates (Leaders of Asia series)
Ho Chi Minh / by Milton Osborne (Leaders of Asia series)
Problems in play: first book of bridge problems / by Denis Priest
Quadrant: twenty-five years / edited by Peter Coleman, Lee Shrubb, Vivian Smith
Ecology of marine parasites / by Klaus Rohde (Australian ecology series)
The birthday gift: a novel / by Thomas Shapcott
The mark of Cain: the stigma theory of crime and social deviance / by S. Giora Shoham, Giora Rahav
Zhu De (Chu Teh) / by Shum Kui-kwong (Leaders of Asia series)
Brisbane lines / by Donald Greenfield, Alan Moir
Wines & wineries of Western Australia / by James Halliday
Wines & wineries of Victoria / by James Halliday
Selected poems, 1960–1980 / by Andrew Taylor
Jiang Jie-shi (1887–1975) / by J.S. Gregory (Leaders of Asia series)
Faith of our fathers / stories by Spiro Zavos
Kaddish: and other poems / by Fay Zwicky
Peter Sculthorpe: his music and ideas, 1929–1979 / by Michael Hannan
Dove / novel by Barbara Hanrahan
Sounds real: radio in every day life / by C.S. Higgins, P.D. Moss
Tunku Abdul Rahman / by A.M. Healy (Leaders of Asia series)
From subservience to strike: industrial relations in the banking industry / by John Hill
Conflict and coal: a case study of industrial relations in the open-cut coal mining industry of central Queensland / by Kevin Hince
Norfolk Island: an outline of its history, 1774–1981 / by Merval Hoare (3rd ed)
Manning Clark and Australian history, 1915–1963 / by Stephen Holt
Memories of a signaller: the first world war, 1914–1919 / by Harold Hinckfuss

1983

The decline of Western Hill / novel by Graham Jackson
The roof of Queensland / by Grahame Walsh
The changing role of fathers? / by Graeme Russell
Miss Peabody's inheritance / novel by Elizabeth Jolley
Who is she? / edited by Shirley Walker on women in literature
Too much order with too little law / by Frank Brennan

Environmental philosophy: a collection of readings / edited by Robert Elliot, Arran Gare
Seals of the world / by Judith E. King (2nd ed)
Australian academic libraries in the seventies: essays in honour of Dietrich Borchardt / edited by Harrison Bryan, John Horacek
A descant for gossips / novel by Thea Astley
Valencies / science fiction by Rory Barnes and Damien Broderick
Mining and Australia / edited by W.H. Richmond, P.C. Sharma
The Big strikes: Queensland 1889–1965 / edited by D.J. Murphy
Unnatural lives: studies in Australian fiction about the convicts, from James Tucker to Patrick White / by Laurie Hergenhan
Searching for Aboriginal languages: memoirs of a field worker / by Bob Dixon
Adolf Bastian and the psychic unity of mankind: the foundations of anthropology in nineteenth century Germany / by Klaus-Peter Koepping
Vice in a vicious society: crime and convicts in mid-nineteenth-century New South Wales / by Michael Sturma
A different drummer: the story of E.J. Banfield, the beachcomber of Dunk Island / by Michael Noonan
Problems in play: second book of bridge problems / by Denis Priest
Let justice be done: the foreign policy of Dr H.V. Evatt / by Alan Renouf
Sticks that kill: a novel / by Trevor Shearston
Beef in Japan: politics, production, marketing & trade / by John W. Longworth
Subjecting and objecting: an essay in objectivity / by Max Deutscher
Future tense?: technology in Australia / edited by Stephen Hill, Ron Johnston
The Australian Imperial Force in France during the main German offensive, 1918 / by C.E.W. Bean (Official history of Australia in the war of 1914–1918 vol 5)
The Australian Imperial Force in France during the Allied offensive, 1918 / by C.E.W. Bean (Official history of Australia in the war of 1914–1918 vol 6)
Social idealism and the problem of objectivity / by Tronn Overend
International security in the Southeast Asian and Southwest Pacific region / edited by T.B. Millar
Colonial sunset: Australia and Papua New Guinea, 1970–74 / by L.W. Johnson
Systems ecology: an introduction to ecological modelling / by R.L. Kitching
Nora aus der Fremde / by Keith Leopold
Primitive mythology: the mythic world of the Australian and Papuan natives / by Lucien Levy-Bruhl, translated by Brian Elliott
The Australian Ballet: twenty-one years / by Charles Lisner
A tragic vision: the novels of Patrick White / by A.M. McCulloch
The passing guest: a life of Henry Kingsley / by J.S.D. Mellick

Broken canoe: conversations and observations in Micronesia / by Ann Nakano, photos by Tim Porter
The monsoon collection / by Ninotchka Rosca (Asian and Pacific writing series)
Welcome!: poems / by Thomas Shapcott
Insects on grain legumes in northern Australia: a survey of potential pests and their enemies / by Merle Shepard, R.J. Lawn, Margaret A. Schneider
Ben Hall: bushranger / by D.J. Shiel
Sex as bait: Eve, Casanova, and Don Juan / by S. Giora Shoham
Slavery, bondage, and dependency in Southeast Asia / edited by Anthony Reid, with Jennifer Brewster
The strength of tradition: stories of the immigrant presence in Australia, 1970–81 / edited by R.F. Holt
A history of modern Thailand, 1767–1942 / by B.J. Terwiel
The turbulent dream: passion and politics in the poetry of W.B. Yeats / by Geoffrey Thurley
The observatory: selected poems of Dimitris Tsaloumas / translated by Philip Grundy
The grasses of southern Queensland / by J.C. Tothill, J.B. Hacker, illustrated by J.B. Hacker
Farewell in June: four Russian plays / by A. Vampilov, translated by Kevin Windle, Amanda Metcalf (Contemporary Russian writing series)
The mass media in Australia / by J.S. Western and Colin A. Hughes (2nd ed)
Africa and after / stories by Victor Kelleher

1984

The observatory: selected poems of Dimitris Tsaloumas / translated by Philip Grundy (2nd ed)
The team: Australian Army advisers in Vietnam 1962–1972 / by Ian McNeill
At the other end of Australia: the Commonwealth and the Northern Territory, 1911–1978 / by P.F. Donovan
Loving daughters / novel by Olga Masters
Bearded ladies: stories / by Kate Grenville
Neither justice nor reason: a legal and anthropological analysis of Aboriginal land rights / by Marc Gumbert
Nine Australian progressives: vitalism in bourgeois social thought, 1890–1960 / by Michael Roe
From 1915 to the early 1980s: a history of Queensland / by Ross Fitzgerald
The Rudd family / by Steele Rudd
A city selection / by Steele Rudd
Palomino / novel by Elizabeth Jolley
A toddler in the family: a practical Australian guide for parents / by Jean Ferguson, Rowena Solomon

Timber and iron: houses in North Queensland mining settlements, 1861–1920 / by Peter Bell
The goori goori bird: from a legend of the Bidjara People of the Upper Warrego / by Grahame L. Walsh, illustrated by John Morrison
Samuel Walker Griffith / by Roger B. Joyce
The day the river / poems by Cornelis Vleeskens
Slow tennis: poems: 1980–1983 / by Gary Catalano
Christopher Brennan / edited with an introduction and notes by Terry Sturm (Portable Australian authors series)
Queenslanders / by Hugh Lunn
Oh lucky country / novel by Rosa R. Cappiello, translated with an introduction by Gaetano Rando
Johannes Bjelke-Petersen: a political biography / by Hugh Lunn (2nd ed)
Kicking the habit: four Australian therapeutic communities / by Charlotte Carr–Gregg
Environmental impact assessment: a practical guide / by Colin F. Porter (Australian environment series)
Marginal manager: the changing role of supervisors in Australia / by Peter Gilmour, Russell D. Lansbury
Mantle of Christ: a history of the Sydney Central Methodist Mission / by Don Wright
Bring the monkey / by Miles Franklin, with an introduction by Bronwen Levy
Ways of exchange: the Enga Tee of Papua New Guinea / by D.K. Feil
A history of philosophy in Australia / by S.A. Grave
Death is a good solution: the convict experience in early Australia / by A.W. Baker
Adventurous spirits: Australian migrant society in pre-cession Fiji / by John Young
Walking the dog: and other stories / by Marian Eldrige
Left at the post / poems by Evan Jones
The beast of heaven / novel by Victor Kelleher
This river is in the south / poems by Philip Mead
Industrial relations in the air: Australian airline pilots / by Nicholas Blain
Blue pencil warriors: censorship and propaganda in World War II / by John Hilvert
Informed professional judgement: a guide to evaluation in post-secondary education / by Ernest Roe, Rod McDonald
Aboriginal pathways in Southeast Queensland and the Richmond River / by J.G. Steele
The anatomy of accounting / by A.D. Barton (3rd ed)
Eighty plus: outgrowing the myths of old age / by Eena Job
Aung San / by Aung San Suu Kyi (Leaders of Asia series)

Gandhi / by Hugh Owen (Leaders of Asia series)
Zhou Enlai / by Merrilyn Fitzpatrick (Leaders of Asia series)
Mao Zedong / by Paul Rule (Leaders of Asia series)
Religion in Aboriginal Australia: an anthology / edited by Max Charlesworth [et al]
Containers of classical Greece: a handbook of shapes / by M.G. Kanowski
Insect ecology / by E.G. Matthews and R.L. Kitching, with colour photographs by Densey Clyne (Australian ecology series)
The experiential dimension of psychology / by Alan Richardson
One foot on the ladder: origins and outcomes of girls' secondary schooling in South Australia / by Alison Mackinnon
In their own right: the rise to power of Joh's Nationals / by Alan Metcalfe
The Australian Imperial Force in Sinai and Palestine, 1914–1918 / by H.S. Gullett (Official history of Australia in the war of 1914–1918 vol 7)
The Australian Flying Corps in the western and eastern theatres of war, 1914–1918 / by F.M. Cutlack (Official history of Australia in the war of 1914–1918 vol 8)

1985

A question of survival: Quakers in Australia in the nineteenth century / by William Nicolle Oats
Farm policy in Australia / by R.K. Hefford
Coal in Queensland: the late nineteenth century 1875 to 1900 / by R.L. Whitmore
Gender, politics and fiction: twentieth century Australian women's novels / edited by Carole Ferrier
University of Queensland: a portrait / compiled by the Information Office
Hawthorne's influence on Dickens and George Eliot / by Edward Stokes
A place of light & learning: the University of Queensland's first seventy-five years / by Malcolm I. Thomis
Nothing seemed impossible: women's education and social change in South Australia, 1875–1915 / by Helen Jones
Aboriginal music: education for living: cross-cultural experiences from South Australia / by Catherine J. Ellis
The defeat of distance: Qantas 1919–1939 / by John Gunn
Nest of traitors: the Petrov Affair / by Nicholas Whitlam, John Stubbs
Fending off forgetfulness: a practical guide to improving memory / by Eena Job
Holiday sea sonnets / by John Blight
The book of epigrams / poems by Dimitris Tsaloumas, translated by Philip Grundy
The blood vote / novel by Jack Lindsay

From fear to friendship: Australia's policies towards the People's Republic of China, 1966–1982 / by Edmund S.K. Fung, Colin Mackerras
Sallyanne Atkinson's Brisbane guide (rev ed)
Plant life of the Great Barrier Reef and adjacent shores / by A.B Cribb, J.W. Cribb
The gentrification of inner Melbourne: a political geography of inner city housing / by William Stewart Logan
Illywhacker / novel by Peter Carey
Australian war strategy, 1939–1945: a documentary history / by John Robertson, John McCarthy
Abdul Haris Nasution: a political biography / by C.L.M. Penders, Ulf Sundhaussen
Seashore ecology / by Thomas Carefoot, adapted for Australian conditions by Rodney D. Simpson (Australian ecology series)
Agro-research for the semi-arid tropics: northwest Australia / edited by Russell C. Muchow
Horsewhip the doctor: tales from our medical past / by Ross Patrick
Paul McLean / by Malcolm McGregor
Foxybaby / novel by Elizabeth Jolley
A long time dying / fiction by Olga Masters
Spanning two centuries: historic bridges of Australia / by Colin O'Connor
Didane the koala: from a legend of the Bidjara People of the Upper Warrego / by Grahame L. Walsh, illustrated by John Morrison
The Kangaroo keepers / edited by H.J. Lavery
The war diaries of Kenneth Slessor: official Australian correspondent, 1940–1944 / edited by Clement Semmler
Vietnam: a reporter's war / by Hugh Lunn
Scribbling in the dark / memoir by Barry Oakley

1986

White lies / novel by Trevor Shearston
Strange country: a study of Randolph Stow / by Anthony J. Hassall
Travelling / poems by Andrew Taylor
St Clair: three narratives / poems by John A. Scott
Headlands: prose sketches / by Bruce Beaver
The Australian short story: an anthology from the 1890s to the 1980s / edited and introduced by Laurie Hergenhan (Portable Australian authors series)
Writing of the 1890s: short stories, verse & essays / edited by Leon Cantrell (rev ed, Portable Australian authors series)
Vernacular dreams / stories by Angelo Loukakis
Threshold approach in urban, regional and environmental planning: theory & practice / by Jersy Kozlowski

Planning with the environment: introduction to the threshold approach / by Jerzy Kozlowski, Greg Hill, Johanna Rosier
Commercial media in Australia: economics, ownership, technology, and regulation / by Allan Brown
A sense of place in the new literatures in English / edited by Peggy Nightingale
Marxist policies today in socialist and capitalist countries / edited by Edwin Dowdy
Planning and federalism: Australian and Canadian experience / by Kenneth Wiltshire
Disorganized crime / by Richard Hall
A touch of healing: speeches / by Sir Zelman Cowen, (3 vols 1977–1982)
Mr. Chairman: a guide to meeting procedure, ceremonial procedure and forms of address, with specimen meetings and standing orders / by Marjorie Puregger (5th ed)
The moving shadow problem: stories / by Peter Murphy
Australian soils: the human impact / edited by J.S. Russell, R.F. Isbell
Reviewing academic performance: approaches to the evaluation of departments and individuals / by Ernest Roe, Rod McDonald, Ingrid Moses
Contemporary Australian poetry / selected and translated by Dimitris Tsaloumas (dual text English, Greek)
Asbestos: its human cost / by Jock McCulloch
The soldiers' story: the battle at Xa Long Tan, Vietnam, 18 August 1966 / by Terry Burstall
Serpentine futures / poems by Lewis Packer
Image in the clay / play by David Ireland (2nd ed)
Dreamhouse / novel by Kate Grenville
Nearer by far / poems by Richard Kelly Tipping
Latitudes: new writing from the North / stories edited by Susan Johnson and Mary Roberts
The pleasure of their company / memoir by Alister Kershaw
Blue days / a YA novel by Donna Sharp
The other side of the family / YA novel by Maureen Pople
An introduction to the Australian economy / by R.K. Hefford [et al] (2nd end)
The beast of heaven / YA edition, by Victor Kelleher
A Steele Rudd selection: the best Dad and Dave stories with other Rudd classics / chosen by Frank Moorhouse
Point of departure: the autobiography of Jean Devanny / edited by Carole Ferrier
The last mountain: a life in Papua New Guinea / by Ian Downs, illustrations by Ian Ottley
A shifting town: glass plate images of Clermont and its people / by G.C.

Pullar, compiled by Richard and Marguerite Stringer, text by Marguerite Stringer
Parasite lives: papers on parasites, their hosts and their associations to honour J.F.A. Sprent / edited by Mary Cremin, Colin Dobson, Douglas E. Moorhouse
James Duhig / by T.P. Boland
High times in the middle of nowhere: the misadventures of Murray Laurence, compulsive traveller
Captives: Australian army nurses in Japanese prison camps / by Catherine Kenny
Great rail non-journeys of Australia / by Colin Taylor
The sky between the trees / YA novel by James Preston
Te kaihau = The windeater / stories by Keri Hulme
Bliss: the screenplay / by Peter Carey, Ray Lawrence

1987

Politics of the High Court: a study of the judicial branch of government in Australia / by Brian Galligan
Journey through darkness: the writing of V.S. Naipaul / by Peggy Nightingale
A great and powerful friend: a study of Australian and American relations between 1900 and 1975 / by Norman Harper
Challenging horizons: Qantas 1939–1954 / by John Gunn
Travel dice / poems by Thomas Shapcott
The devil in nature / poems by Silvana Gardner
A formula for glass / poems by Michael Sariban
Robert D. FitzGerald / edited with an introduction by Julian Croft (Portable Australian authors series)
Catherine Helen Spence / edited with an introduction by Helen Thomson (Portable Australian authors series)
McKenzie's boots / YA novel by Michael Noonan
Amy's children / novel by Olga Masters
The extra / memoir by Hal Porter
Ecology of mangroves / by Patricia Hutchings, Peter Saenger (Australian ecology series)
Self possession / novel by Marion Halligan
Circles of faces: stories / by Mary Dadswell
King Wally: the story of Wally Lewis / by Adrian McGregor
The Royal Australian Navy, 1914–1918 / Arthur W. Jose ; with introduction by Ross Lamont (Official history of Australia in the war of 1914–1918 vol 9)
The Australians at Rabaul: the capture and administration of the German possessions in the southern Pacific / by S.S. Mackenzie, with introduction

by Hank Nelson and Michael Piggott (Official history of Australia in the war of 1914–1918 vol 10)
The wild dogs: stories / by Peter Skrzynecki
A season of grannies / YA novel by James Grieve
Working in the arts: a guide for enterprise, employment and assistance / by Keith Windschuttle
The boys from Bondi / YA novel by Alan Collins
Reading Australian poetry / by Andrew Taylor
Sporting injuries: indispensable for players, coaches, teachers, parents and all fitness enthusiasts / by Peter Dornan, Richard Dunn, drawings by Peter Dornan
In Australia, or, The old selection / play by Steele Rudd, edited by Richard Fotheringham
From the frontier: a pictorial history of Queensland to 1920 / by Duncan Waterson, Maurice French
The First Fleet marines, 1786–1792 / by John Moore
Tropical visions / by John Millington
The war despatches of Kenneth Slessor, official Australian correspondent, 1940–1944 / edited by Clement Semmler
Training and working dogs for quiet confident control of stock / by Scott Lithgow, artwork and appendix by Don Morris
On our selection / by Steele Rudd making the 4 vol complete edition with The Old Homestead, The Rudd Family and A City Selection
Summer press / YA novel by Rosemary Dobson
Dislocations / stories by Janette Turner Hospital
Real lies / stories by Craig McGregor
The estuary / novel by Georgia Savage
Collected poems / by Michael Dransfield, edited by Rodney Hall
A history of health & medicine in Queensland, 1824–1960 / by Ross Patrick
Women in the university: a policy report / report of the University of Queensland Senate Working Party on the Status of Women, edited by Brian G. Wilson, Eileen M. Byrne
Rain / poems by Susan Afterman
Borderline / novel by Janette Turner Hospital
The traveller: stories of two continents / by Victor Kelleher (new ed)
Evening under lamplight: selected stories of David Campbell / with a foreword by David Malouf (rev ed)
Shabbytown calendar / poems by Thomas Shapcott (new ed)
Coloring book of Australian birds / by Jan Bryant

1988

Race relations in colonial Queensland: a history of exclusion, exploitation,

and extermination / by Raymond Evans, Kay Saunders, Kathryn Cronin (2nd ed)
Fringe-dwellers and welfare: the Aboriginal response to bureaucracy / by Jeff Collmann
A very small insurance policy: the politics of Australian involvement in Vietnam, 1954–1967 / by Glen St. J. Barclay
Oscar and Lucinda / novel by Peter Carey
The red flag riots: a study of intolerance / by Raymond Evans
Australian marketing casebook / by Peter Gilmour, David L. Rados, Donald M.T. Gibson (2nd ed)
James McAuley: poetry, essays and personal commentary / edited by Leonie Kramer (UQP Australian authors series)
The Literature Board: a brief history / by Thomas Shapcott
Falcon drinking: the English poems / by Dimitris Tsaloumas
Fresh linen: sixty prose poems 1980–1986 / by Gary Catalano
New Caledonia: essays in nationalism and dependency / edited by Michael Spencer, Alan Ward, John Connell
Lonely summers / YA novel by Nora Dugon
Jondaryan station: the relationship between pastoral capital and pastoral labour, 1840–1890 / by Jan Walker
Academic staff evaluation and development: a university case study / by Ingrid Moses
Turns of phrase: young Queensland writers / edited by Lawrie Ryan, Ross Clark
Norfolk Island: an outline of its history, 1774–1987 / by Merval Hoare (4th ed)
Selected poems 1960–1985 / by Andrew Taylor (rev ed)
The universities of Australia / introduction by John Ward
The heroic life of Al Capsella / YA novel by Judith Clarke
Pioneer aviator: the remarkable life of Lores Bonney / by Terry Gwynn-Jones
Australia felix, or, Harlequin laughing jackass and the magic bat: a pantomime / by Garnet Walch, edited by Veronica Kelly
Separation, divorce, and after / by Imogen McNamara, Jenny Morrison (2nd ed)
Brisbane, our town: a century of photographs / by Helen Dash
Joan makes history / novel by Kate Grenville
Em's story: a novel / by Victor Kelleher
The living hothouse / stories by Marion Halligan
The road to Fitzgerald: revelations of corruption spanning four decades / by Phil Dickie
The Barbarians: a soldier's New Guinea diary / by Peter Pinney
Charmed lives / poems by Bruce Beaver
1988 and all that: new views of Australia's past / edited by George Shaw

Miles Franklin: the story of a famous Australian / by Marjorie Barnard
Tribute: selected stories of Katharine Susannah Prichard / edited by Ric Throssell
Pelican Creek / YA novel by Maureen Pople
Lawrence Hargrave: aviation pioneer, inventor and explorer / by W. Hudson Shaw, Olaf Ruhen
Love poems and other revolutionary actions / by Bobbi Sykes
The Australian literary calendar 1989 / photographs by Brendan Hennessy, text and bibliography Kate Ahearne
Beyond the echo: multicultural women's writing / edited by Sneja Gunew, Jan Mahyuddin
Regards to the Czar / stories by Margaret Coombs
The inheritors / YA novel by Jill Dobson
The motorcycle cafe / stories by Matthew Condon
Discovering coastal Queensland: the complete guide to the Queensland coast, Great Barrier Reef, Stradbroke, Moreton, and Fraser Islands / Sunmap, produced under the direction of the Surveyor-General by the Department of Geographic Information with the support of the Great Barrier Reef Marine Park Authority
Under Berlin: new poems 1988 / by John Tranter
Charades / novel by Janette Turner Hospital
The rose fancier / stories by Olga Masters
Nettie Palmer: her private journal Fourteen Years, poems, reviews and literary essays / edited by Vivian Smith (UQP Australian authors series)
The house by water: new and selected poems / by Judith Rodriguez
High corridors: Qantas, 1954–1970 / by John Gunn

1989

Labor in Queensland: from the 1880s to 1988 / by Ross Fitzgerald, Harold Thornton
Black words, white page: Aboriginal literature 1929–1988 / by Adam Shoemaker (UQP studies in Australian literature series)
Literature and the Aborigine in Australia / by J. J. Healy (new ed, UQP studies in Australian literature series)
Share markets and portfolio theory: readings and Australian evidence / edited by Ray Ball [et al]
Encounters in place: outsiders and Aboriginal Australians, 1606–1985 / by D.J. Mulvaney
The tilted cross / novel by Hal Porter
Women in rural Australia / edited by Kerry James
The shearers' war: the story of the 1891 shearers' strike / by Stuart Svensen
The press in colonial Queensland: a social and political history, 1845–1875 / by Denis Cryle

Enemy aliens: internment and the homefront experience in Australia, 1914–1920 / by Gerhard Fischer
The sporting image: a pictorial history of Queenslanders at play / by Max Howell, Reet Howell, David W. Brown
Australia's women: a documentary history: from a selection of personal letters, diary entries, pamphlets, official records, government and police reports, speeches and radio talks / compiled by Kay Daniels, Mary Murnane (2nd ed)
Australian English: the language of a new society / edited by Peter Collins, David Blair
Singles: shorter works, 1981–1986 / poems by John A. Scott
The Torres Strait: people and history / by John Singe (2nd ed)
On all fronts: Australian stories of World War II / edited by J.T. Laird
Utah and Queensland coal: a study in the micro political economy of modern capitalism and the state / by Brian Galligan
Blockade: the Queensland loans affair 1920 to 1924 / by Tom Cochrane
Traditional architecture in the Gilbert Islands: a cultural perspective / by John Hockings
Long white cloud / YA novel by James G. Porter
Heartland / novel by Angelika Fremd
Colonial voices: letters, diaries, journalism and other accounts of nineteenth-century Australia / edited by Elizabeth Webby (UQP Australian authors series)
Poetry and gender: statements and essays in Australian women's poetry and poetics / edited by David Brooks, Brenda Walker (UQP studies in Australian literature series)
China's rural development miracle, with international comparisons: papers presented at an International Symposium held at Beijing, China, 25–29 October, 1987 / edited by John W. Longworth
Wally and the Broncos / by Adrian McGregor
Working the system: government in Queensland / by Peter Coaldrake
Collected poems / by Charles Buckmaster, edited by Simon MacDonald
Selected poems, 1956–1988 / by Thomas Shapcott
Australia during the war / by Ernest Scott, with introduction by Michael McKernan (Official history of Australia in the war of 1914–1918 vol 11)
The boy on the lake: stories of the supernatural / YA fiction by Judith Clarke
The woman at the window / stories by Marian Eldridge
Barbeque of the primitives / poems by Philip Salom
The shipwreck party / stories by Liam Davison
Winter vision / novel by Geoff Page
The road to Fitzgerald and beyond / by Phil Dickie (2nd ed)
We survived: a mother's story of Japanese captivity / by Nell van de Graaff, with drawings by the author

Eight voices of the eighties: stories, journalism and criticism by Australian women writiers / edited by Gillian Whitlock (UQP Australian authors series)
Homecoming: three novellas / by John Clanchy
By the line / novel by Thomas Keneally
Charles & Elsa Chauvel: movie pioneers / by Susanne Chauvel Carlsson
My heart, my country: the story of Dorothea Mackellar / by Adrienne Howley
Merryll of the stones / novel by Brian Caswell
Portrait of a young forger: Marian Pretzel's memoir of his adventures and survival in war-time Europe
The great secondhand supper / YA novel by Greg Bastian
Over the top with Jim: Hugh Lunn's tap-dancing, bugle-blowing memoir of a well-spent boyhood
Driving too fast / poems by Dorothy Porter
City to city / stories by Laurie Clancy
Flawless jade / novel by Barbara Hanrahan
Forward: the history of the 2nd/14th Light Horse (Queensland Mounted Infantry) / by Joan Starr, Christopher Sweeney
On a wing and a prayer: great Australian air stories / by Terry Gwynn-Jones
Exiles undaunted: the Irish rebels, Kevin and Eva O'Doherty / by Ross & Heather Patrick
The gentle art of beachcombing: a collection of writings / by E.J. Banfield, edited by Michael Noonan
Aboriginality: contemporary Aboriginal paintings & prints / by Jennifer Isaacs

1990

Paperbark: a collection of black Australian writings / edited by Jack Davis [et al] (UQP Black Australian writers series)
Up rode the troopers: the black police in Queensland / by Bill Rosser
The Premiers of Queensland / edited by Denis Murphy, Roger Joyce, Margaret Cribb (rev ed)
Strange country: a study of Randolph Stow / by Anthony J. Hassall (rev ed, UQP studies in Australian literature series)
The folly of spring: a study of John Shaw Neilson's poetry / by Cliff Hanna (UQP studies in Australian literature series)
A body of water: a year's notebook / by Beverley Farmer
Before the interval: Australian mythology and feature films, 1930–1960 / by Bruce Molloy
Clare Street / YA novel Nora Dugon
The troubled eyes of women / stories by C.B. Christesen
A history of the Pacific islands / by I.C. Campbell

Wrong face in the mirror: an autobiography of race and identity / by Lolo Houbein
Ask me / poems by Fay Zwicky
The road to Summering / YA novel by Maureen Pople
The house in the rainforest / YA novel by Sophie Masson
One of the family: telling the story of a violent childhood and the healing beyond / by Pearlie McNeill
The riches of ancient Australia: a journey into prehistory / by Josephine Flood
The honey-ant men's love song and other Aboriginal song poems / edited by R.M.W. Dixon, Martin Duwell
The tiger in the tiger pit / novel by Janette Turner Hospital
Norman Lindsay on art, life and literature / edited by Keith Wingrove
Al Capsella and the watchdogs / YA novel by Judith Clarke
Heads and chairs: managing academic departments / by Ingrid Moses, Ernest Roe
A guide to herbaceous and shrub legumes of Queensland / by J.B. Hacker
A soldier returns: a Long Tan veteran discovers the other side of Vietnam / by Terry Burstall
Race and politics in Fiji / by Robert Norton (2nd ed)
Queensland images: in film and television / edited by Jonathan Dawson, Bruce Molley
Troppo man / novel by Gerard Lee
Collected poems / by Jennifer Rankin, edited by Judith Rodriguez
Reporting home: Olga Masters: her writings as a journalist / selected by Deirdre Coleman
Flight of the albatross / YA novel by Deborah Savage
Corruption and reform: the Fitzgerald vision / edited by Scott Prasser, Rae Wear, John Nethercote
Holocaust Island / poems by Graeme Dixon (UQP Black Australian writers series)
Parnassus mad ward: Michael Dransfield and the new Australian poetry / by Livio Dobrez (UQP studies in Australian literature series)
Imagined lives: a study of David Malouf / by Philip Neilsen (UQP studies in Australian literature series)
Johnno, short stories, poems, essays and interview / by David Malouf, edited by James Tulip (UQP Australian authors series)
Visitants, episodes from other novels, poems, stories, interviews, and essays / by Randolph Stow, edited by Anthony J. Hassall (UQP Australian authors series)
Isobars / stories by Janette Turner Hospital
Exotic pleasures / selected stories by Peter Carey
Wintering / novel by Victor Kelleher

The patchwork hero / YA novel by Michael Noonan
The December boys / YA novel by Michael Noonan
Fineflour / stories by Gillian Mears
Headliners: Craig McGregor's social portraits
Robert Adamson selected poems 1970–1989
Greg Chappell: cricket's incomparable artist / by Adrian McGregor
The glass cannon: a Bougainville diary 1944–45 / by Peter Pinney
The overlander songbook / compiled and illustrated by Ron Edwards

1991

Coal in Queensland: from federation to the twenties, 1900 to 1925 / by R.L. Whitmore
Australian Aboriginal languages: a general introduction / by Barry J. Blake (2nd ed)
The constitutions of the Australian states / by R.D. Lumb (5th ed)
Political crossroads: the 1989 Queensland election / edited by Rosemary Whip, Colin A. Hughes
Innocent cities / novel by Jack Hodgins
Flame and shadow: a study of Judith Wright's poetry / by Shirley Walker (UQP studies in Australian literature series)
Son of Alyandabu: my fight for Aboriginal rights / by Joe McGinness (UQP Black Australian writers series)
Counting backwards: and other stories / by Suzanne Edgar
Words of our country: stories, place names and vocabulary in Yidiny, the Aboriginal language of the Cairns-Yarrabah region / compiled and edited by R.M.W. Dixon, with flora identification and interpretation by Tony Irvine
Simply the best: the 1990 Kangaroos / by Adrian McGregor
The edge of the rainforest / YA novel by James G. Porter
The empire of grass: twenty-eight poems: 1983–1989 / by Gary Catalano
New and selected poems 1960–1990 / by Bruce Beaver
Time to go / YA novel by Jill Dobson
The romantic lives of Louise Mack / by Nancy Phelan
The madding of Daniel O'Hooligan / novel by Peter Wear
Struggle of memory / novel by Joan Dugdale
The big steal: screenplay / by David Parker, with a foreword by David Williamson
Sweetie: the screenplay / by Gerard Lee & Jane Campion
The life and opinions of Tom Collins: a study of the works of Joseph Furphy / by Julian Croft (UQP studies in Australian literature series)
Caprice: a stockman's daughter / by Doris Pilkington — Nugi Garimara (UQP Black Australian writers series)
The ivory swing / novel by Janette Turner Hospital

The tax inspector / novel by Peter Carey
John Shaw Neilson, poetry, autobiography and correspondence / edited by Cliff Hanna (UQP Australian authors series)
Tansy / YA novel by Margaret Trist
Sooner or later / YA novel by Sophie Masson
Once were warriors / novel by Alan Duff
Proud to be a rebel: the life and times of Emma Miller / by Pam Young
Voices from the river / novel by Victor Kelleher
Kenneth Slessor: poetry, essays, war despatches, war diaries, journalism, autobiographical material and letters / edited by Dennis Haskell (UQP Australian authors series)
Neighbours: multicultural writing of the 1980s / edited by R.F. Holt
Olga Masters: a lot of living: the compelling biography of this much loved writer / by Julie Lewis
Robert Dunne, 1830–1917, Archbishop of Brisbane / by Neil J. Byrne
Usher / novel by Matthew Condon
Rookwood / YA novel by Dorothy Porter
Folds in the map / poems by Andrew Taylor
Here is their spirit: a history of the Australian War Memorial 1917–1990 / by Michael McKernan
In a different light: Australian artists working in Italy / by Peter & Susan Ward
A peculiar people: William Lane's Australian Utopians in Paraguay / by Gavin Souter (3rd ed)
Accidentally in transit / the further misadventures of Murray Laurence, compulsive traveller; maps by Janet Laurence, Michael Snape
High times in the middle of nowhere: the misadventures of Murray Laurence, compulsive traveller (rev ed)
Portrait of a dog: and other classical bagatelles / poems by Dimitris Tsaloumas, with illustrations by Michael Winters
The observatory / poems by Dimitris Tsaloumas (3rd ed)
What God wants / stories by Lily Brett, illustrations by David Rankin
A dream of stars / YA novel by Brian Caswell
The Creeklanders / by Ian Ottley
Komninos / poems by Komninos
Pictures on the margin: memoirs / by Clement Semmler
Leaving the snow country / YA novel by Diana Noonan

1992

The Petrie family: building colonial Brisbane / by Dimity Dornan, Denis Cryle
Russia and the fifth continent: aspects of Russian-Australian relations / edited by John McNair, Thomas Poole

Sojourners: the epic story of China's centuries-old relationship with Australia: flowers and the wide sea / by Eric Rolls
Tom Petrie's reminiscences of early Queensland / by Constance Campbell Petrie, with an introduction by Mark Cryle
One day at a time: a Vietnam diary / by D.J. Dennis
The devils' garden: Solomon Islands war diary, 1945 / by Peter Pinney
Making the legend: the war writings of C.E.W. Bean / selected by Denis Winter
Gender, politics and fiction: twentieth century Australian women's novels / edited by Carole Ferrier (2nd ed, UQP studies in Australian literature series)
On a clear day / poems by Joanne Burns
Bush ballads, poems, stories and journalism / by A.B. "Banjo" Paterson, edited by Clement Semmler (UQP Australian authors series)
Flying low: a novel / by Geoffrey Dutton
Crossfire / YA novel by James Moloney
The Australian short story: a collection 1890s–1990s / edited and introduced by Laurie Hergenhan (2nd ed, UQP Australian authors series)
Eagle and emu: German-Australian writing 1930–1990 / by Manfred Jurgensen
By the seats of their pants: more great Australian air stories / by Terry Gwynn-Jones
Images of Australia: an introductory reader in Australian studies / edited by Gillian Whitlock, David Carter (Open Learning series)
Land rights Queensland style: the struggle for Aboriginal self-management / by Frank Brennan
Akhenaten / poems by Dorothy Porter
The seal woman / novel by Beverley Farmer
Good night Mr Moon / novel by Barbara Hanrahan
The sixth sense / stories by Lolo Houbein
Black life: poems / by Jack Davis (UQP Black Australian writers series)
A long way to Tipperary / YA novel by Sue Gough
Things could be worse / stories by Lily Brett, illustrated by David Rankin
Iris in her garden: eight stories / by Barbara Hanrahan, with relief etchings by the author
Midnight voices / stories by Patricia Pengilley
Relative strangers / YA novel by Maureen Pople
Brief encounters: YA short stories / compiled by Barbara Ker Wilson
Breaking glass: a novel in two parts / by John Clanchy
The last magician / novel by Janette Turner Hospital
The genesis of sport in Queensland: from the dreamtime to federation / by Reet A. Howell, Maxwell L. Howell
Passion / stories by Nick Earls

A blaze of summer / YA novel by Sophie Masson
Head over heels / memoir by Hugh Lunn
Over forty in Broken Hill: unusual encounters outback & beyond / by Jack Hodgins
Springfield / novel by Marian Eldridge
Jumping at the moon / stories by Venero Armanno
Boundary conditions: the poetry of Gwen Harwood / by Jennifer Strauss (UQP studies in Australian literature series)
Fabricating the self: the fictions of Jessica Anderson / by Elaine Barry (UQP studies in Australian literature series)
Broken dreams / memoir by Bill Dodd (UQP Black Australian writers series)
The glass inferno / novel by Angelika Fremd
Al Capsella on holidays / YA novel by Judith Clarke
No regrets / memoir by Mabel Edmund (UQP Black Australian writers series)
Poems 1959–89 / by David Malouf
Selected poems, 1939–1990 / by John Blight
Country childhoods / stories edited by Geoffrey Dutton
Micky darlin' / novel by Victor Kelleher
Unbranded / novel by Herb Wharton (UQP Black Australian writers series)
A cage of butterflies / YA novel by Brian Caswell
The ALS guide to Australian writers: a bibliography 1963–1990 / edited by Martin Duwell, Laurie Hergenhan; associate editors Marianne Ehrhardt, Carol Hetherington (UQP studies in Australian literature series)
Red roses / stories by Ania Walwicz
Xavier Herbert: episodes from Capricornia, Poor fellow my country and other fiction, nonfiction and letters / edited by Frances de Groen, Peter Pierce (UQP Australian authors series)
Proof: the screenplay / by Jocelyn Moorhouse
My brilliant career: the screenplay / by Eleanor Witcombe
The sea coast of Bohemia: literary life in Sydney's Roaring Twenties / by Peter Kirkpatrick
Australia's frontline: remembering the 1939–45 war / by Libby Connors [et al]
The unique continent: an introductory reader in Australian environmental studies / edited by Jeremy Smith (Open Learning series)
Keeping them honest: democratic reform in Queensland / edited by Andrew Hede, Scott Prasser, Mark Neylan
The Australian economy in the Japanese Mirror / by Kyoko Sheridan
Good company / memoir by Henry "Jo" Gullett
Aboriginality: contemporary Aboriginal paintings & prints / by Jennifer Isaacs (rev ed)

Concise history of Australia / by Russel Ward, maps, diagrams and drawings by Mark Ward (rev ed)
A guide to the Great Court / produced by Media and Information Services, edited by Brian D. Pascoe (rev ed)
Wilder shores: women's travel stories of Australia & beyond / edited by Robin Lucas, Clare Forster
Michael and me and the sun / memoir by Barbara Hanrahan
One night out stealing / novel by Alan Duff
Lies & alibis / YA novel by Gregory Bastian
Jim & me / by Hugh Lunn, edited by Barbara Ker Wilson
Inky Stephensen: wild man of letters / by Craig Munro (2nd ed)
From bees to buzz-bombs: Robert Raymond's boyhood-to-blitz memoirs

1993

Henry Kendall: poetry, prose & selected correspondence / edited by Michael Ackland (UQP Australian authors series)
The witch number / YA novel by Dorothy Porter
The watcher on the cast-iron balcony / memoir by Hal Porter
The riches of ancient Australia: an indispensable guide for exploring prehistoric Australia / by Josephine Flood (2nd ed)
Hennessy / YA novel by Vincent Banville
A question of leadership: Paul Keating political fighter / by Michael Gordon
Australian marketing casebook / by Peter Gilmour, David L. Rados (3rd ed)
Water pollution: causes and effects in Australia and New Zealand / by D.W. Connell (3rd ed)
Unnatural lives: studies in Australian convict fiction / by Laurie Hergenhan (new ed) (UQP studies in Australian literature series)
Race relations in colonial Queensland: a history of exclusion, exploitation, and extermination / by Raymond Evans, Kay Saunders, Kathryn Cronin (3rd ed)
Faces of culture: explorations in anthropology / edited by Jenny Hughes (Open Learning series)
Mabo: a judicial revolution: the Aboriginal land rights decision and its impact on Australian law / edited by M. A. Stephenson, Suri Ratnapala
Finwood & Lisa / YAF novel by Barbara Wels
The distribution of voice / poems by Martin Harrison
Waiting: a comedy of errors and expectations: the screenplay / by Jackie McKimmie
Martin Johnston: selected poems & prose / edited by John Tranter (UQP Australian authors series)
Poems 1970–1992 / by Fay Zwicky
Mike / by Brian Caswell (UQP storybridge series)

The magic palace / by Mavis Scott, illustrated by Mike Spoor (UQP storybridge series)
Green Slime / by John Fairbairn, illustrated by Rosemary Allen (UQP storybridge series)
Winning streak / YA novel by Donna Sharp
Atomic fiction: the novels of David Ireland / by Ken Gelder (UQP studies in Australian literature series)
Helplessly tangled in female arms and legs: Elizabeth Jolley's fictions / by Paul Salzman (UQP studies in Australian literature series)
Musica ficta / novel by Anne Kennedy
Soundings / novel by Liam Davison
But the dead are many / novel by Frank Hardy
Fred & Olive's blessed lino / by Hugh Lunn, illustrated by David Mackintosh
The scent of eucalyptus / by Barbara Hanrahan
The barge / poems by Dimitris Tsaloumas
Dougy / YA novel by James Moloney
The emperor Wally Lewis / by Adrian McGregor
Mathematics and gender / edited by Elizabeth Fennema, Gilah C. Leder
Paul Keating: a question of leadership / by Michael Gordon (2nd ed)
Mister Maloga / by Nancy Cato (rev ed)
Lives on fire / novel by Rosie Scott
Uncertain beginnings: debates in Australian studies / edited by Gillian Whitlock, Gail Reekie
The name's still Charlie / by Olwyn Green
Tin dog, damper & dust / memoir by Don Munday
My kind of people: achievement, identity and Aboriginality / by Wayne Coolwell (UQP Black Australian writers series)
Sweet water — stolen land / novel by Philip McLaren (UQP Black Australian writers series)
At the Florida / poems by John Tranter
The gripping beast / novel by Joan Dugdale
Eating dog: travel stories / by Gerard Lee
Ferretabilia: life and times of Nation Review / edited by Richard Walsh
Clarrie Grimmett: the Bradman of spin / by Ashley Mallett
Martin Offiah: a blaze of glory / by David Lawrenson
Work at home: the domestic division of labour / by Janeen Baxter
From forest to sea: Australia's changing environment / by Eric Rolls
The Ern Malley affair / by Michael Heyward; introduction by Robert Hughes
George Robertson: a publishing life in letters / by Anthony Barker (2nd ed)
Queen of love: and other stories / by Rosie Scott
Going home: sequel to The boys from Bondi / YA novel by Alan Collins
Wyrd / YA novel by Sue Gough

The road to anywhere / the travel writings of Peter Pinney, selected by John Borthwick
War on the homefront: state intervention in Queensland 1938–1948 / by Kay Saunders
Encounters with Australian artists / by Janet Hawley
Tradition and change: contemporary art of Asia and the Pacific / edited by Caroline Turner
Vietnam: the Australian dilemma / by Terry Burstall
Behind barbed wire: internment in Australia during World War II / by Margaret Bevege
Scribbling in the dark / memoir by Barry Oakley (2nd ed)
Conned! / by Eve Mumewa D. Fesl (UQP Black Australian writers series)
Canoes of the dead / YA novel by David Kelly
Blind luck / novel by Mandy Sayer
Selected poems 1973–1992 / by Gary Catalano
Isaac Isaacs / by Sir Zelman Cowen (2nd ed)
Outback / by Lawrie Kavanagh, illustrated by Hugh Sawrey
The sting in the Wattle : Australian satirical verse / edited by Philip Neilsen
Winning streak / YA novel by Donna Sharp

1994

Glory days / novel by Rosie Scott
My cousin Clarette: and other YA stories / by Budge Wilson
On the edge: women's experiences of Queensland / edited by Gail Reekie
No ordinary childhood: Barbara Corbett's celebration of a charmed life in the 1920s, photographs of Dora Creek by her father Malcolm McDonald 1880–1956
Aboriginal Australia: an introductory reader in Aboriginal studies / edited by Colin Bourke, Eleanor Bourke, Bill Edwards (Open Learning series)
A migrant's story: the struggle and success of an Italian-Australian, 1920s–1960s / by Osvaldo Bonutto (2nd ed)
The last call of the bugle: the long road to Kapyong / by Jack Gallaway
25 April 1915: the inevitable tragedy / by Denis Winter
Raphael Cilento: a biography / by Fedora Gould Fisher
Gracey / YA novel by James Moloney
Anima: and other poems / by Bruce Beaver
The wild sweet flowers: Alvie Skerritt stories / by Marian Eldridge
The Highgate Hill mob / by John Fairbairn (UQP storybridge series)
This world, this place / poems by Pamela Brown
The great fairytale robbery / by Eric Scott (UQP storybridge series)
Small ecstasies / stories by Moya Costello
Sally Marshall's not an alien / by Amanda McKay (UQP storybridge series)

Mr Hornbeam's treasure hunt / written and illustrated by Louise Elliott (UQP storybridge series)
Flesh and blood / YA novel by Vivienne Bon
Janet Frame: subversive fictions / by Gina Mercer
Dancing on hot macadam: Peter Carey's fiction / by Anthony J. Hassall (UQP studies in Australian literature series)
The scandalous Penton: a biography of Brian Penton / by Patrick Buckridge
Australia: republic or monarchy?: legal and constitutional issues / edited by M.A. Stephenson, Clive Turner
Dangerous redheads / YA novel by Louise Elliott
Out in the open: an autobiography / by Geoffrey Dutton
My Bundjalung people / by Ruby Langford Ginibi (UQP Black Australian writers series)
Dreamslip / YA novel by Brian Caswell
Passenger on a ferry / poems by Jena Woodhouse
The white woman / novel by Liam Davison
The flying damper / by Jean Chapman (UQP storybridge series)
The confessions of a beachcomber / by E.J. Banfield, with an introduction by Michael Noonan
Voyage from shame: the Cowra breakout and afterwards / by Harry Gordon (2nd ed)
Australia and the Olympic Games / by Harry Gordon
The finish line: a long march by bicycle through China and Australia / by Sang Ye, translated by Nicholas Jose, Sue Trevaskes
Angels twenty / memoir by Ted Park
Oodgeroo / by Kathie Cochrane, with contribution by Judith Wright, illustrations by Ron Hurley
The grocer's daughter / picture book by Nigel Gray, illustrated by David Mackintosh
The bunyip and the night / picture book by Mark Nestor Svendsen, illustrated by Annmarie Scott, David Mackintosh [et al]
Red Ted: the life of E.G. Theodore / by Ross Fitzgerald
Patrick White: selected writings / edited by Alan Lawson (UQP Australian authors series)
The ancient guild of tycoons / novel by Matthew Condon
Christina Stead: selected fiction and nonfiction / edited by R.G. Geering, A. Segerberg (UQP Australian authors series)
One siren or another / poems by Andrea Sherwood
That shining band: a study of Australian colonial verse tradition / by Michael Ackland (UQP studies in Australian literature series)
Wallflowers and witches: women and culture in Australia 1910–1945 / edited by Maryanne Dever
The First humans: human origins and history to 10,000 BC / general editor

Goran Burenhult, foreword by J. Peter White (Illustrated history of humankind series)
People of the Stone Age: hunter-gatherers and early farmers / general editor Goran Burenhult, foreword by J. Peter White (Illustrated history of humankind series)
New World and Pacific civilizations: cultures of America, Asia, and the Pacific / general editor Goran Burenhult, foreword by Gordon R. Willey (Illustrated history of humankind series)
Old World civilizations: the rise of cities and states / general editor Goran Burenhult, foreword by Barry Cunliffe (Illustrated history of humankind series)
Bridge of triangles / novel by John Muk Muk Burke (UQP Black Australian writers series)
The unusual life of Tristan Smith / novel by Peter Carey
Collected Stories / by Peter Carey
Holding on / YA novel by Donna Sharp
Friend of my heart / YA fiction by Judith Clarke
Metis: the octopus and the olive tree / YA fiction by Jena Woodhouse
Lisdalia / by Brian Caswell (UQP storybridge series)
Little Eva at Moonlight Creek: and other Aboriginal song poems / edited by Martin Duwell, R.M.W. Dixon
Hands up!: who enjoyed their schooldays / YA stories compiled by Barbara Ker Wilson
The day before yesterday / by Barbara Corbett, illustrated by Louise Elliott (UQP storybridge series)
Changing places: Australian writers in Europe 1960s–1990s / edited by Laurie Hergenhan, Irmtraud Petersson (UQP Australian authors series)
The circumference of the knowable world / travel stories by John Borthwick
Columbus' blindness: and other essays / edited by Cassandra Pybus
Once were warriors / novel by Alan Duff (2nd ed)
A letter to our son / nonfiction by Peter Carey
Cattle camp: Murrie drovers and their stories / by Herb Wharton (UQP Black Australian writers series)
The Brisbane Customs House / by Malcolm I. Thomis

1995

Traditional peoples today: continuity and change in the modern world / general editor Goran Burenhult, foreword by Marvin Harris (Illustrated history of humankind series)
Komninos by the kupful / poems by Komninos
Caden walaa! / picture book by Karin Calley, with Guugu Yimithirr translation by Noel Pearson
Water bombs: a book of poems for teenagers / by Steven Herrick

Elements of horseshoeing / by J.A. Springhall (3rd ed)
People, places and policies: aspects of Queensland government administration 1859–1920 / edited by Kay Cohen, Kenneth Wiltshire
No place for a nervous lady: voices from the Australian bush / edited by Lucy Frost
Kundi Dan: Dan Leahy's life among the highlanders of Papua New Guinea / by John Fowke
Childe and Australia: archaeology, politics and ideas / edited by Peter Gathercole, T. H. Irving, Gregory
Beyond the big run: station life in Australia's last frontier / by Charlie Schultz, Darrell Lewis
Selected poems / by John A. Scott
Sandstone / poems by Andrew Taylor
M. Barnard Eldershaw: Plaque with laurel, essays, reviews & correspondence / edited by Maryanne Dever (UQP Australian authors series)
A reader's guide to contemporary Australian poetry / by Geoff Page
Oodgeroo: a tribute / edited by Adam Shoemaker
Looking out for Ollie / by Sharon Montey (UQP storybridge series)
Lone bandits / YA novel by Louise Elliott
Moonbird / by Robin Stewart (UQP storybridge series)
Nightmares in paradise / YA stories compiled by Robyn Sheahan
The night bees / by Anthony Holcroft (UQP storybridge series)
Days with Gran / picture book by Catherine Farthing-Knight, designed & illustrated by Anne-Maree Althaus
Just a prostitute / by Marianne Wood
Brides of Christ. Episode 3, Ambrose: the screenplay / by John Alsop, Sue Smith
From Italy to Ingham: Italians in North Queensland / by William A. Douglass
Mabo: the native title legislation / edited by M.A. Stephenson
Swashbuckler / by James Moloney (UQP storybridge series)
Tasha's witch / by Natalie Jane Prior (UQP storybridge series)
More about the mob / by John Fairbairn (UQP storybridge series)
The sky is blue with clouds like fishbones / by Michelle Mee (UQP storybridge series)
Panic stations / YA fiction by Judith Clarke
The city of home / poems by Thomas Shapcott
Australian melodramas: Thomas Keneally's fiction / by Peter Pierce (UQP studies in Australian literature series)
Deucalion / YA novel by Brian Caswell
Yesterday's heroes / YA novel by Natalie Jane Prior
No casual traveller: Hartley Grattan and Australia-US connections / by Laurie Hergenhan
Spies like us / memoir by Hugh Lunn

Goss: a political biography / by Jamie Walker
The lifestyles of previous tenants / stories by Barbara Wels
On our selection: the original Dad & Dave stories / by Steele Rudd
Dad & Dave — On our selection: the screenplay / by George Whaley
Collected stories 1970–1995 / by Janette Turner Hospital
Paradise to paranoia: new Queensland writing / stories edited by Nigel Krauth, Robyn Sheahan
Joshua / YA novel by Alan Collins
The news they didn't use / YA novel by Stephen Measday
The house on River Terrace / YA novel by James Moloney
The house in the light / novel by Beverley Farmer
Movie dreams / novel by Rosie Scott
One land, one nation: Mabo — towards 2001 / by Frank Brennan
Pig with a view / by Pamela Platt (UQP storybridge series)
Maddie / by Brian Caswell (UQP storybridge series)
The big bazoohley / by Peter Carey (UQP storybridge series)
Theory and reality: federal ideas in Australia, England and Europe / S. Rufus Davis
The lives of the saints / stories by Edward Berridge
The white garden / novel by Carmel Bird
Wandjuk Marika: life story / as told to Jennifer Isaacs
In with the tide: memoirs of a storyteller / by Michael Noonan
In search of Steele Rudd: author of the classic Dad & Dave stories / by Richard Fotheringham
The place where the planes take off / picture book by Steven Herrick, illustrated by Annmarie Scott
Grandma Ollie / picture book by Frank Moffatt
Harry Oakman's what flowers when: the complete guide to flowering times in tropical and subtropical gardens
Quirky gardens / by Jennifer Isaacs
The over the top with Jim album / by Hugh Lunn, research by Helen Dash, designed & illustrated by David Mackintosh
The sausage tree / memoir by Rosalie Medcraft & Valda Gee (UQP Black Australian writers series)

1996

Collected stories / by Olga Masters
Colonial Queensland: perspectives on a frontier society / by Bill Thorpe
Pacific Highway boo-blooz: country poems / by Mudrooroo (UQP Black Australian writers series)
Follow the rabbit-proof fence / by Doris Pilkington — Nugi Garimara (UQP Black Australian writers series)
A woman's voice: conversations with Australian poets / by Jenny Digby

Penelope's knees / poems by Joanne Burns
A net full of honey / YA novel by Estelle Runcie Pinney
Dyirbal song poetry: the oral literature of an Australian rainforest people / by R.M.W. Dixon, Grace Koch
Red hot notes / stories edited by Carmel Bird
Brave new world: Dr H.V. Evatt and Australian foreign policy, 1941–1949 / edited by David Day
"And what books do you read?": new studies in Australian literature: essays presented to Laurie Hergenhan celebrating his contribution to the study of Australian literature and marking the occasion of his retirement / edited by Irmtraud Petersson, Martin Duwell
Fabricating the self: the fictions of Jessica Anderson / by Elaine Barry (rev ed) (UQP studies in Australian literature series)
The sun is rising / YA novel by Sophie Masson
A veritable dynamo: Lloyd Ross and Australian Labour 1901–1987 / by Stephen Holt
Almost Wednesday / YA novel by James Roy
The banshee and the bullocky: tales of my uncle Arch / Bill Scott, illustrated by Ron Edwards
Pelicans & chihuahuas: and other urban legends / by Bill Scott talking about folklore
Collected stories / by Beverley Farmer
Eclipse / poems by Bobbi Sykes
The descendant / novel by Joan Dugdale
The Australian yarn: the definitive collection / edited by Ron Edwards, illustrated by the author
The copper crucible: a novel / by Betty Collins (unexpurgated edition, edited by Ian Syson)
A man and his camel / picture book by Jo Bertini
West End shuffle / YA novel by Natalie Jane Prior
The footy club: inside the Brisbane Bears / by Ross Fitzgerald, with Andrew Berkman
Balancing act: being a stepmother / by Robin Lucas
Pieces of heaven: in the South Seas / memoir by Nancy Phelan
Accidental grace / poems by Judith Beveridge
Harry Oakman's shrubs: the complete guide to shrubs for tropical and subtropical gardens
Harry Oakman's tropical and subtropical gardening: the complete guide
A true believer: Paul Keating / by Michael Gordon (new ed)
The white rajah: a dynastic intrigue / by Cassandra Pybus
Warrigal's way / by Warrigal Anderson (UQP Black Australian writers series)
In the quietness of my aunt's house, Bad blood: two novellas / by Joanne Carroll

See through / fiction by Neil Boyack & Simon Colvey
Autographs: contemporary Australian autobiography / edited by Gillian Whitlock (UQP Australian authors series)
Writing on the backs of the blacks / by Mari Rhydwen
The year the dragon came / by Sang Ye, edited by Linda Jaivin with several other translators
Flame and shadow: a study of Judith Wright's poetry / by Shirley Walker (rev ed, UQP studies in Australian literature series)
The 1890s: Australian literature and literary culture / edited by Ken Stewart (UQP studies in Australian literature series)
After January / YA novel by Nick Earls
Bindi / by John Fairbairn (UQP storybridge series)
The rock 'n' roll rainforest / by Pamela Platt (UQP storybridge series)
Monster magic / by Cecily Matthews (UQP storybridge series)
Favourite live thing / by Jean Chapman (UQP storybridge series)
Love, ghosts & nose hair / YA poetry by Stephen Herrick
Asturias / YA fiction by Brian Caswell
Wild blue yonder / flying stories by Terry Gwynn-Jones
Where ya' been mate / stories by Herb Wharton (UQP Black Australian Writers series)
Not without dust and heat: a journey into learning and teaching / by Maxwell Howell
Unwanted aliens: Japanese internment in Australia / by Yuriko Nagata
Edward Koiki Mabo: his life and struggle for land rights / by Noel Loos & Koiki Mabo
Citizens: continuing the epic story of China's centuries-old relationship with Australia ...: flowers and the wide sea / by Eric Rolls
Dreaming in urban areas / poems by Lisa Bellear (UQP Black Australian writers series)
Wild blue yonder: flying stories of amazement and wonder / by Terry Gwynn-Jones
Overland: from Kelly country to the Gulf / by Lawrie Kavanagh, illustrated by Hugh Sawrey
Heaven, where the bachelors sit / memoir by Gerard Windsor
The viewfinder / poems by Anthony Lawrence
New and selected poems, 1971–1993 / by Laurie Duggan
Betty and Bala and the proper big pumpkin / picture book by Lorraine Berolah, LilyJane Collins & Noel Cristaudo, with illustrations by Noel Cristaudo
Original sin / YA stories compiled & edited by Robyn Sheahan
A bridge to Wiseman's Cove / YA novel by James Moloney
The figures of Julian Ashcroft / picture book by Gary Crew, illustrated by Hans de Haas

Streetwise / YA novel by John Maddocks
The good liar / by Gregory Maguire (UQP storybridge series)
Imagined lives: a study of David Malouf / by Philip Neilsen (rev ed, UQP Studies in Australian literature series)
Boundary conditions: the poetry of Gwen Harwood / by Jennifer Strauss (rev ed, UQP studies in Australian literature series)
The Recollections of Geoffry Hamlyn / by Henry Kingsley, edited by Stanton Mellick, Patrick Morgan, Paul Eggert (Academy Editions of Australian literature)

1997

Astronauts, lost souls & dragons / by Diana Giese
Henry Handel Richardson: The getting of wisdom, stories, selected prose & correspondence / edited by Susan Lever & Catherine Pratt (UQP Australian authors series)
The killing of Mud-eye / YA novel by Celeste Walters
Daughters & fathers / edited by Carmel Bird
Thomas Carr: Archbishop of Melbourne / by Tom Boland
Collected stories / by Marion Halligan
Our land is our life: land rights — past, present and future / edited by Galarrwuy Yunupingu
Kenneth Slessor — critical readings / edited by Philip Mead (UQP studies in Australian literature series)
Relax Max! / by Brian Caswell, illustrated by Kurt Hedridge (UQP storybridge series)
A celebration of food & wine: of flesh, of fish, of fowl / by Eric Rolls
Plains of promise / novel by Alexis Wright (UQP Black Australian writers series)
The news on aliens / YA novel by Stephen Measday
Through the doorway / by Julia Holland (UQP storybridge series)
Fred Paterson: the people's champion / by Ross Fitzgerald
Talking about Celia ... / by Jeanie Bell (UQP Black Australian writers series)
Mary Martin: a double life: Australia-India 1915–1973 / by Julie Lewis
The ALS guide to Australian writers: a bibliography 1963–1995 / edited by Martin Duwell (rev ed) (UQP studies in Australian literature series)
London calling / YA novel by Natalie Jane Prior
A celebration of food & wine: of grain, of grape, of Gethsemane / by Eric Rolls
The way we civilise: Aboriginal Affairs — the untold story / by Rosalind Kidd
Abiding interests / by Gough Whitlam
My life, my love, my lasagne / by Steven Herrick (UQP storybridge series)
Only the heart / YA novel by Brian Caswell, David Phu An Chiem

A celebration of food & wine: of fruit, of vegetables, of vulgar herbs, of sugar and spice / by Eric Rolls
Jack Maggs / novel by Peter Carey
Collected stories / by Gillian Mears
Trivia man / by Laurine Croasdale (UQP storybridge series)
Steam pigs / novel by Melissa Lucashenko (UQP Black Australian writers series)
Along came the sky / novel by R.D. Lappan
Here comes the night / YA novel by Sue Gough
Collected stories / by Thea Astley
Paradise mislaid: in search of the Australian tribe of Paraguay / by Anne Whitehead
The Mayne inheritance / by Rosamond Siemon
One less fish / picture book by Kim Toft & Alan Sheather
The Australian short story collection / edited by Laurie Hergenhan
The N.Z. short story collection / edited by Marion McLeod & Bill Manhire

1998

Child of the Kulaks / memoir by Alex Saranin
Oscar & Lucinda / film edition, by Peter Carey
Coming of age: charter for a new Australia / by David Solomon
Too far everywhere: the romantic heroine in 19th C. Australia / by Fiona Giles (UQP studies in Australian literature series)
Dancing on hot macadam: Peter Carey's fiction / by Anthony J. Hassall (new ed, UQP studies in Australian literature series)
Aboriginal Australia: an introductory reader in Australian studies / by Colin Bourke, Eleanor Bourke & Bill Edwards (new ed, Open learning series)
On the brink: Australian universities confronting their future / by Peter Coaldrake
Red golf balls / YA novel by Laurine Croasdale
A place like this / YA novel by Steven Herrick
Till apples grow on an orange tree / memoir by Cassandra Pybus
New and selected poems / by Anthony Lawrence
Oscar & Lucinda: the screenplay / by Laura Jones from Peter Carey's novel
Tee Dee and the collectors / by Brian Caswell (Alien Zones series)
Messengers of the Great Orff / by Brian Caswell (Alien Zones series)
Gladiators in the holo-colosseum / by Brian Caswell (Alien Zones series)
Gargantua / by Brian Caswell (Alien Zones series)
Journal of Annie Baxter Dawbin / edited by Lucy Frost (Academy Editions of Australian literature)
Maurice Guest / by Henry Handel Richardson, edited by Bruce Steele, Clive Probyn (Academy Editions of Australian literature)

Keen as mustard: Britain's horrific chemical warfare experiments in Australia / by Bridget Goodwin
A celebration of food & wine / by Eric Rolls (one volume ed)
Celebration of the senses / by Eric Rolls (new ed)
Full moon racing / YA novel by James Roy
Killing Darcy / YA novel by Melissa Lucashenko
Setting out on the voyage / memoir by Nancy Phelan (new ed)
Black angels, red blood / novel by Steven McCarthy (UQP Black Australian writers series)
Barbara Hanrahan: diaries 1960–91 / edited by Elaine Lindsay
Buzzard breath & brains / by James Moloney (UQP storybridge series)
Woman and herself: a critical study of the works of Barbara Hanrahan / by Annette Stewart (UQP studies in Australian literature series)
Judah Waten: fiction, memoir, criticism /edited by David Carter (UQP Australian authors series)
If the truth be known / by Jackie Huggins (UQP Black Australian writers series)
UQP: the Writer's Press 1948–98 / edited by Craig Munro
The vigilant heart / poems by Catherine Bateson
Poetry to the rescue / by Steven Herrick (UQP storybridge series)
The Australian guide to chairing meetings / by Marjorie Puregger (new ed)
Legislating Liberty: a bill of rights for Australia? / by Frank Brennan
The moment made marvellous: poetry anthology / edited by Tom Shapcott
The view from Ararat / YA fiction by Brian Caswell
The soldiers' story / memoirs by Terry Burstall (combined ed)
Johnno / novel by David Malouf (special anniversary ed)
The Gift of story / edited by Marion Halligan, Rosanne Fitzgibbon
Land window poems / by John Graham (UQP Black Australian writers series)
Wildest dreams: a selective memoir / by Michael Wilding
When darkness falls / by John Bodey (UQP Black Australian writers series)
The fat man in history / by Peter Carey (special anniversary ed)
Xavier Herbert: a biography / by Frances de Groen
The Queen of Bohemia / memoir by Dulcie Deamer, edited by Peter Kirkpatrick
Angela / YA novel by James Moloney
The harbour / poems by Dimitris Tsaloumas

Appendix II
Fryer Library UQP Archive

The University of Queensland Press Archive in Fryer Library, University of Queensland, consists of 324 boxes of records. The papers document the history of the Press from about 1965, the time of UQP's expansion from a university publications outlet into a fully fledged publishing house, and they supplement the earlier records held at the university archives. It is a growing collection, with the University of Queensland Press regularly adding more records.

The archive consists of the following records series:

Production files

Correspondence

Publishing meetings (minutes, agendas, etc.)

Australian Literature Board

Miscellaneous files

They show UQP's development into the largest and most significant university press in Australia, with a reputation for innovative excellence in both scholarly and general publishing. In the last decade, UQP has specialised in Australian studies. The archive, particularly the production files and correspondence series, shows the background to numerous award-winning publications. Included are files for some of the great recent success stories of Australian publishing, such as Peter Carey's *Oscar and Lucinda*. There are also extensive files for the widely-praised Australian literature series: Paperback Poets, Poets on Record, Australian Authors, and Studies in Australian Literature. As well, there are administrative files, such as the records of publishing meetings.

What follows is a summary guide to the University of Queensland Press Archive, collection number UQFL 198, in Fryer Library. A full inventory of the collection can be obtained in print format in the Fryer Library, or on the World Wide Web (at http://www.library.uq.edu.au/fryer).

Production files

The production files are at present the largest group of records in the archive. They consist of typescripts, typesetting instructions, proof copies, corrections, galley proofs, production notes, cover designs, correspondence, printing plates, artwork, photographs, printing requisitions, title page layout samples, and manuscript appraisal forms.

There are files from the following Australian literature series:

From the Paperback Poets series, the files include those relating to: *The Inspector of Tides* by Michael Dransfield; *Poems from Murrumbeena* by R.A. Simpson; *Condition Red* by Vicki Viidikas; *A Soapbox Omnibus* by Rodney Hall; *Creekwater Journal* by Robert Gray; *Airship* by Roger McDonald; files from Peter Skrzynecki, Peter Kocan, and Philip Roberts; *Two Poets: Paperback Poets 5*, by Geoff Page and Philip Roberts; *The Cool Change* by Andrew Taylor; *New Devil, New Parish* by Alan Wearne; *Heaven in a Way* by Rodney Hall; *Begin with Walking* by Thomas Shapcott; and *Soft Riots* by Richard Tipping.

The files from the Poets on Record series include those relating to R.D. Fitzgerald, Douglas Stewart, Rosemary Dobson, A.D. Hope and Bruce Beaver.

From the Australian Authors series, the files include those for *Kenneth Slessor* edited by Dennis Haskell; *Johnno, short stories, poems, essays and interview* by David Malouf, edited by James Tulip; and *A.B. "Banjo" Paterson* edited by Clement Semmler.

From the Studies in Australian Literature series, the files include those for *Strange Country: a study of Randolph Stow* by Anthony J. Hassall; *Unnatural Lives: studies in Australian fiction about the convicts, from James Tucker to Patrick White* by Laurie Hergenhan; *Boundary Conditions: the Poetry of Gwen Harwood* by Jennifer Strauss; *The life and opinions of Tom Collins: a study of the works of Joseph Furphy* by Julian Croft; and *Flame and Shadow: a study of Judith Wright's poetry* by Shirley Walker.

Also included in the archive are files from the UQP Black Australian Writers series, and from the series Australian Public Figures and Australian Public Issues on tape.

There are numerous other production files, including the following:

Peter Carey. There are files relating to *The Fat Man in History, The Unusual Life of Tristan Smith*, and a large group of files for *The Tax Inspector*.

Olga Masters. There are 2 boxes of files relating to *The Rose Fancier.*

David Malouf. Includes files relating to *Johnno*.

Thomas Shapcott. There are files relating to *Begin with Walking, Contemporary American and Australian poetry, Focus on Charles Blackman, Inwards to the Sun*, and *Birthday Gift*.

John Manifold. Files relating to *Op 8; Poems.*

Michael Dransfield. Files relating to *The Inspector of Tides*.

Janette Turner Hospital. Cover design and files for *Charades*, and files for *Isobars, Dislocations*, and *The Ivory Swing*.
Nancy Cato. Files relating to *Mister Maloga*.
Judith Rodriguez. Files relating to *Water Life*.
Ross Fitzgerald. Files relating to *From the Dreaming to 1915: a History of Queensland*.
Denis Murphy. Files relating to *T.J. Ryan: a Political Biography*.

The writers in the above list are all represented in other Fryer Library manuscript collections, as well as the University of Queensland Press Archive. Details of these manuscript collections are given later.

There are also four parcels of cover designs and artwork, and a sub-series of control cards, which give production schedules, printing information and financial details for specific publications.

In addition, there is a sub-series of manuscript appraisal forms, which detail the financial options for each publication, as well as printing specifications. Some of the many publications represented in this group are *Oscar and Lucinda* and *Exotic Pleasures*, by Peter Carey; *Isobars, Dislocations, The Ivory Swing, Borderline* and *Charades* by Janette Turner Hospital; and *Palomino* and *Foxybaby* by Elizabeth Jolley.

There is also a group of printouts with statistics for publishing and sales from 1980 to 1984.

Correspondence

The correspondence files fall into two broad groups of production and administration. In the first category, some examples of files are:

- correspondence relating to *The Fat Man in History* by Peter Carey: 1974–75. This was UQP's first Peter Carey publication and it launched Peter Carey's literary career.
- correspondence between Michael Dransfield and Roger McDonald, poetry editor: 1969–70. Roger McDonald, editor at UQP 1969–76, is described in *The Oxford Companion to Australian Literature* as a "university press employee of significance in Australian literary and publishing history."
- correspondence relating to *Bicycle and other Poems* by David Malouf: 1973–74. (*Bicycle and other Poems* was Malouf's first publication with UQP, in 1970.) Also correspondence relating to Malouf's first novel *Johnno*.

There is also correspondence with agents, freelance editors and publishing houses, as well as correspondence relating to rejected and projected manuscripts. The correspondence files relating to rejected manuscripts make up at present 18 boxes.

In addition, there will be editorial files available, relating to UQP titles up until the 1980s. These will be subject to some access restrictions.

Publishing meetings (minutes, agendas, etc.)

There are at present 3 boxes of files in this series, covering the period 1983–91. They document UQP's monthly publication meetings, which began in 1983 and superseded the publications committee meetings. The minutes for the meetings of the external publications committee are held in the university archives.

The publishing meetings minutes will be subject to some access restrictions.

Literature Board of the Australia Council

UQP has consistently been a leading recipient of Literature Board assistance, and has published *The Literature Board: a Brief History* by Thomas Shapcott. The records relating to the Literature Board comprise 3 boxes. There are applications for publishing subsidies, 1979–84; claims, 1979 and previous; and correspondence, 1973–78.

Miscellaneous files

A variety of records is included in this series, such as blurbs, memos, and copies of contracts.

Writers represented in the UQP Archive and in other Fryer Library manuscript collections

Fryer Library is the Special Collections Department of the University of Queensland Library. It has an extensive Australian studies collection of published and unpublished material, including a large number of manuscript collections from leading Australian authors. Among these are a number of UQP authors. Users of the UQP Archive may also wish to consult some of the collections briefly described below. Full inventories for these collections are available in print format from the Fryer Library, or on the World Wide Web (at http://www.library.uq.edu.au/fryer).

Astley, Thea. Papers from 1950 onwards. There are 15 boxes, including manuscript drafts for *A Descant for Gossips, The Slow Natives, A Kindness Cup, Hunting the Wild Pineapple, Beachmasters, Reaching Tin River, Vanishing Points, It's Raining in Mango, Coda* and *The Multiple Effects of Rainshadow.*

Blight, John. 19 boxes of papers, 1920–84. Includes correspondence, drafts of poems, and family photographs.

Carey, Peter. 80 boxes of papers, including manuscripts for *Bliss, Illywhacker, Oscar and Lucinda, Until the End of the World* (screenplay), *War Crimes, The Tax Inspector* and *The Unusual Life of Tristan Smith*; also correspondence, notebooks, and research materials.

Cato, Nancy. 4 boxes of papers, including correspondence and manuscript drafts of *Brown Sugar, Queen Trucanini* and *The Heart of the Continent.*

Dransfield, Michael. Includes typescript (photocopied) of *Memoirs of a Velvet Urinal.*

Fitzgerald, Ross. 17 boxes. Include research materials, manuscripts and proofs for publications; correspondence, and personal papers.

Hanger, Eunice. The Hanger Collection of Australian Playscripts comprises some 2000 unpublished playscripts. There are also 15 boxes of papers, which mainly relate to Eunice Hanger's career as a lecturer in drama at the University of Queensland Department of English.

Hospital, Janette Turner. 13 boxes of personal papers and literary drafts, including proofs and manuscripts for *The Last Magician, Charades, Oyster, Dislocations, Isobars* and *The Tiger in the Tiger Pit.*

Malouf, David. 1 box of manuscript drafts of *Child's Play, Fly away Peter* and *An Imaginary Life.*

Manifold, John. 3 boxes of typescript poems, songs, short stories, articles and plays.

Masters, Olga. 10 boxes of papers, including correspondence (mainly with UQP), manuscript and typescript drafts of *Amy's Children, The Home Girls, A Long Time Dying, A Working Man's Castle* (play), *A Very Dull Place* and personal papers.

Murphy, Denis. 119 boxes of research material from publications by Denis Murphy and personal papers.

Noonuccal, Oodgeroo. 59 boxes of personal papers, including correspondence and photographs; drafts of poems; and papers relating to Oodgeroo's political and professional activities.

Rodriguez, Judith. 8 boxes, mainly correspondence, with some manuscript drafts of poems by Judith Rodriguez and others.

Shapcott, Thomas. 53 boxes of correspondence, manuscript poems, Literature Board records, photographs, manuscripts and proofs including those for *Hotel Bellevue, The Golden Orb, What You Own: Stories, Summer Carol, Mr. Edmund, His Master's Ghost, Theatre of Darkness: Lillian Nordica as opera.*

Wearne, Alan. 21 boxes of papers including correspondence, notebooks, literary drafts including those for *The Nightmarkets, Nothing but Thunder* and *The Lovemakers.*

Wharton, Herb. 7 boxes; drafts of *Unbranded, Where ya been, mate?* and *Cattle Camp: Murrie drovers and their stories.*

Index